So Far, So Good

So Far, So Good

THE AUTOBIOGRAPHY

Paul Eddington

Hodder & Stoughton

First published in Great Britain in 1995 by Hodder and Stoughton,
a division of Hodder Headline PLC.

10 9 8 7 6 5 4 3 2 1

A CIP catalogue record for this title is
available from the British Library

ISBN 0 340 63837 0

Typeset by Hewer Text Composition Services, Edinburgh
Printed and bound in Great Britain by
Mackays of Chatham PLC

Hodder and Stoughton Ltd
A Division of Hodder Headline PLC
338 Euston Road
London NW1 3BH

To Toby, Hugo, Dominic, Gemma,
my grandson Tom and my dearest Tricia

Contents

1 A Quaker Catholic   1
2 Short Commons   17
3 Every Night Something Awful   33
4 Adventures in Rep   51
5 The Pause Magnificent   65
6 Riding through the Glen   83
7 The Great White Way   99
8 A Good Life   117
9 Very Droll, Minister   139
10 The Corridors of Power   155
11 'You'll be Marvellous!'   177
12 G & S in Oz   195
13 Home   211

Acknowledgements

It was my niece, Charlotte Barratt, who first gave me the feeling that I ought to write this. In fact she asked me to because she wanted to know more about my, and therefore her, family background. I had brushed aside previous suggestions on the grounds that I was a) too young b) too busy and c) so rich that I need not bother. None of these objections now apply.

Some years later it was my agent, Paul Lyon-Maris, who gave me the necessary kick-start. "You have led an interesting life," he said sternly, "and it is your duty to do so."

Having given in, it was my wife who did all the research I was too lazy to do, which means most of it, but above all I must thank Rowena Webb of Hodder and Stoughton who encouraged, cajoled and inspired feelings of guilt in me in equal measure. She visited me frequently and clearly knows the way to an actor's heart; she allowed me to read passages aloud to her and usually gave a most flattering appearance of enjoying them.

Finally, my most heartfelt thanks to the medical team which has kept me going all this while. Foremost amongst them is Trish Garibaldinos and her dedicated colleagues at St John's in St Thomas's. Their philosophy, I believe, is that if they do so for long enough there is every chance of my dying of something else, and they may well succeed.

1

A Quaker Catholic

My wife says that I am a born worrier. If she is right, which she usually is, I started worrying on Saturday, 18 June 1927. This was the hundred and twelfth anniversary of the battle of Waterloo and to me, of course, it is quite a worrying thought that there may well have been people alive on my birthday who were so before that battle was fought.

Had I but known, I had more than that to worry about. Temperamentally my parents were far apart and, although I have no doubt that on their wedding day they must have appeared to their guests to be an attractive couple, it is perhaps surprising that their marriage lasted as long as it did.

My father had had a troubled start. His own father had been a moderately successful watercolourist who lived with his large family, the product of two marriages, in a house on the outskirts of Worcester. But by the time my father was eleven both his parents were dead – in my grandfather's case, it was hinted, from drink. He had startled Worcester by living *la vie de bohème* to the full, causing shock-waves to ripple through the teetotal Quaker community from which he was impeccably descended.

He had been born William Clark, of the shoemaking family in Somerset, but on discovering that there was already a painter of the same name he added his mother's maiden name to his own. To this day there are some members of the family who refer to him without irony as 'The great W.C.'. The Clarks and the Eddingtons had been amongst the first members of the Society of Friends when it was formed in the mid-seventeenth century, so my grandfather's distinctly un-Quakerly behaviour was regarded with some disfavour, particularly by my half-aunts. My father told me that on some nights

I

he and his younger brother would watch from their bedroom window as their father's guests were carried out and put into the horse-drawn cabs which had called to take them home, and which would then rattle off over the cobblestones under the yellow gas lamps. The half-aunts would breathe a sigh of relief behind their bedroom doors, which they had locked against possible intruders – rather unnecessarily, I thought unkindly when I first met them. Perhaps I was prejudiced, because a wall of disapproval always seemed to me to exist between them and our part of the family. My grandmother Eddington, a lively and, I believe, humorous person, had been my grandfather's 'housekeeper' and it was a second marriage for both of them. Amongst the Clark-Eddingtons there was much pursing of lips and drawing aside of black bombazine skirts.

My father would have liked to be a painter himself, but after he had left the Friends' School at Sidcot, a co-educational Quaker boarding school in Somerset at which his own father had been educated, he was apprenticed to an engineering draughtsman – Good at Drawing was the thinking, I expect. It was an apprenticeship that he loathed and in the summer of 1914, as soon as war began to loom, he enlisted enthusiastically in the Honourable Artillery Company.

Much of the next four years was spent in the mud and blood of northern France, but, like many of his contemporaries who survived, he was extremely reticent about his experiences. He had had a bout of trench fever and then a whiff of gas at Ypres, but Armistice Day found him relatively intact, in body at least. I have spoken to people who knew him as a young man and they remembered him as amusing, charming, full of jokes and fun and a wonderful extemporiser on the piano, but by the time I knew him nearly all of that had gone. He was charming, certainly, courteous, tall – six feet was tall in those days – ironic and kindly but in common with many of his generation he carried with him an air of wistfulness.

Although I only caught fleeting glimpses of it at the time, it became clear to me many years later that his one consuming passion, his great compensation, was not art nor women nor drink, but gambling. At first it was horses and later, when I suppose he began to feel uneasy in the company of his financial betters, the dogs. On only one occasion do I remember what must have been the aftermath of one of his rare wins. He stood at the kitchen table and threw up his hands, and the air was filled with huge, white, fluttering fivers, symbols then of a breathtaking opulence, each one a week's wages for a skilled worker.

It was clearly a happy occasion and I joined in his laughter, although even then I was uneasily aware of my mother's and my sister's more subdued reaction. My mother always protected me with what must have been heroic ingenuity, but a seed of bitterness had been planted in my sister which took her many years to uproot.

My father drifted from job to job as our circumstances gradually reduced. At one time he set up as an interior decorator and I remember going with my sister to a children's fancy dress party, she as Jill and I as Jack, seriously encumbered by the kitchen pail, my trousers being made from Evelyn Laye's old cushion covers. Forty years later I found myself seated next to Evelyn on an Equity committee and had the fun of being able to tell her. The winner of the fancy dress competition at that party was Adolf Hitler, whose mother had dressed him in a brown mac and wellington boots; the brilliant simplicity of the concept took the edge off even my jealousy.

This tenuous brush with celebrity was not my only one; in 1935 we went to the Ideal Homes Exhibition at Earl's Court and, as she swept superbly through a backstage area with a sheaf of flowers and a retinue of attendants, I caught a glimpse of the gorgeous Jessie Matthews. Then one day my father came back from work to say that he had actually seen the Prince of Wales. 'I was so close I could have touched him!' he exclaimed. I was baffled as to why, given such a golden and unrepeatable opportunity, he had not done so.

For my mother, glimpses of high life were particularly poignant; she had been born at Leek in Staffordshire, in the workhouse. Workhouses were an essential part of the structure of Victorian and Edwardian social services, but to the poor of the time they were symbols of degradation and shame, traps from which the poverty of the destitute allowed no escape. Children were separated from their unmarried mothers, husbands were segregated from wives and, although the physical welfare of the inmates was adequate and strictly supervised, workhouses were places of such universal dread that, although they were abolished soon after the Second World War, I have known old people who would refuse a bed in the local hospital because they remembered that it had once been the workhouse. None of these considerations affected my mother's infancy, however. The Leek workhouse, and the one at Worcester to which she later moved, represented home – a place of comfort, not to say luxury. My grandparents were its master and mistress.

My grandfather was technically, of course, a despot, but nevertheless a benevolent one and to the inmates the Roberts family was regarded as little less than royal. Throughout her childhood my mother was surrounded by adulation, respect and an entourage of devoted attendants, all drawn from the impoverished residents. Until the time she was married she had never been allowed to tie her own shoelaces, had never made a pot of tea or boiled an egg. It is easy to believe that in those days, when domestic virtues were supreme and a young wife was expected to be her husband's housekeeper, my parents' marriage must have been under something of a strain from the start.

My maternal grandparents were both Irish Catholics: he a small, dark man from Waterford, where Welsh names such as Roberts are not uncommon, and she a flame-haired beauty from Cork. Out of curiosity I once made an attempt to trace their ancestry. This is not easy with Southern Irish people because all the records used to be kept in Dublin in the Four Courts, a building which was burnt down during the Troubles; with Roland Roberts I drew a blank. Fortunately I had no such trouble with Alice McKernan; carefully concealed during her lifetime was the fact that she was the daughter of an immigrant greengrocer from South Shields in County Durham. She was, however, as regal in manner as befitted the mistress of the workhouse, and would seldom condescend to leave her own home. 'Now, Mrs Roberts, I'm not coming to tea with you until you have been to tea with me,' an acquaintance would say to my grandmother. 'Well,' she would reply, 'I much regret that we shall not be able to have tea together again!' She would never, I was told, wear a pair of kid gloves twice; after one wearing they would be peeled off and given to the cook – no doubt another of the pauper inmates.

My grandparents' relationship suffered from at least two substantial handicaps. My grandfather had a roving eye (when they first met, my wife was the object of his keenly interested attentions and he was then over eighty, his second wife having only recently insisted on his giving up his racing bicycle), and it was possibly in response to this aggravation that my grandmother had taken discreetly to the bottle – which may in its turn, I suppose, explain why she was so reluctant to leave the security of her own home. She managed to retain appearances for some time, though increasingly dishevelled and incoherent, until one night, before her startled guests, she slid quietly beneath the table. My grandfather, as was then the common practice, eventually had her 'put away' and a few years later she died in the Powick Lunatic Asylum, halfway between Malvern and Worcester. One of my earliest memories is of being lifted on to a starched white bed, tightly tucked in, to be embraced by an old, old woman.

My mother's first job when she came to London as a girl to seek work was at the Savoy Hotel where she was a cashier in the restaurant, managed then by Santarelli, 'that prince of restaurateurs', as Sir Hugh Wontner described him to me recently. It was on a trip home to Worcester that she met my father who, gallantly and typically, helped her with her luggage. Whether there was any friction between the families over religion I do not know, but it was certainly necessary for my mother to obtain dispensation from the bishop before they could marry, and the terms of the dispensation, as was usual, were that any children must be brought up as Roman Catholics.

The first home that I recall was a rented flat in Boundary Road, North-west London, memorable for me only because it was there that my mother once discovered me sitting in my bath eating a bar of Lifebuoy soap. The texture was firm but yielding, the taste agreeably tangy and the sensation it caused even more so. It must have been about this time too that I first experienced a feeling of vertigo, my pram, pushed no doubt by a vivacious hand, shooting over the kerb and going into free fall for six or so inches.

We never owned anywhere we lived in, but things must have got a bit better because later we moved to a pleasant house, with a garden, in nearby Alexandra Road. The district had started life as one in which prosperous Victorian gentlemen had kept their mistresses and, although it seems unlikely that anyone would have told me, from somewhere I heard that Edward VII had been accustomed to visit Lily Langtry at a house just down the road. Apparently he entered through a discreet door in the high outer wall and ascended to the front door by steps concealed within a frosted glass tunnel. The district has now regained its grandeur, at least in terms of property values, and has quite possibly added a touch of respectability, but at the time we lived there its gentility was decidedly shabby.

We became such inveterate flat-dwellers that for years afterwards I was convinced that number 61 Alexandra Road was a flat, but I may have been mistaken because there was a basement kitchen and certainly the garden was ours. I remember, too, lying in bed on a summer's morning listening to the pigeons cooing under the eaves, with that irritating way pigeons have of breaking off in mid-coo. It must have been in this house that we took in a series of lodgers or paying guests (they were known as PGs) out of economic necessity. It was certainly in this house that my mother sought to establish a kind of salon. Mother had no means, of course, to subsidise young artists or anything like that, but she had acquired a talent for making her surroundings agreeable, with the white walls and primary colours which were beginning to be fashionable and which did not involve great expense. Together with a great number of people in those inter-war years she was passionately interested in music, painting, literature, religion and politics, especially the last, which I believe had originally been stimulated by a highly significant incident during her early upbringing.

Soon after the turn of the century, when she was very young, there was a great deal of industrial unrest which in Staffordshire came to a climax with a march by the unemployed on the Leek workhouse, which probably symbolised for them all that was hateful about the Establishment's attitude to society. My grandfather chained the iron gates and turned the fire hoses on the marchers. My mother's Irishness had no doubt already prepared the ground (she was always instinctively 'agin the government'), and the sight of those ragged people being tumbled contemptuously in the dirt awoke in her a hostility to injustice and poverty which never left her.

Ours at that time was a house which my parents' friends were glad to visit, and within the walls of which the topics of the day were vigorously discussed. Every month or so there would be a small party to which a prominent exponent of his or her subject would be invited to speak to our friends. I remember the saintly John Fletcher of the Quakers; I believe Father D'Arcy, the famous Jesuit, came to speak; and – on separate occasions, I imagine – a member of the Communist Party and a leading Fascist visited us.

My own participation in these activities was almost wholly confined to going round afterwards and finishing up the dregs in the sherry glasses. On one unfortunate occasion I collected a few cigarette butts and smoked them in a clay pipe. Much anxious knocking on the lavatory door. 'Are you sure you're all right in there, Paul?' 'Yes, thank you,' came my faint and wholly misleading reply.

It appears to me that the success or otherwise of a convent education depends very largely on the order of nuns in whose establishment this takes place. I mean no disrespect (fans of *Yes Minister* will recognise the insincerity) but the nuns of, say, St Vincent de Paul or the Poor Clares were used to teaching ignorant peasants who could only be roused from their spiritual torpor by visions of hellfire and eternal damnation. My mother had been the victim of a French fundamentalist order for whose members the fear of sex, amongst other things, loomed large. She used to wear a rather saucily low-cut blouse, she told me, and was frequently told to pin it up. '*Mettez un épingle, Ma'moiselle!*' was the oft-repeated cry, and a friend at boarding school was not permitted to take a bath without first donning a mackintosh cape, lest the sight of her own naked body inspire lustful thoughts.

I went to my own first school in London at the age of three, and I had the great good fortune for it to be the Holy Child convent, on the north side of Cavendish Square.

The Holy Child order was not like the one my mother had experienced. The convent itself no longer exists, but the twin neo-classical buildings in which it was housed remain. They are joined by a bridge on which, high above the passers-by, is a statue which made a deep impression on me then and continues to do so now. It is a Mother and Child by Jacob Epstein. The mother stands, her hands resting on her son's shoulders, her eyes cast down in love and sorrow, while the child, arms outspread in anticipation of the cross, gazes before him, wide-eyed and grave. Their garments are pressed against their bodies and, although the group is very nearly life-sized, the impression is that it is held in place by the wind alone. It is a remarkable work of art, unknown to most Londoners. All the more remarkable, if it is true, is the fact that the nuns had commissioned it from this highly controversial and presumably non-believing American Jew and that he had, moreover, donated it to the order.

Although I have done a good deal of hard work in my time it has never held much appeal for me, and its absence is no doubt responsible for many of the warm feelings I hold for the Holy Child nuns. Mother Gerard, in whose study I spent much of my time looking at the birds in the square and playing with her kitten, seemed fond of me and I reciprocated her feelings.

Cavendish Square was the first step in my erratic and nomadic education. Between us, my sister Shirley and I attended at least sixteen different schools. At some stage during my childhood my parents separated. My sister and I continued to live with my mother and although we still saw my father, we trailed around the country with her since she was constantly on the move in search of employment. It was not until I began to write this book and really to think about the past that I appreciated the remarkable way in which I seemed to accept the ups and downs and the giddy swerves that outlined my childhood. From about 1931, when I was four, until I left school in 1943 my sister and I lived a life of severe turmoil and unrest and frightening insecurity. And yet, although I can clearly remember all those ups and downs, they seemed not to have touched me. My sister Shirley, being three years older, was touched by them most painfully and it must surely have been an extra irritation to see me apparently rising above things. Children are notoriously capable of absorbing life's shocks, and I simply carried on as if everything were normal.

It was not until about the age of fifteen that my mother told me, in answer I suppose to a question, that her marriage to my father was at an end. The news cannot have come as a surprise, for my father had not lived with us for many years. I suspect that my myopia had had a psychological basis: I did not want to know the truth and had, all those years, suppressed the obvious all along.

Meanwhile, I went to the cinema as often as I could and enjoyed films promiscuously, except those which showed, however comically, marital conflict. These I hated and they left me shaking and frightened. Separation from my mother was the hideous shadow lurking round the corner, and as long as that could be kept at bay all was comparatively well.

As I've mentioned, schools came and went in rapid succession. Some forty years later, replete with celebrity and finding myself in Birmingham, where I learnt that Mother Gerard was now the Reverend Mother of the Holy Child convent in Moseley, I decided to call on her. How gratifying for her, I felt, to be visited by such a famous star, and how pleasant for me to witness her gratification. She did not immediately recognise me, and was not able to remember the infant Paul. She did not in fact remember me at all and was not aware that the person who was visiting her was in any way celebrated. That may have been the only lesson she ever taught me.

I recall a brief sojourn with the nuns of St Vincent de Paul, with their dramatic winged head-dresses. Catholicism had evidently given us an entrée into a social circle somewhat above our own and I remember some rather grand acquaintances and even grander parties, although these last were, alas, wasted on me. I was never a very jolly joiner-in and at one party – could it have been in Mayfair and could I have possibly heard that it was at the house of the Duchess of something? – I discovered a dish of the most delicious chipolata sausages and retired with them under the table, only to be unmasked in mid-munch and hauled out by my hostess to join the party and stop being so miserable.

Another little friend whom I ungratefully found extremely tiresome was the son of Mrs, later Dame, Vera Laughton-Matthews. She was then head of the Sea Rangers and later, during the Second World War, became head of the WRNS and was known as the Queen Bee. Her husband was Something in the City but spent much of his time making model ships in the cellar. Their son Peter – I think he later became an admiral – was always telephoning to try to get me to come round and play. Such invitations taxed my ingenuity to resist without giving offence: clearly I was an unsociable child, and it is no wonder that I had few friends.

On the whole I preferred adult company and I loved my mother's old friends, most of whom remained mine and my wife's after my mother's early death. In addition to these I was entertained by the PGs, one of whom was a young lady whom I interrupted while she was taking a bath. Having been instructed by my mother to wash my hands I strolled into the bathroom and did so. I then dried them on the nearest available towel, to be alarmed by a horrified cry from the bath: 'But that's my *body* towel!' I puzzled over this social blunder for years; what on earth could either she or I have done to her towel that would make any difference to anything?

Another lodger became a friend and remained one for the rest of her life. Gwynedd Lewis was reading for the Bar. In all but actual gender, Gwynedd – there was no formality and we called her Gwynedd straightaway – was an extremely hearty young man and she blew through our house like a great, jolly gale. Her laugh rattled the plates, and if my father did not take rapid evasive action she was liable to greet him with a shout and a disabling clap on the back.

One of our lodgers brought with her a pet green parrot which I adopted when she left to take a job abroad. I believe parrots are one-person birds and it was fortunate for my mother and sister that Lorita had chosen me, as they both suffered from a feather phobia. She was apparently a native of South America and I hoped, romantically, that she had belonged to a sailor and that the words she spoke consisted of Spanish indecencies. During the school holidays she was my constant companion, rocketing round the garden on the handlebars of my fairy cycle or crouching for hours on end, her claws digging into my naked shoulder, while I whispered endearments in the direction of what I hoped was her ear. One day she stooped confidentially and, putting her beak close to my own ear, made a long whispered but, alas, incoherent speech in return.

Lorita had discovered how to lift the hasp of her cage door and took great pleasure in stepping carefully out, climbing on to the top and waiting for my mother to come in and recoil in horror. Should she fail to appear, Lorita would make her way upstairs to my sister's room where, it seemed obvious to me, she was hoping to find Shirley in bed. If she was lucky, Lorita would then climb up on to the bed and advance towards her victim, smiling wickedly until my sister's screams brought help.

This was all splendid entertainment and it occurs to me now that the malice was not, perhaps, all on Lorita's side. Sardonic and intelligent as I believe she was, her black eye missed little and she could hardly fail to have noticed the hostility which existed between me and Shirley. I was Mummy's Darling and took every advantage of the fact; my sister, understandably, took every advantage in return and, until I discovered that she suffered from a cigarette-end phobia as well as a feather one, my only defence was to cry tearfully for Mummy.

Meanwhile I continued my odyssey through the local schools, of which most provide only fleeting memories. After my whistle-stop acquaintance with the St Vincent de Pauls there was a term at the Montessori school in Regent's Park, where I was taught how to tie shoelaces and guess the number of beans in a bottle (surprisingly useful at garden fêtes in later life), and then a bracing encounter with real life at an LCC council school. This last made a strong impression on me because of the Empire Day celebrations. These took place on the playground and consisted mostly, as far as I could see, of marching round and saluting the flag. I was extremely reluctant to make a fool of myself doing the former and, since it was obvious that if I were to take part I was in danger of making a fool of everyone else as well, I was allowed to skip the marching part. At the time I was a fervent republican, so of course standing to attention and saluting the flag was out of the question as well. This was not taken by the staff in quite such a tolerant spirit and, as I sat cross-legged on the concrete, I was aware of being surrounded by a posse, as it were, of embarrassed adults. I felt like a stubborn weed in a thicket of stout oaks. Unable to rouse any response, as a last resort they tried lifting me by the elbows in an attempt to shake me to attention; but it was to no avail, and eventually I think they simply gave up.

It must have been one of our frequent periods of financial embarrassment that sent us to the council school, because we children were brought up in our mother's Roman Catholic faith. Our place of worship at that time was the church in Quex Road in Kilburn in North London – an enormous place, it seemed then, with a large crucifix suspended over the nave. We were diligent worshippers and I myself was particularly devout, being heavily influenced by the glorious ritual, the richly embroidered robes, the candles and the incense. In those days Mass was said in Latin, all but the sermon being in this mysterious secret language.

I made considerable efforts to learn the catechism, I fasted conscientiously before Holy Communion and with tremendous self-denial I did not chew the Host after it, letting it slowly dissolve in my mouth. I took part with enthusiasm in all the high days and holy days and I knelt by my bed every night to say my prayers.

Once in bed, though, I had a problem; I was unaware of the Doctrine of Invincible Ignorance and I worried long and hard over the fate of all the poor, teeming blacks of Africa who, it seemed clear to me, would be consigned to the Everlasting Bonfire unless they all immediately became Catholics. The confessional too had its problems; I was so supernaturally good that there was very little for me to confess. Sex, of course, is a weapon which a priest can wield with deadly effect in those close confines, but if I was aware of it at all I did not associate its stirrings with guilt. The only guilt I felt was in my failure to produce anything that might interest the shadowy figure behind the wire mesh on the other side of the darkened box. My weekly claim that I had been rude to my parents and felt jealous of a little friend began to sound somewhat repetitive even to me. My interlocutor would eventually cut me short, order me to say a certain number of Hail Marys and release me, purged.

I expect my angelic good looks did me no harm, and one happy day I was invited to place my foot on the bottom rung of a ladder which could have led me in time, I suppose, all the way to Rome; I was asked to be an altar boy. In my scarlet cassock and white lace cotta, I have to admit that I presented a picture of both innocence and piety. In fact an actual picture still exists, and a close inspection of it reveals a stout pair of shiny black boots and a Kirby grip. The hope of ever being able to perform the bishop's blessing was, I realised, remote, but there did exist just a possibility that I might be allowed to ring the little bell which tells the congregation that it must avert its gaze from the Host, or even – and this I did want very much – to swing the censer, with its rattling chains and the intoxicating puff of perfumed smoke at the end of each graceful arc. But, alas, there was a move of home or some other change in our circumstances and I never did achieve that ambition.

One summer holiday, leaving my father behind and taking with us Marie, one of our best friends, we rented, I think for ten shillings (fifty pence) a week, a cottage in Cornwall.

It was not just any cottage, but the one on the end of the little mole which juts into the harbour at Polperro, a picture of which is often placed in the middle of art shop windows.

It was the beginning of what was for me a period of ecstasy. The summers of one's childhood are always long and hot, but that year the cliché was true. Daily we packed a picnic hamper and made our way to the sea where we spent long, hot hours clambering about on the extraordinarily painful, barnacle-covered rocks, exploring the (smugglers', of course) cave at the back or just sitting in the surf. The tiny cove we always went to is a mile or so east of Polperro so we almost always had it to ourselves, and in any case we felt we had to leave the village during the day to avoid the tourists – or 'trippers', as we called them.

Dull days were few, or seemed so. On one such, our dear friend Marie offered to take my sister and me down to the quayside and see if the Puckey brothers might not be persuaded to take us on a trip round the bell-buoy, which could be heard tolling eerily, the sound coming and going with each gust of wind. At Polperro the harbour mouth is long and narrow and little can be seen of the sea, which on that day looked as grey and unexciting as everything else. The brothers looked doubtful. 'Well,' one of them said at length, 'it be all right for we, if it be all right for thee.' We said we thought it would be all right for us, they took our sixpence and we clambered aboard.

Emerging into the open sea, we suddenly found ourselves in the middle of a boiling frenzy. Climbing up what seemed to me to be enormous waves, we shot down on the far sides as we toiled our way to the buoy. As they lashed me to the mast, I understood the Puckey brothers' hesitation. Marie and Shirley clung to their seat in the stern, both looking extremely anxious and my sister decidedly green. The brothers had three tries at getting round the buoy. They succeeded at last and we raced home, past rocks with teeth like rip-saws. I am sure that for my sister that trip laid the foundations of a lifelong aversion to travel.

A year or so later we returned to Polperro. We had had to give up the cottage on the mole, but a retired Free Church clergyman who had taken a fancy to my mother had built a minute bungalow – we actually called it a 'hut' – on the cliff path, halfway to 'our' beach, and this we rented one winter. One day a genuine flying circus arrived on the field behind our hut. To my good fortune, the parish priest was among the spectators and he offered my sister and me a joy-ride. Shirley withdrew hastily, but I thought the matter over carefully and decided that, as I was with the priest, I might well be under some form of divine protection and that, in any case, if the worst were to come to the worst he might just have time to administer the Last Rites before we hit the ground. I accepted his offer with gratitude.

It was an open biplane and I was able to look down on my sister as she stood in her green beret and khaki shorts gazing upwards, her white face and aghast expression diminishing as we rose. The leather-helmeted pilot turned in his forward cockpit and shouted something; the priest put his mouth close to my ear and shouted in his turn. Did I want to loop-the-loop? I felt I had pressed divine providence hard enough and declined. My mother was gazing at the scene out of the kitchen window all this time and would have been as horrified as my sister had she known what I was up to – as indeed she was when at last I made my triumphant way home.

Of our return to London I have no recollection whatsoever, and it must have been during the following months that our family finally broke into its component pieces. For me this period will always be associated with Rusty, a much-loved liver and white spaniel who possessed in abundance all the charm and absurdity of his breed. I can understand now the impossibility of keeping pets given that our lives were about to become so highly mobile, but mature judgements are not available to children. I returned home one day and, instead of my dog leaping to greet me, the house was silent and empty. Rusty, I learnt, had been 'given a good home'. I was stunned with dismay and incomprehension.

My parents' dilemma must have been poignant. To explain that they were no longer going to live together and that the family was on the move would have seemed out of the question and, self-absorbed as most children are, it was years before I could forgive them for what I felt at the time was such a gross betrayal.

How long I spent at the Warren School in Maldon, on the estuary of the river Blackwater in Essex, or how I came to be there I cannot now remember. It was a tiny private school run by two women friends, and as I appeared to be the sole boarder I suppose some special influence must have been at work. I do not know whether I learnt anything there and I certainly do not remember any lessons. I do recollect how kind they were to me – and that must have been kind indeed, because it was the first time I had ever been sent away by myself and I was clearly on the brink of being very unhappy in consequence.

The magic panacea was their boat. They went sailing every weekend, and they took me with them. We sailed round the buoy in the estuary and they made me perform some sort of initiation ceremony which involved my having to drink a tumbler of the river water. Nowadays no doubt the ordeal would fell one like an ox, but then it was tremendous fun. The dear ladies promised that as soon as I could swim across Maldon's murky municipal pond they would take me on the boat for a whole weekend, and the thrilling prospect of actually sleeping in a bunk on board kept me hard at work. Alas, I was taken away again before I had learnt to swim.

Miraculously, Mother got a job back in Cornwall, managing a musty, dusty, old-fashioned hotel in Penzance. My presence was tolerated, apparently – but only just, I should think, because I found the speaking tubes which were on every landing quite irresistible. I would unplug the whistle, listen for a moment to the voices in the kitchen far below, and then blow down the tube before running to escape the answering bellow.

I was sent – temporarily of course, as always – to a large boys' school in the town. This establishment recommended itself to me immediately because it had an orchestra, which must have been more than competent because I heard them play, amongst other things, the overture to *La Traviata*. It was the first piece of serious music I had ever heard 'live', and it ravished me. The head boy of the time took a kindly interest in me, and a few years ago (by then he was a retired doctor) he made himself known to me. I heard him say, without quite taking it in at the time, that he remembered my mother well. 'We all felt very sorry for her,' he said. I wondered afterwards what he could have meant. With the self-centredness of childhood I hadn't realised that other people had problems as well.

Soon, however, my peripatetic education had moved on again.

2

Short Commons

It was 1937. I was sitting in a sunlit garden. On the bench beside me was the person who was going to have a decisive influence on the rest of my life. Arthur Johnstone was a ruddy-complexioned man with small glasses and a tuft of white hair – one of his nicknames was 'Tufty' – and he was wearing what he always wore: a thick, snuff-coloured tweed suit, rather short in the leg. His trousers had turn-ups, of course, and were braced halfway up his chest. Completing this ensemble was a white Viyella shirt with an Oxford University tie, and on his small feet he wore brown boots. I was too engrossed in working out the few simple sums he had given me to notice all this, but I can describe him with some confidence because, except for one occasion when I remember him in cricket whites, his appearance never varied. I completed my calculations and some time later learnt that I was now enrolled as a pupil at the Friends' School, Sibford Ferris, seven miles west of Banbury in Oxfordshire.

My mother's Catholicism had been wearing thin over the years and the Pope's passive attitude towards the Fascist regime in Germany, where Hitler was now Chancellor, and towards Franco in Spain, was becoming increasingly unacceptable so far as she was concerned. A rigid structure such as Roman Catholicism is likely, I imagine, to become unstable when one of its principal props is removed, and for my mother the edifice was rapidly reduced to rubble. Because of our domestic circumstances it was now necessary for me to be sent to boarding school and, resisting the offers of well-to-do Catholic friends who were even prepared, I believe, to pay for me to be sent to Downside, she consulted the Quaker who had sometimes spoken at my parents' discussion evenings.

By good fortune, John Fletcher was a member of what was then the Friends' Education Committee and, partly because my father and grandfather had attended a Friends' school and I might therefore be considered a 'Birthright Friend' (a form of membership which does not exist now), I was able to get some form of bursary. Sibford had been founded in 1844 as what surely must have been one of the country's first co-educational boarding schools, and the intention of its founders was that it should cater for the needs of the less academically inclined children of poorer Friends. What this meant in practical terms was that I only cost whoever paid my fees a very few shillings a week.

Apparently there was no bed available at the school, so for the first term I boarded with a Quaker family in the village, the Lambs, to whom I was distantly related, and experienced my first taste of genuine country life. Notwithstanding my months in Cornwall, I approached this with urban disdain. What was so soon to become a fascinating part of rural history, a way of life that had not changed for hundreds of years, was for me a cumbersome and inconvenient way of getting through the day. Judging by the speed with which it disappeared the moment that electricity and running water were laid on, the local population felt much the same.

I suppose the most noticeable thing, during the day, was the fact that all domestic water was drawn from the well set in the grassy bank at the edge of the road in front of the house. That and the privy down the garden, which was a single-holer with a noisome and menacing space beneath it. The school's head gardener, Mr Green, told me that when he had first arrived there, before the turn of the century (he showed me the smock he wore at the time), one of his duties every holiday was to clean out and whitewash the long, low chamber beneath the boys' lavatories. One day, as he was putting the final touches to his dreadful work, he looked up from his crouching position to find out why everything had suddenly gone dark. One of the maids, feeling a sudden need, had dashed across the playground and sat down immediately above him. Whitewash brush in hand, it was a temptation that Mr Green felt unable to resist. I knew them both, and they had not spoken to each other for nearly half a century.

At night the downstairs rooms in the Lambs' house, like most houses in the village, were lit by oil lamps, and the bedrooms by candlelight. If you washed, which I did as seldom as possible, you did so in a bowl with a ewer and a slop pail. Baths were taken once a week in a sort of zinc coffin in front of the parlour fire. The beds were made of feathers, and when you jumped in you sank like a stone into a kind of feather canyon, perhaps warmed in the winter by a stoneware hot water bottle. For me, the winters were unbelievably cold; it was not unusual on a winter morning to find the water in the bowl frozen over.

On my first Sunday Viv Lamb, the son of the house, invited me to go mushroom-picking with him. Whether or not we found any mushrooms I cannot remember, because the event was quite overshadowed for me by an ominous summons the next day to see the headmaster at my earliest convenience – meaning immediately. It appeared that, although for that term I was living in the village, I was technically (the technicality was not explained to me) a boarder. As a boarder I was naturally expected to take part in all the Sunday activities of the rest of the school, which included hymn practice, Meeting for Worship at eleven, an afternoon walk or supervised 'pig drive' for the juniors and, after tea, Evening Meeting.

It was an interview calculated, I am sure, to instil in me a respect for A.J.'s authority. He appeared to be genuinely outraged by what he interpreted as my casual attitude. His ruddy complexion flushed purple, his eyes grew even smaller behind their gold-rimmed spectacles and his tuft of white hair quivered with anger. It would be understating the case to write that I was dismayed; I was appalled and terrified. I had never, as a tenderly reared ten-year-old, been confronted by adult rage, particularly directed towards myself, and it set the tone of our relationship for the future. During the next six years I was unable to approach or be approached by Arthur Johnstone, to hear his name spoken or even to see it written, without experiencing a tremor of dread.

I should certainly have felt a sympathy for and possibly a keen interest in the headmaster had I known that he was an ex-jailbird, as was his senior master, Mr Parkin. A.J. had been a conscientious objector in the First World War and had eventually found himself breaking stones on Dartmoor. The saintly Mr Parkin was already in uniform when he decided that it was his duty as a Christian to refuse military service. Had he already been at the Western Front, for which he was destined, he might well have been shot, as were many others. As it was, he was thrown into Oxford jail where an attempt was made to certify him insane.

Something about my interview with A.J. which baffled me and gave me much food for thought was its injustice. He must have thought that my sensibilities were well worth sacrificing to his bullying, and successful, attempt to cow me at the outset. A cloud formed over my head. But it was only a small cloud, and for the most part the rest of the firmament was blue. It became a matter of pride to me that I never wrote a weepy letter home. I daresay that one reason for this was the fact that 'home' was a somewhat vague concept and my school was providing me with almost my first taste of stability. A.J. was, of course, a substantial fly in the ointment, but a considerable compensation was that, although he was unpopular with most of the staff and with people in the district, he ran a good and happy establishment.

The fact that Sibford was a Quaker school was in no way a disadvantage so far as I was concerned. Quite apart from my mother's quarrel with the Pope, in which I joined heartily, I had reached an age when one begins to question accepted attitudes, and amongst other things I wondered what on earth people thought they were up to worshipping in a tongue of which they had no comprehension; the bulk of the Mass was said in those days in Latin. Then there was all that standing up, sitting down, kneeling and crossing oneself. I can understand now the worldwide usefulness of a lingua franca and the need that most people feel for ritual but by then, to me, it seemed merely absurd.

A Friends' Meeting for Worship is a very different matter, and came to me like a breath of fresh air. Basically, it consists of an hour during which you sit in silence, 'waiting on the Lord'. Should the wait be fruitful and you have an irresistible urge to share the thoughts which have come to you, you stand up and do so. Clearly, this way of doing things is wide open to abuse and sometimes it is abused, usually by one who has perhaps wandered into the Meeting House from the street, but it is surprising how rarely this happens.

At Sibford all the pupils, whose ages ranged from nine to sixteen, were required to attend the hour-long meeting from eleven to twelve every Sunday morning. The girls sat on one side and the boys on the other, and the tedium of having to sit still for an hour was considerably relieved by the opportunity it offered to make covert signals to people you fancied on the other side.

On two occasions we had unbelievable luck. One of the Lamb family was Joshua, a white-bearded, patriarchal figure who was very deaf. (His hobby, incidentally, was cultivating weeds; he grew beds of dead nettles, and cow parsley nine feet tall.) On two separate Sundays he rose to his feet to minister to the meeting while old Mrs Winter, whose frail voice we children used to mock cruelly, was already speaking. She had no alternative but to subside, making a feeble attempt to pick up the thread after Joshua had sat down.

At one Meeting a boy called Cole achieved instant heroic stature by standing up and saying that he could not for the life of him see why very young children were forced to submit to this ordeal. 'A boy behind me,' he said languidly, 'has spent the last fifteen minutes trying to force a large moth down my collar.' The boys behind Cole then tried to make themselves invisible and silent glee exploded amongst the rest of the school, not lessened by the fact that, because it was a privileged occasion, the headmaster could do nothing but turn purple.

Not long afterwards the school was divided and only the seniors were required to attend the full Meeting, but I have always been grateful for the opportunity of acquiring the ability to sit still for long periods without fidgeting. To attract attention on the stage, being still is second only to waving a white handkerchief – a lesson which some restless performers take a lifetime to learn.

Quakers have always had a lively concern for the plight of refugees, especially children, and the first I saw arrived to stay one night only and then to pass on. They were victims of the Spanish Civil War. World war was coming closer, with many alarms and false starts. One of my mother's peregrinations for the sake of employment had taken her to a flat in Percy Street in central London, and one holiday I leaned out of the window to hear the news boys at the corner of Tottenham Court Road shouting the news of Munich. 'Peace,' they cried. 'Peace!'

Refugee children came flooding into the school, mostly German Jews but with a sprinkling from eastern Europe. On the whole they were nine-day wonders and were rapidly assimilated; we were fascinated by the effort of teaching them English and finding out about their backgrounds. Their adventures escaping from the Nazis were of course thrilling, but it was impossible to avoid the tragedy of their situation. The Society of Friends had a large number of contacts and in some quarters a good deal of influence, but frequently they were unable to do more than go to a family and say, 'We can take one of the children.' I remember well the day that Gerhardt arrived. He was nine years old, unable to speak any English and had with him only what he was wearing, which included, I recall, a pair of grey lederhosen with green trimmings. He had had to say goodbye to his parents, brothers, sisters, aunts and uncles. His story was replicated dozens and dozens of times. To this day I find it difficult to speak of those children.

War was declared on Sunday, 3 September 1939. My sister had not then defected from Catholicism and was at church. After Guernica and Warsaw it was generally believed that the outbreak of war would be followed immediately by a devastating blitzkrieg which would certainly flatten London and probably most of the larger British cities. It was only natural, therefore, that some Civil Defence expert should choose the moment after Mr Chamberlain's broadcast announcement to test the capital's air raid sirens. Shirley arrived home late, exhausted and panic-stricken, as did many other Londoners. No doubt too precious to be exposed to similar dangers, I heard the broadcast in Weston-super-Mare, the guest of some generous neighbours in London who had taken a house there in order to escape those anticipated raids.

Weston was, and is, a charming West Country seaside resort renowned for its spectacular sunsets, which I believe Turner enjoyed painting. The tide goes out a mile and leaves a vast mud plain and the sunsets are indeed picturesque, if you like the ominous feel of the end of an early autumn day emphasised by blood-red sky. I detested it, and was unable to look at a Turner for many years without a shudder.

I am afraid I was an ungrateful guest, even though my host did his best to cheer me up. 'Surely you don't want to go back to London, with bombs raining down and people being blown to bits all over the place!' If my Mummy was going to be blown to bits I most certainly wanted to be there with her, but he did not understand. I am ashamed to admit that, with the utter unscrupulousness of childhood, I used to lock myself in the lavatory and write pleading letters to my mother upon which I actually dropped tears. The tears were real enough, but I used them quite deliberately in order to make clear my hatred of exile. I must have hurt her dreadfully and the guilt has not left me. Luckily for everyone concerned, the holidays were soon over and I was able to return to my more acceptable exile in Oxfordshire.

Homesickness was the miserable price one paid for the fun, adventure and companionship of the rest of school life; everyone suffered from it, and it lasted about three or four days. Curiously, the normal, cold-hearted cruelty of children did not show itself at the start of term. I suppose that because homesickness was such a universal affliction there was an instinctive feeling that the idea of teasing one's fellows for being tearful was somehow improper. Whatever the reason, I cannot remember ever seeing that sort of bullying take place. When the three-day moratorium had expired, however, normal bullying resumed. There was all the petty unpleasantness that this implies, some of it not much more than teasing, especially of the new boys. The feeling of superiority that this induced, which was quite foreign to us until then, was pleasantly inflating.

There was also, however, bullying of a more serious nature. For several terms a group of the senior boys formed a gang which roamed the school after hours, picking on smaller boys to whom they had taken a dislike. Armed with cricket stumps, they would then march their victims to a small, dark storeroom at the end of one of the corridors, where some beating and other unpleasantness took place. I managed to avoid the worst of this by the adroit use of invective, and it was then that I first understood the power of The Word. I was once cornered by one of the bullies and it was clear to both of us that I could neither fight him nor escape. I really had no alternative but to rely on speech. I abused and insulted him until I was almost out of breath, including his family and friends in my contempt and dwelling at length on his squat form, his very noticeable squint and his bad breath. What I said was largely invention but some part of it must have hit on a secret feeling of inadequacy because he gradually began to look a little sheepish, shuffled a bit, glanced away and at length sloped off. Whatever the ethics of the matter it did my morale no end of good, and I was not too much troubled by bullies ever again.

My friend Mike Farr was a great help in all this. Nobody troubled him much either, partly because he was a big chap anyway and carried with him a careless 'Do your worst!' air, and partly because he was clearly a person of high principles. When, later on, he was appointed head boy he wrestled for a time with his conscience and then caused an unprecedented sensation by resigning 'because it was undemocratic'.

The idea of bullying was and is wholly detestable to me. I do not know whether it was my mother's political interests or the spectacle of our refugees – the ultimate victims of bullying – or even something else, but the sight of it can turn me from a mild, entirely non-violent person into something highly combustible. I simply cannot and do not tolerate it, and I am enormously thankful that it is at last becoming a matter of public concern. Mike and I decided that when we reached the top of the school we would stamp out bullying, and one of my proudest feelings is that on the whole, and so far as we could tell, we did.

It was at about this time that my mother came, all too briefly, into her own. She was appointed manageress of an extremely smart restaurant which was part of a block of flats in Chelsea called Chesil Court. The building belonged to the London Electricity Company, which had built it as a showcase for the benefits of all things electric. Many features of No.4, the flat that went with the job, were possessed by few households then: underfloor central heating, cable radio, a refrigerator in the kitchen, and a sybaritic dream of a bathroom with a mirror heated to stop it steaming over, heated towel-rails of course and, almost defying my credulity, a specially heated area just where one stepped out of the bath.

On a day of sadness and anxiety, because it was the end of the holidays, I took a last long, luxurious hot bath. As I was drying myself I paused. 'No,' I thought, 'that was not the last bath of the holidays. I will be Master of my Fate!' I ran a second one, returning later in the day, extremely clean, to my spartan school.

On arrival a summons awaited me. I was to present myself forthwith at the headmaster's study. I went pale. The term had not even started. What on earth could A.J.'s spies have seen me doing during the holidays?

'Eddington, are you a peer of the realm?'

'No, sir,' I stammered as I tried desperately to fathom his meaning.

'How curious,' he said. 'You wrote me a letter informing me of your time of arrival at Banbury station and signed yourself: Eddington.'

'Yes, sir,' I replied shakily.

'Why, pray?'

'I don't know, sir.'

'Is that the way you usually sign your letters?'

And so the little game went on. It might have all been quite friendly and amusing had he not already spent a great deal of time and effort frightening us.

Spartan the school certainly was, and it grew much more so as the war went on. The Little Dining Hall was where the juniors ate, and a messy place it could be. We used to call the brown sugar we had at breakfast 'sand' and the ceiling was stained with the scraps of butter we flicked up when we thought the staff were not looking. How longingly we gazed up during the coming years when the weekly butter ration was about the size of the average matchbox! The first margarine I saw was grey, and crumbled when cut. I decided I would never ever eat margarine – a resolution which did not last long.

Catering was in the hands of the headmaster's wife, and Mrs Johnstone was regarded by the pupils as incompetent in this respect. No doubt two hundred and fifty hungry young people would make such a judgement of anyone in charge of their nourishment, but the facts speak for themselves. All the meals were poor, but supper was perhaps the most depressing meal of the day. During the hungriest part of the war it consisted of an enamel jug of watery cocoa and a trayful of pieces of bread and marge. Other meals were larger but not much more imaginative. Everyone else's food always looked better. The staff, a member of whom was required to sit at the head of each table in the dining hall, were, with an extraordinary disregard for psychology, served an entirely different menu, cooked separately – a circumstance which I believe embarrassed them as much as it outraged us. Children adopted various stratagems in order to vary their diet. Some declared themselves to be Jewish for a term, others vegetarian, but it did not seem to make a great deal of difference. On the last day of term we sometimes had an egg for breakfast, but I do not remember seeing one at any other time.

We were, as a result of all this, ravenously hungry. It is difficult to believe at this remove, but on more than one occasion parties of us slipped out of school to scavenge in the surrounding fields. Carrots were wonderful, beetroot fine, turnips less so and raw potatoes quite unacceptable. We tried them all without doing much to relieve our pangs. Actually it is little wonder that we were underfed. Only recently my old friend Mike Farr told me that, when he was head boy, he came across the caretaker shovelling into the boiler piles of out-of-date ration books. The burden of wartime hunger was also exacerbated by A.J.'s lunatic obsession with fresh air. Dormitory windows had to remain open at all times. This was all very well in the summer but winter was another matter, and I have a vivid recollection of helping another boy carry his top blanket to the stairwell in order to shake off the snow.

One holiday, my alarmed mother took me to a doctor who diagnosed clinical undernourishment. In later years X-rays revealed that, like nearly half my generation, I was also suffering from TB. For the rest of that holiday, the summer term and the holiday following that, six months in all, I was sent to stay with my lovely 'Auntie' Hilda, one of my mother's childhood friends, in her beautiful (rented) Queen Anne house near Malvern. I was put on a special diet which included a daily quart of milk. Every morning I used to shut myself in the cold, slate-shelved pantry and make myself a deliciously sickening drink with the cream off the top of the two pints of milk and, dug out of sacks in the corner, some cocoa and brown sugar. Luckily my Auntie Hilda was an unscrupulous black marketeer.

My dislike of Hilda's husband, my 'Uncle' John, was mutual. For some reason he seemed to disapprove of me and to placate him I managed to find a temporary job with a local farmer, mucking out the pigs, helping with the harvest and so on. It was extremely hard work, but it earned approval all round and I soon got used to the smell of pig muck. I even helped drive a cow to Worcester market one day. The farmer had agreed to pay me fifteen shillings (75 pence) a week but when, on my return to school, I presented him with a scrupulously made out time sheet and a polite request for three pounds he simply laughed. He glanced in an amused way at my figures, tore the paper in half and handed me a ten-shilling note. It was not the first time that I had been disillusioned by adult behaviour.

Six months away from school did little for me academically, and on my return I suffered the additional humiliation of being taken away from my late classmates and placed with the – despised, of course – juniors below me. Mathematics was particularly trying. This subject was taught by A.J. himself, and he hit on a clever way of emphasising and illustrating my stupidity in this department. I have what I then felt to be the misfortune to be distantly related to Sir Arthur Eddington, who was at that time Professor of Astronomy at Cambridge and one of the foremost physicists in the world. A.J. would dash off a theorem, turn from the blackboard bristling with malicious amusement and say, 'Eddington will, of course, tell us what it is that X is equal to!' The iron curtain in my mind had long since fallen with a clang and I could do no more than blush and stammer, at which A.J. would turn back to the blackboard with a sigh and dash it off again at double the speed. That did not help, and I would then be put into detention with extra work for Saturday afternoon.

At fifteen I made the mistake of falling in love, and the mistake was compounded by the fact that Ruth was only thirteen. Looking back, I can see that Sex must have been a hideous and ever-present worry for the staff but so far as I know, they had little to worry about. There was the usual smutty talk and tentative experimentation in the dormitories but, when compared with the horror stories one hears now about some single-sex boarding schools, it was really very innocent. By the law of averages we must have had our quota of homosexuals, but romantic interest was for most of us focused exclusively on members of the opposite sex. 'Truth and Honour, Freedom and Courtesy,' was the school's motto, quoted from Chaucer's Knight, and there is no doubt that it was those sentiments which governed our relations with the girls we fancied. We were chivalrous to a degree, and for a boy to touch a girl's breast on the outside of her stout school uniform was considered the ultimate in abandoned libertarianism.

Ruth was a lovely girl: tall and willowy, her fair hair touched with auburn, she had hazel eyes and the most enchanting freckles. Her voice was low and husky, and even from this distance in time I feel I was extremely lucky to have attracted her attention. After many courtly preliminaries we formalised our relationship by agreeing to become 'friends'. This was a state well recognised by our schoolfellows and, I think, by the staff.

Not by A.J. I was summoned to his study and confronted by what A.J. described as his extreme distaste for the spectacle of someone as senior as myself walking about with a girl so very junior. And not simply walking. He hinted at other activities which were entirely unacceptable in any establishment with a firm religious basis and insisted that these activities must be terminated forthwith, as must any connection whatsoever with the girl in question. With a prurient curl of the lip he lectured me at some length on purity of both mind and body.

I was dismayed and above all disgusted but, as usual when challenged by A.J., overwhelmed by a feeling of helplessness. It was not a court of law. He was not required to present any evidence. It was simply to be thus, and there was no appeal.

I suppose that to some people all this may appear a little absurd; we were children, and both my friend and I are now drawing our old age pensions, but I expect that she was as deeply wounded as I, and when I look back on the matter I feel the same pain and anger. That Sunday I attended Evening Meeting as usual, sitting in the front row of the gallery exactly opposite A.J. Throughout that time of spiritual refreshment I directed towards him such a concentrated beam of hatred that I was surprised he did not drop dead on the spot.

It might be wondered that I still think of my school with affection and gratitude, but A.J. was by no means the whole story and even he had at least one supremely redeeming feature: he had a keen appreciation and wide knowledge of classical music. The principal way in which he communicated this knowledge was by way of record concerts held in one of the rooms in the Old School next to his own house in the village, using the latest technology: a pile of seventy-eights and a wind-up gramophone. He would give a short talk on, say, Beethoven's Fifth and then play the records. The concerts were for the Seniors only and were cleverly arranged to take place a little later than any of the other school activities, so that, quite apart from any aesthetic pleasure that the music might give us, we had the agreeable sensation of privilege.

It was an unforgettable experience to walk the quarter-mile back to our dormitories on 'the hill' after everyone else had gone to bed, one's head filled with the greatest music in the world. The air was crystal-clear five hundred feet up there on top of the Cotswolds and, with no artificial light because of the blackout, the stars shone with a brilliance that would be difficult to find now.

The headmistress, the austere Miss Burgess, taught us English, and at her hands I was seized by a passion for Shakespeare which has fortunately never left me. She also directed the school play, and it must have been her production of *The Wind in the Willows* that entranced me and reconciled me to the Boarding School Experience at the end of my first term, much as music had warmed me to the school in Penzance. I was later recruited for some of the plays myself and discovered that being on a stage and making people laugh was the most tremendous fun and actually, it seemed to me, rather easy.

Some of our, quite legitimate, activities were extra-curricular and some of the ones which were not were, we flattered ourselves, unknown to the authorities. Halfway up the village street lived Joe Canning and his family. Joe was a smallholder who kept a few cows in a meadow on the other side of the street. He had a milk round and a charming tenor voice and was an essential performer at all the local functions. Why his wife Min was so wonderfully hospitable I do not know. We did help the Cannings with some of the haymaking and rounding up the cattle (milking I never quite mastered), and we did take a hand now and again churning illicit butter, with lookouts posted up and down the street in case the Min of Ag and Fish made an unwelcome appearance, but we would spend hours of our spare time sitting in the Cannings' kitchen, arguing and drinking tea. Joe was a combative and eloquent political polemicist. There had been a time when I could not have enough sugar in a cup of tea, but at this time both tea and sugar were rationed, of course. 'You come up yere and drink my bloody tea,' he would say in his ripe Oxfordshire accent, 'and you drink it without any bloody sugar!' I have since become so sensitive to sugar in tea that I can tell if a cup has not been washed properly. Joe also taught us to smoke Woodbines and how to blow the most expert smoke rings. I am now a dedicated member of the anti-smoking lobby but, curiously, the ability to blow smoke rings has stood me in good stead. In Noël Coward's *Private Lives*, at one point the hero has to spend some time on the stage alone doing just that. I do not suppose that there are many actors apart from Coward and myself who have been able to do so.

Nocturnal visits to the Cannings were not my only extra-mural activity. Seated on the saddle of one of the day boys' bicycles while he stood on the pedals, I tore down a frighteningly steep hill and then trudged up the opposite side of the valley to a pub called The Gate Hangs High. There I threw a football sweater over my shoulders, the sleeves knotted at the wrist, and slipped a quart bottle of beer down each sleeve. Another quart went into each blazer pocket and I held one more in each hand. We then returned to our club behind the boys' common room and had one or two wicked drinks. Naturally we exaggerated the effects of our orgy considerably and my talent for histrionics was exploited to the full; the dormitory was much amused.

Unfortunately, the sister of one of the members of the dormitory was head girl. She saw it as her duty to report the matter to Miss Burgess, who relayed it to A.J. Again I found myself on the carpet. For once, perhaps because this time I really was guilty, I fearlessly and emphatically protested my innocence. 'Beer, certainly,' I said, with an appearance of transparency, 'But, sir,' I went on cleverly, 'ginger beer, sir. Ginger beer.' To my amazement he seemed to believe me, saying that I was very wicked and must never do it again. Not even a thousand lines. In a vain attempt to instil in me a sense of responsibility I had not long before been made a prefect, and I have reflected since that I probably had him at a severe disadvantage. As a recently elected member of the Headmasters' Conference he could hardly be seen to sack someone for drunkenness. Not from a Quaker school. Not a prefect.

The dangers of smoking were not as well recognised as they are today. An occasional cigarette was tolerated at home, and I had told my mother all about the Cannings; she had in fact given me a lighter for my fourteenth birthday, and one term she sent me back to school with a packet of twenty. 'I know very well that you are going to smoke, and I would rather know how many,' she said.

On the first day of that term A.J. gave the assembled school a stimulating lecture on the general deportment he expected of us in the coming days, during the course of which he said he knew that some of us intended to smoke cigarettes and he expected those who possesed a stock to surrender them. He dwelt at some length on the honour of the school and on the beauty of truthfulness. Despite many outward appearances there must have been in me a serious core, and I took an appeal to my honour and truthfulness seriously. Dutifully I surrendered my packet. I was a little disappointed not to be congratulated on my honesty, but after lunch A.J. once again demonstrated his capacity to astonish.

At one end of the dining hall was a raised platform on which stood the staff table and a lectern. From this lectern A.J. delivered to the assembled school a stinging and lengthy public anathema on my disgraceful conduct, a rebuke which fell just short of ignominious expulsion. I do not know what the effect on my schoolfellows was, but I myself decided that in future appeals to my honour would be treated with caution.

The war ground on. For most of us it was not the exciting experience that some people imagine. Not enough food was its main feature, followed by drabness. Even if new clothes and fresh paint had been obtainable the use of them would have been frowned upon. On the counter of every shop was a large notice headed 'NO' above a comprehensive list of the goods of which they were out of stock. The headmaster caused some amusement one day when he lectured us on our excessive use of lavatory paper which our brave merchant seamen had risked their lives to bring across the submarine-infested ocean. Next Sunday night, during the Evening Meeting, we were abruptly reminded of the horrors of war when a Lancaster bomber crashed in a nearby field during a snowstorm and caught fire, its bombs exploding and its machine guns rattling for the next half-hour. The rear gunner was trapped in the upraised tail and those who witnessed it were unwilling to talk about it.

Paradoxically, I often associate long, lazy summer days with the rattle of machine gun fire. We sat at our lessons in the hot weather, the long concertina doors of the classrooms drawn back to give a view of Mrs Johnstone's lovingly tended flower beds, the playing fields and the hills beyond while overhead planes towing yellow targets flew back and forth pursued by trainee gunners.

One of our girls, a Dutch Jew who had had the good fortune to escape from the Nazis with her mother, disappeared in the middle of one term. Their house in Southampton had been bombed and her mother killed. By this time the restaurant at Chesil Court in Chelsea had closed its doors and our sybaritic life there had come to an end. I went flat-hunting with my mother one day, and when we reached the address there was simply a hole in the ground. Each floor projected about two feet from the wall of the house next door, ornaments still standing on a mantelshelf, a wardrobe leaning out, the clothes in it hanging over the void.

We went to live in part of a house near Sloane Square, and every night during the air raids we crouched in a space under the stairs which we shared with a Franco-Indian family. Elsewhere, of course, people were much closer to the dangers, not just the discomforts, of war.

It did not occur to me that I might be horribly wounded, but I did think I might be killed; indeed, the possibility seemed very real as the bombs crashed and thundered all round us. One device that the Germans used on the bigger bombs was apparently designed to frighten, and it worked very well. A kind of whistle attached to one fin, it produced a terrifying noise like an express train tearing down at you from the skies, ending in a crash which shook the whole district and a sound as though a giant hand was tearing down the entire glass front of Peter Jones's department store. Each morning I was amazed to find Peter Jones still intact.

The end of my school career marched steadily closer. I ought to have been deeply apprehensive, but for some reason I remained calm. I had enjoyed being at Sibford very much but, having been educated for thirteen years, I felt ready to do something else. What that something was I had simply no idea.

A.J. helped, in a negative sort of way. I received the summons to his study.

'Eddington,' he began, 'what are you going to do when you leave school?'

'I don't know, sir.'

'I think you have sufficient mathematical ability to enter a bank.'

It would be understating the case to say that I was astounded.

Quite apart from the fact that my School Certificate results were embarassingly modest, A.J. had himself poured liberal measures of scorn on my mathematical abilities almost from the moment of my arrival.

'Have you considered banking?' he continued.

'No, sir.' For the first time in our acquaintance I was firm.

'No?' He seemed surprised himself.

'No, sir.'

There was no more to be said, so I left.

3

Every Night Something Awful

The year was 1943, and the world was my oyster. It was the middle of the war, so in theory there should have been a wide choice of work. But I was very aware of the danger of becoming trapped by the comparative poverty in which my parents had found themselves, so there was at least one criterion which I felt had to be met: whatever job I took would have to offer the prospect, however distant, of earning a comfortable amount of cash.

Mother and I were living at the time in a minute bedsitter, with an even smaller spare room for me, in the Edgbaston district of Birmingham. With a sense of timing which I hope and believe I did not inherit, she had fled the London Blitz just in time for the Birmingham one.

Like many in that area the house was divided into small flats, and by a wonderful stroke of luck our neighbours were an extremely congenial group of single women, two of whom became lifelong friends. Ruth Maguire was a highly placed civil servant and Nora Ansell was a cashier, a job she utterly despised. Both women were passionately artistic; Ruth was a keen musician and Nora regarded herself, as we all did, as principally a painter and sculptor. All four of us were in and out of each other's flats, and long and enthralling evenings were spent discussing the latest novels, biographies, paintings and concerts. It was possibly the most pleasant ambience in which my mother and I had found ourselves.

I came in very handy as an artists' model for Nora and her friends, and in consequence my appearance at that time is well documented. The fact that my grandfather had been a painter, together with all this artistic activity, provided me with another job criterion: it must have an aesthetic dimension. I would really have liked to be an artist

33

myself, but I had always understood that the life of a painter involved, to begin with anyway, a certain amount of starving in a garret; as I have said, I did not intend to starve again, in a garret or anywhere else, if I could possibly help it. I was also very interested in both music and architecture, but I had always believed that both those disciplines required a talent for mathematics – and over the years A.J. had drummed into me the belief that a talent for maths was something which I did not possess.

My sister Shirley was at this time working on a farm not far from Birmingham. Lodging there in order to escape the bombs were another couple who became lifelong friends. John and Eirene Peet were both teachers but Eirene was working temporarily as a personnel manager at Lewis's, the big local department store (which had, alas, no connection with the well-known London shop). She suggested that I could probably get a job there in Display, a euphemism for window dressing. I thought that this was not at all a bad idea. I wanted a job that had something to do with art and yet was also commercial; what could be more logical than commercial art? Before too long I found myself a junior member of the Display Department at thirty-five shillings (£1.75) a week.

There is something slightly risible about the job of window dresser but I thought then, and still think, that it is a vastly under-rated calling, bracketed in the public mind with male modelling and ballroom dancing. Imagine the changed appearance of our high streets if the same standards were applied to windows as are applied to theatre design, let alone to pictures or sculpture – with the added discipline that the goods displayed would have to look saleable. Window display is possibly the most accessible form of art in existence, apart from architecture. Like architecture, it can be viewed for nothing, by anybody, with the added advantage that because of its ephemeral nature the exhibition is constantly changing. If window design were recognised as an art form alongside the theatre and ballet, and its practitioners reviewed in the daily newspapers as are actors and painters, our surroundings would be transformed.

At Lewis's Ltd, however, such aesthetic considerations were entirely foreign. For a window dresser there the daily round consisted of pinning material to dummies – 'yardage' it was called – strewing paper flowers around the place and giving orders to the printing department for price cards. Our leader, who bore a close resemblance to Dr Crippen, was Mr Acton, a small, harassed man with greying hair and a Hitler moustache. He and his deputy, a slightly larger man with a flushed face and a ginger moustache, kept order with difficulty. There was a severe manpower shortage and all the male employees were ineligible for the armed services, being either too young or too old, or in some way disabled. There was much bunking off, sending oneself on needless errands and having a quick smoke in corners of the windows invisible to members of the passing public.

I disliked the place heartily, and in ways that must have been extremely irritating I did not take too much trouble to conceal my dislike. There was an attitude of 'We're all terrifically lucky to be members of the most wonderful firm in the world!' that irked particularly and must have been a hangover from the days of the Depression. Attempts were frequently made to boost morale in this way, but they fell on stony ground so far as I was concerned because our friend Eirene had told us the truth about the store. Before the war the assistant general manager, Mr Leek, used to spend his Saturday mornings touring the departments and arbitrarily sacking a few employees in order, presumably, to encourage the others. On Saturdays there would be queues, she said, of anxiety-ridden junior managers outside the staff lavatories. My impression was that the management deeply regretted the fact that they could no longer behave in that way. In only one circumstance could they still do so: if an employee so much as breathed the phrase 'trade union' he or she was instantly dismissed.

My mother's influence and my Quaker upbringing had made me a pacifist, and the first test of my convictions came one day when the under-manager rattled a tin can under our noses and suggested that we should contribute to the Spitfire Fund. I took a deep breath and declined. The shock and bafflement were severe, but in that splendid British way everyone else took a deep breath too and I was written off as a harmless eccentric.

My disillusionment with the idea of a career in commercial art, as represented by Lewis's Display Department, seemed a dismaying development. It was at this moment that an old scholar of Sibford told me that one of the girls with whom I had acted in a school play had decided to be a professional actress, and had started a course at the Royal Academy of Dramatic Art. I have some inkling of the effect of St Paul's experience on the road to Damascus; I knew immediately that I would be a professional actor.

I cannot imagine why I had not thought of it before; acting was the one thing which I had done well at in school and which I had enjoyed, but of course it was not on the curriculum. I do not suppose that it is on the curriculum of many schools which are not specifically designed to teach drama. Neither I nor anyone in my family had any money for a drama school; we were curiously ignorant of the entire world of higher education. I think it was only my sister who had any notion of it at all, managing to send herself to a teacher training college through the influence of our friends at the farm where she worked. I decided that the only way I could reach my destination would be by practical experience, paying my way as I went. Firstly, though, I had to find out a bit more about the stage.

With no money and no time – my nine-to-five job at Lewis's only kept body and soul together – it was a puzzle to know how to go about matters. But nothing now could daunt me, and I knew that if I thought long enough and hard enough I should be shown the way. Clearly I could not become a professional actor without preparation, so perhaps one solution might be to start as an amateur actor. I heard from someone that the best amateur theatre in Birmingham was the Crescent, not far from the city centre. I was told that it was a company of which Laurence Olivier had been a member when in his teens. This was good enough for me, so on my day off I hastened to its shabby doorstep and rang the bell.

'I would like to be an actor, please,' I said to the small, plump man who opened the door.

His eyes widened and he seemed to grow a couple of inches in every direction. He stood back to allow me through. 'Come in, dear,' he breathed.

Thursday night at the Crescent was bar night; for the next few months I decorated the bar but did little else. I had intended that at the very least I should learn the mechanics of stagecraft. As things turned out I just about grasped the fact that stage left and stage right were right and left from the actors' point of view and not that of the audience; that was all.

The members who used the bar were divided into two groups – bar left, as it were, and bar right – and they stood as far from each other as possible. I was recruited to, and made very welcome by, the right-hand group. This was formed by some beautifully dressed and lightly scented men, young and old, and a handful of mostly older women who reminded me a little of our friend Gwynedd Lewis, except that they seemed to lack entirely Gwynedd's lovely sense of boisterous fun. They wore tweed suits, collars and ties and their grey hair was clipped short. Bar left consisted almost exclusively of large, hairy men with handlebar moustaches which were as curly as their pipes. Between puffs they cast what seemed to me malevolent glances towards bar right, to which our group responded with aristocratic disdain.

From time to time over a period of several weeks bar nights were interrupted by special committee meetings of some sort, the nature of which I could never discover. At these times the temperature in the bar rose, with many a muttered aside, and the rate of malevolent glances and scornful responses increased noticeably. It was not until long after I had ceased to be a member that I discovered that it was myself who was the cause of the unrest. The assumption of the bar left party had been that I was not only the darling of the bar rights but the particular darling of the company's producer, the person who had originally given me such a glowing welcome on the doorstep; and that I was, moreover, the latest in a long line of such decorative drones.

This explained why the matter of actually doing some acting had never seemed to arise. True, I was eventually given a minute part as an effeminate policeman in Ivor Novello's *Full House*, which we performed in a tent during an amateur arts festival, but even the small effect that my brief appearance had was diminished by the play's title, which persuaded most passers-by that there was not much point in trying to book seats.

One bar night, a heterosexual couple who evidently felt themselves to be above the fray enquired of me whether, if I really wanted to be an actor, I had thought about ENSA. The Entertainers' National Service Association was a body formed to entertain members of the armed services and generally raise morale by putting on mostly variety shows and concert parties at home and abroad. There was also, however, a Drama Division whose headquarters was at the Theatre Royal, Drury Lane. So, enthusiastically accepting my friends' suggestion, I drew a few pounds out of the Post Office, took a day off from work and bought a return ticket to London.

At the stage door I used the same formula that had proved so successful at the Crescent: 'Please, sir, I would like to be an actor.' I took for granted that it would work, and surprisingly it did. I was directed to a tiny office into which a desk had been crammed and behind which sat a large man with a beard. After a few preliminaries he handed me a copy of *George and Margaret*, a recent West End success, and told me to take it to the canteen and read the love scene between the two young people. Having done so, I was to return and read it to him. I did so, reading the part of the young man while the bearded man read the part of the girl.

Evidently satisfied by what he had heard, he directed me, if I so desired, to report to an address in the garrison town of Colchester the following week and join the company of *Jeannie*, another recent West End success. I would be an assistant to the ASM, the assistant stage manager, the lowest form of theatrical life – and play the part of a waiter in the play. My pay would be five pounds a week, from which thirty-five shillings would be deducted for my keep.

I did so desire. Desire flowed through my veins like flame and I sped back to Edgbaston to be greeted by an admiring circle, as proud and delighted as I was myself. But one small cloud hovered at the back of my mind – trivial enough, no doubt. I was a pacifist. Would I be helping the war effort? Certainly the authorities thought so, but I discovered that if you want to do something badly enough it is always possible to find a very good reason for doing it. I reflected that the members of the Friends' Ambulance Unit did their best to heal soldiers' bodies and that what the soldiers did with their healed bodies after that was their own business. What is good enough for the Quakers, I thought, is certainly good enough for me, and the next morning I returned to Lewis's solely in order to take my leave. I did so without regret, and I expect that the feeling was mutual.

I returned, too, to the Crescent to thank the couple who had given me such good advice and to bid farewell to my bar acquaintances, who had at least provided the place where it was given. I drew the producer aside and thanked him for his help. He drew me a little further aside, clasped me to his bosom and gave me a kiss on the lips, lengthy and wet. I struggled free and ran all the way home, spitting as I went.

The company I joined at Colchester had been touring, more or less together, for about a year and the cast had originally been headed by James Mason. He had not been popular amongst his colleagues for various reasons. He kept himself aloof from the others, never went with them to the pub, they said, and even took his apparent disdain for the whole task to the extent of refusing to take curtain calls, an unforgivable sin in their eyes (and in mine). He was also a pacifist. Matters were exacerbated by the fact that he travelled with his wife, Pamela, who sat every night in the men's dressing room typing replies to James's fan mail. Some of ENSA's actors were elderly members of the profession who had been unable to get any other work, and this evidence of his enormous success made them very uncomfortable.

Mason had been succeeded by Eric Portman, who had played the part in the West End run. He was as popular as Mason had been unpopular; generous and unassuming. Ten pounds a week was the maximum salary, and apparently he used to take everyone to the pub on pay day and spend it all. I imagine that some form of exemption from military service was offered to distinguished actors in return for an annual stint in ENSA – which may, incidentally, have been the last occasion on which government recognised the importance of the arts. But Portman did his stint with good grace.

Leading the company which I joined was David Farrer, who had made several films not long since. He was a large, good-looking man who smoked a pipe, wore tweeds and did his job well and without fuss. Undoubtedly the most flamboyant member of the company was Peter Upcher. Peter was primarily a singer who had made a considerable reputation entertaining the troops in South-eastern Europe during the First World War. Women were not then permitted to travel abroad and Peter had sung the female roles in many a light opera, earning himself the sobriquet 'Balkan Liz'. He was a big man with bright gold hair and copiously rouged cheeks, and most days he wore a sky-blue tweed plus-four suit. We were always a little on edge in case he should commit some indiscretion which would remove him from our midst. This was not so much for Peter's sake as for our own, since we would have had to find an instant replacement, but he usually managed to extricate himself – even on the night he was discovered with a sailor in a Portsmouth telephone box.

The company manager, Ambrose, was decidedly creepy. He was a tall, bony man whose principal article of faith was that soap was harmful to the skin – and to the fingernails, so far as I could see. He carried with him a powerful body odour and in his luggage were two heavy volumes of forensic science, containing horrific photographs of suicides and rapes. One of the actresses, a chirpy Scots girl, was his girlfriend and we could only suppose that she liked all that.

There was a woman stage manager, her deputy, an assistant and a deputy assistant, myself. My job, apart from serving dinner to David Farrer and his leading lady on the Scottish Express, was to stay behind after the show and help to dismantle the scenery. This was no light task. The play had three acts and eleven scenes: there was the kitchen of a stone cottage in Scotland, the rail of a Channel boat, the train dining car, the lobby of a Viennese hotel, the hotel lounge, a restaurant and the kitchen of a flat in Glasgow with the chairs, tables, cutlery, glass, china, linen and ornaments used to furnish them. All this fitted somehow into one lorry and the following day we would collect it, drive on to the next date and set it up again.

We toured the whole of England, Scotland and Wales and my family, when eventually I had one, sometimes used to get quite tired of the fact that we could never go anywhere that I had not been to already.

We took our play to military establishments of every kind, almost all of them for one night only. We visited army camps of every shape and size, airfields and naval bases, both ashore and afloat. I only ever saw one other ENSA show, given in the converted hold of a submarine depot ship in Scapa Flow. It was variety and I thought it was excellent.

Audiences varied considerably and each presented a different problem. The Army tended to rowdiness, with wolf-whistles and pressing invitations to the girls to 'Show us yer tits!' The RAF seemed generally good-natured, but the Navy was considered to be difficult. The first row would be the officers, sleeves heavy with gold lace. They would need to be thoroughly convinced before they laughed, and the seamen behind them made great efforts to suppress their natural liveliness.

Undoubtedly the worst audience was the Pioneer Corps. Half of them consisted of the scourings of the police courts and the other half of eastern European refugees, academics and artists, many of them non-English speakers, so one had the worst of both worlds: 'Show us yer tits!' on the one hand and on the other those who either despised the lack of intellectual content in the play or simply did not understand.

Alcohol occasionally exerted a malign influence on the show. One of our number was a middle-aged woman who played a small part in the first act and then had to wait an hour and a half until she was called upon to play another in the last. When she could, she whiled away the time between acts in the sergeants' mess and quite often made her second entrance very drunk, sometimes losing her teeth in the process. One night she not only got drunk but after the show took a prolonged farewell of a friend against the side of the coach, which gently rocked as we waited to return to our lodgings. One of our problems, or mine anyway, was that for the troops we were entertaining we were a fortnightly event and they usually seized the opportunity to throw a wild party. For us it was every night and we joined in heartily. At seventeen one does not get headaches and hangovers, but by the end of a year I was beginning to look forward to my first glass of ale in the morning in order, I felt, to clear the cobwebs away before loading up the scenery.

Lorna – I think that was her name – was a member of the company who seemed to have no particular function unless, perhaps, it was morale-raising in its simplest form. She was eighteen with blonde hair, blue eyes, a perfect figure, a charming smile – everything, in fact, needed for the show – and her very appearance silenced the wolf-whistlers before they could draw breath.

I had reached an age at which my metabolism was beginning to insist on my finding out about sex. I had indulged in an occasional fumble now and then, but nothing very significant. Once I had even had a romp with one of the company's girls on a bed in the hostel in which we were both staying – 'horseplay', it is called in the police courts – but had become disconcerted when my friend suddenly stopped struggling. Lorna had raised my morale at least as high as that of our audiences, and I felt that it was time I did something about it.

That week we were lodging in a hotel in Southsea and one morning I suggested that we would be much more comfortable chatting in my bedroom than in the lounge. I did so casually, in a way which cleverly disguised my intentions, but even so I was surprised at the readiness with which she agreed. Once in the bedroom I closed the door behind me and advanced on her. She retreated towards the bed, casting an amused glance over her shoulder as she did so. There was a gold-coloured eiderdown on the bed, quilted in a pattern of squares. 'Oh look!' she said with a delighted shriek, 'a pattern of squares!' and laughed in what I thought was a decidedly hysterical manner. I paused, frozen.

I knew that it was not necessary to be in love with someone in order to have sex with them. I did not love Lorna, for instance, but I had a feeling that if I made love to a woman she would almost inevitably fall in love with me. I have to admit that up to now I had looked on this possibility with some complacency, but with Lorna's wild laughter ringing in my ears a feeling of unease crept over me. Suppose she fell in love with me and turned out to be insane? A mad woman, hopelessly infatuated with me! The prospect was an uninviting one and there she was, flushed and expectant and standing by my bed. Laughing.

At that very moment the gong sounded for lunch, providing an admittedly rather feeble way out of my dilemma. 'I say, lunch, what!' I bleated. 'Shouldn't we, er, sort of go down?' Wet Sunday afternoons in the school library discovering P. G. Wodehouse had not, after all, been wasted. It was not until years later that I discovered that Lorna was at the centre of a web of devil-worshippers. I congratulated myself on a lucky escape. I could so easily have been turned into a toad.

A lodging house in Oswestry provided me with the next opportunity to lose my virginity, and this time I seized it without hesitation. It was another girl in the company who, with an enthusiasm which enchanted me, took me on my course of instruction, congratulating me on my manly prowess and my thoughtful use of a condom and suggesting with infinite tact and delicacy that the next time (there was going to be a next time!) I might do my best to make love to her, if at all possible, for something more than fifteen seconds. She was a Bristol girl, and like many of her fellow citizens possessed that striking combination of black hair and blue eyes and the creamy complexion that often goes with it. It is true that at twenty she may have been a little old for me, but neither of us felt that to be a bar.

The consequence, which could have been foreseen by anyone less green than myself, was that it was I who fell in love with her – and with all my heart.

We were somewhere in the Midlands when I received a summons to register for my 'medical', the first step to military service. Understandably, no one was given any assistance to register as a conscientious objector, but I happened to know that one could do so and, a little nervously, I took my place in the queue. There was no fuss and in the tolerant British tradition I was registered as a bona fide CO until proved otherwise. How much easier for an idealistic teenager to be shot; how hard to be tolerated. It did rather take the wind out of one's sails.

We were due to tour the south coast and, although we were not aware of it, D-Day was looming and we had to be provided with special identity cards to give us access to restricted areas. These were green instead of the normal buff and had to contain a photograph, so on our next visit to London I made my way to ENSA's own studio in one of the little rooms under the stage of the Theatre Royal.

It was the time when London was experiencing a very heavy bombardment from the first flying bombs, the V1s or 'doodlebugs', the nickname no doubt invented by the Ministry of Information to defuse some of the horror. One day I saw from the top of my bus a street in which every house had been destroyed; it was lined on either side with coffins. The nickname seemed to me to emphasise the horror rather than diminish it. There were so many V1s that the authorities had given up sounding the sirens every time there was an attack, and at the exit from Covent Garden tube station there was simply a small red notice which read: AN ALERT IS IN PROGRESS.

I sat on my stool in the studio and the young woman photographer told me to sit slightly sideways and then look straight at the camera. As I did so the Imminent Danger bells rang out all over the theatre. The corridors were immediately thronged with a chattering crowd as everyone left whatever they were doing in order to take cover. The distant drone became a thundering roar as the bomb approached, sounding like fifty ill-maintained motorcycles without silencers. The bombs were designed so that when they reached their destination, roughly London, they simply circled until they ran out of fuel. Our bomb began its circle and the roar lessened slightly, rising again as it returned.

This was evidently all in the day's work for my photographer. 'Keep quite still,' she said above the noise. I stared at the lens, trying to look brave. Suddenly there was complete silence and the V1 began its descent. The camera went click, to be followed by an enormous explosion a couple of streets away.

It is pleasant for me to think that I took some of my first steps as a professional actor at the Theatre Royal Drury Lane on one of the most famous stages in the world when we performed our play on tour there, even though to a dark and apparently empty auditorium. It cannot have been quite empty as the production was approved, and one warm April evening found us crammed into a third-class railway compartment on our way to Scotland.

The journey to Thurso, changing trains at Inverness, seemed endless and in fact took twenty-four hours, growing colder and colder as we travelled north. By daylight Thurso seemed like the end of the world, windswept and desolate. The last straw for some of my colleagues on the stage management was the fact that draught Bass was impossible to obtain, indeed had never been heard of. The next morning we boarded the *Earl of Zetland* and set out across the Pentland Firth for Stromness.

It was a glorious sunny day with rainbows playing round the bows and the sea was flat calm, an extremely rare phenomenon since the Pentland Firth is notorious as one of the roughest stretches of water in the world. The islands were low and green and Stromness harbour looked like a port one might find in the Adriatic, white houses clustered round the landing-stage, some rising straight out of the water.

When we arrived, a petty officer from one of the many naval establishments around Scapa Flow befriended the deputy stage manager and myself and invited us for a drink in the POs' mess when we visited his camp. In due course we did so, accepting a modest glass of beer. I drank mine quickly, as one of my duties was that of callboy. Before I left, however, he pressed me to join him in an illicit drop of naval rum. Mere politeness led me to agree and he poured me a generous tot – about half a tumblerful in fact. Time was getting on and I knew that the garrison theatre was about twenty minutes' brisk walk away on the other side of the huge camp, so I knocked back my rum and set off. I knocked on the door of the girls' dressing room and attempted to say, 'Half an hour, please,' but what came out was a mere suggestion of the right words. I pulled myself together and tried again at the men's dressing room door, with not very much more success.

Serving dinner on the Flying Scotsman was something of a nightmare. At the end of the show David Farrer said, 'Are you all right?'

'Perfectly,' I replied with dignity.

'I think you're drunk,' he said.

Some stars would have demanded my instant dismissal; I was lucky indeed that he was such a kindly man.

Later that night I have a recollection of going to yet another petty officers' mess about the size of the Albert Hall, where craggy old POs rose in turn to recite, through a haze of blue smoke, 'Dangerous Dan McGrew' and 'The Green Eye of the Little Yellow God'. I believe my girlfriend had to put me to bed.

Another night we did the show on an island which was little more than a bar of sand, with an RAF camp at one end and a fishermen's pub at the other. Only recently the island had been in the front line, suffering raids from German torpedo boats, and many of the men stationed there had served prolonged periods without leave. In consequence it was felt necessary to spirit the female members of the cast away the moment the curtain was down and place them under armed guard in the pub. We were thrown, as it were, to the sergeants' mess. During the course of the evening one of the sergeants made a beeline for me and engaged me deep in conversation. He was a small, plumpish man, not unlike the artistic director of the Crescent Theatre.

'Come to my cabin,' he kept saying.

'No.'

'Why not?'

'I'm not like that.'

'What do you mean?'

'I've got a girlfriend.' I had, too – she was under armed guard at the other end of the island.

'Well, so have I,' said the sergeant. 'Be modern!'

On one of the other islands I had a more sobering experience. Again, the island was a bar of sand, but this time with an army camp at one end and a sort of village hall at the other. It was the opening night of a man who had come to replace one of the actors in a major supporting role, that of a smooth foreign aristocrat determined to have his wicked way with the heroine. He had been rehearsing with us for the usual two weeks but confessed to me that he was finding things very difficult. He explained that it was a long time since he had appeared on a stage, having been filming in Hollywood for the past ten years. I was deeply impressed. A real Hollywood star! He certainly looked the part: tall, handsome, with beautifully cut tweeds and a splendid voice.

When the play started it quickly became apparent that the difficulty he had mentioned to me was in fact a severe case of stage fright. He had attempted to overcome this by slipping into the gents at the half-hour and drinking a quarter bottle of gin. He made his first entrance and stood there rooted to the spot, paralysed with fear and alcohol. He was unable either to move or to speak, and we watched from the wings with anguish as the prompter gave him the line. He repeated it slowly and stopped. He was given the next line and stopped again, and every one of his lines was dictated in the same way until at the end of the scene he was manoeuvred into the dressing room where attempts were made to revive him. The nightmare routine was repeated in subsequent scenes, and when he made his final exit he fell like a tree and was carried to his room.

Until then I had been living a dream, thrilled and proud to be an absolutely bona fide Professional Actor. I now felt bitterly ashamed; the reason for my colleague's collapse was transparently clear, and I was sure that everyone in the audience would now be feeling the deepest contempt for my new profession. The hall emptied at the end of the show and we on the stage management set about demolishing the set. Two young officers had stayed behind with a jeep to give us a lift to the camp for the obligatory party. I knew that there was only one exit and I realised that our still-unconscious drunk would have to be carried out under their noses. I begged them not to wait. They told me that it was half a mile to the camp. 'Good heavens,' I cried, 'It'll do us good! We've been stuck indoors all day.' No. They courteously insisted on waiting, and I have to confess that when the man was eventually carried out I was unable to face the scene and hid round the corner.

Up at the heavily blacked-out officers' mess I found myself, as luck would have it, sharing a drink with the commanding officer.

'Well, young man,' he said, 'and what branch of the services will you be joining?'

'I don't think I shall be joining any, sir,' I replied.

'Oh really,' he said. 'Why not?'

'I expect I shall be exempt, sir.'

'What, on medical grounds?' he probed.

'No, sir.' This capped the entire nightmare evening. 'I have registered as a conscientious objector.'

Beneath the small blue light hanging over the bar the CO's face took on a purplish tinge and I waited in trepidation for the roof of the Nissen hut to fall. I would not have been all that surprised if he had ordered an armed guard to escort me from the camp.

'Don't agree with you,' he said at last. He seemed to be in some difficulty himself. 'Don't agree with you. Admire your stand.'

I think I grew up several years in those few moments. Later, when I had calmed down and was able to think quietly about the matter, I wondered to myself in what other country in the world could such a conversion have taken place. France? The USA? At seventeen one is always right and I did not think then that I was wrong, but I did appreciate for the first time that people who did not think as I did could hold opinions with equal sincerity, and would be prepared to go to any lengths to preserve a society which would tolerate mine.

The war in Europe ended in May, for us in a flurry of snow. It did not make a great deal of difference materially except for the exhilaration of being able to turn on a light at night. No one who has not spent six years creeping about at night by the glimmer of a torch can appreciate the thrill of seeing street lighting.

On our last night in the Shetland Isles we played at the RAF camp at Sumburgh Head, on the southernmost tip of the main island. They gave us a lovely party, with dancing, but during it I felt increasingly unwell. My girlfriend called the MO who got me to bed in the camp hospital, and I bade her farewell. She said she would collect me in the morning and we would fly back to London. It was ten years before I saw her again.

The next day the doctor said I had a touch of flu, a touch of pneumonia (can one have a touch of pneumonia?) and a touch of one or two other things. In short, I was to stay where I was, and I spent an idyllic day in a small room at the head of an inlet, which I could see through the large window at the end of my warm, comfortable bed. I was ill enough not to want to move but not so ill as to be in any distress. The sky was blue and the water crystal-clear, as it is round those shores, and all day I watched the waves as they crashed up the inlet, sparkling in the sun. Whenever I feel stressed I often think of that scene.

The following day I was put into an ambulance and taken on the long, winding coast road to the military hospital in Lerwick. This had been converted from the old grammar school and I was given a bed in what had been a classroom overlooking the harbour. One of the first things I saw was a U-boat being brought in under the White Ensign. Because the war had ended and the number of troops had been scaled down, the hospital was almost empty. My ward had only one other patient in it, a diminutive, red-haired officer from a Scottish regiment who was looking forward with keen anticipation to being part of the army of occupation in Germany, where he would be able to requisition any number of luxury cars and have any German woman who took his fancy. I think he expected me to turn green with envy, and conversation was not easy. Luckily for me, though perhaps not for Germany, he was discharged after a couple of days and I had the more agreeable task of entertaining Matron, who was bored with so little to do.

She was unable to get out of her mind the terrible night when the *Royal Oak* was torpedoed in Scapa Flow and went down. She told me that the hospital was as empty as it was now, and that immediately she heard the news she had telephoned her opposite number at the naval hospital to offer her services. There the wards were full and casualties were stacked in the corridors. She told me that she had not been able to take any of them because that was a naval hospital and

47

this was a military one. She had met a member of my profession once before, when she had been matron of a hospital in the Middle East. 'A Mr Coward,' she said. 'He had come out to entertain the troops and went down with acute appendicitis. Oh, never again!' she added with feeling. 'Up days before he should have been, and round all the wards showing everybody his scar.'

After two weeks of this not unpleasant limbo I was discharged. I was looking forward to being wafted home by plane – I had not flown since my maiden trip in Cornwall – but instead I was put on a large passenger ship and sent off to Aberdeen to get the train. This time the Pentland Firth lived up to its evil reputation. The mattress on my bunk was just three inches short of the bunk itself, and as the boat pitched down the enormous rollers my feet would crash against the bulkhead. I then waited in fearful anticipation for the boat to rise up the other side of the wave and for my head to do the same. The whole effect was exacerbated by the fact that the man with whom I was sharing a cabin was copiously sick all night, in a basin just by my right ear.

I rose early and went on deck to get some air. I was leaning on the rail, breathing deeply, when there was a large disturbance just astern of us and, like Leviathan, a submarine rose to the surface. It was an appalling sight and I had to remind myself sharply that the European war was over.

At home I entered another sort of limbo. The *Jeannie* company had gone off to the Far East, but much as I would have liked to join them I was unable to do so because I had to wait for my tribunal, at which the judge would decide whether or not I was a genuine conscientious objector.

There were several categories of CO. If you were quite clearly a saint, your name was allowed to remain on the register without qualification. If you were obviously trying it on – and I believe a large number of people registered simply to get a few months' deferment – you were struck off and sent again for a medical. Most fell somewhere in between and were directed into some form of non-combatant service, down the coal mines or on the land.

I spent my time mustering support. You were allowed to present letters, the purpose of which was to testify to your sincerity, and one witness in person. I was lucky indeed to recruit as my witness my old senior master, Eric Parkin, the one who had done time in Oxford jail in the first World War, and I had some impressive letters, one of them from Major Sir George Dunbar, late of the Indian Army. Sir George had been one of my mother's clients at the Chesil Court restaurant and was typical of the many aristocrats of slender means who lived in the Chelsea of that time. The burden of his letter was that I was a bloody fool but there was, alas, no doubt of my sincerity. I had with some difficulty extracted one from Henry Oscar, the head of ENSA's Drama Division, who said that although it was not ENSA's policy to assist anyone who was attempting to evade conscription, the organisation would, however, have me back if the judge so directed.

I knew what would happen if the judge simply struck me off the register; I would be directed to attend a medical, I would refuse, committing an offence in the process, and would have to go to jail. Having served my sentence I would again be directed, would refuse again and be jailed again. This was no mere speculation but had happened to several people. I wondered whether he would try to trip me up with biblical quotations or trick questions, and remembered Lytton Strachey's tribunal in the the First World War when he had been asked by the judge what he would do should a German soldier rush in and attempt to rape his sister. 'I would interpose my body between them,' he had said.

The day came and I found myself at the back of a large school gymnasium. In front of us was a long trestle table with the judge presiding, flanked by a selection of Birmingham city worthies. I looked at the judge with some awe; I had been told that, some years before, as a barrister, he had led the unsuccessful defence in what I knew as the Blazing Car Mystery. I watched as he dealt first with about a dozen Christadelphians.

My sister and her husband became Christadelphians, and I know them to be good and loving people who live a far more Christian life than I do myself and whose knowledge of the Bible would leave most scholars far behind. I have to say, however, that the youths I saw that day were not very impressive. They all mumbled exactly the same thing as if having learnt it by heart, and the one witness they shared repeated it. They all spoke with the same broad Birmingham accent and, while there was of course nothing wrong with that, I felt it did not help them. The judge briskly sent them all to work on the land or down the mines.

I was proud to be an actor, and when it came to my turn I spoke up loudly, clearly and with an educated voice. There was an almost audible sigh of relief. 'Damn fool, but at least he's One of Us,' seemed to be the feeling. Outrageously unfair, I know, but I would hardly have been human not to have taken a little comfort from it.

'Well, Eddington, and what exactly are your objections to military service?' asked the judge without preamble.

Well, put like that I had not the faintest idea. I gulped, and I actually heard the sound rebound from the wall behind his head.

'Are they religious?' he asked helpfully.

Relief swept over me. 'Yes!' I said gratefully, and we proceeded from there.

Amongst other things he referred to Henry Oscar's letter. 'Are you willing to go to the Far East to rejoin your company?'

Was I not! There were several things working in my favour, the inaudibility and Birmingham accents of my predecessors being two of them, but the over-riding factor must have been the fact that the war was virtually over. True, it was rumbling on in the Far East and the atom bomb had yet to be dropped, but it was obvious that the end was in sight and so the accusation of cowardice – so easy to level, so difficult to refute – was not made. I emerged from the tribunal triumphant, ready to resume my march to fame and fortune.

The first thing I did was to send a telegram to Henry Oscar in order to relieve him of the anxiety he must have been feeling: I was free to return, I told him. Curiously, there was no response. I sent another. Silence. I decided that some misunderstanding must have taken place which could only be resolved by a more personal approach, so I took the train to London and made my way to Drury Lane.

They were very sorry, they told me, but there were no vacancies and, with great regret, ENSA would have to dispense with my services. Theatrical promises, I learnt that day, are promises that do not, after all, have to be kept.

Disillusioned, I returned home, thinking anxiously not only about my future, but of my poor girlfriend hacking her way through the jungle. I was in a considerable quandary. By law, the only job I was permitted to do was in ENSA; yet ENSA had refused to employ me. Neither I nor my family had any money and my mother was in no position to support me. I was just a vast cuckoo in her nest. I thought long and hard and eventually I pulled myself together and sent a letter to the Ministry of Labour and National Service, telling them that until ENSA could find a place for me I would have to find my own job.

4

Adventures in Rep

⋙⋘

Birmingham is celebrated for many things and amongst the most celebrated is the Birmingham Rep, the second oldest repertory theatre in the country. The repertory movement was started in Liverpool by Miss Horniman, heiress of the tea-importing family, at the turn of the century, and her initiative was followed in 1913 by that of Sir Barry Jackson, whose money came from a Midlands chain of grocery shops and who in the 1940s was still running the Rep.

It is to the repertory movement that Britain owes its dominance of the world of stage acting. At its most active the movement boasted several hundred theatrical companies up and down the country which turned out a different play every week, or in Birmingham's case every four weeks. With the luxury of four weeks' playing, and therefore four weeks' rehearsal – as much as the normal West End play gets – and with Sir Barry's artistically enlightened policy, Birmingham had managed to achieve a standard comparable to the best that British theatre had to offer.

It was to the Rep, therefore, that I gravitated, where I bearded a man called Peter Streuli. I was so full of life and energy and confidence that Mr Streuli simply did not have a chance. I felt that to achieve my ends I could have burst through a three-foot-thick concrete wall without difficulty, and I did not so much ask for a job as demand one. I was only moderately surprised when he succumbed almost immediately and did in fact make me an offer.

At that time the Rep supported a school of acting and some of the graduates of this school, under Sir Barry's aegis, were about to set off on a six-month tour of schools in the Midlands. One of their number had fallen out leaving a vacancy. They were touring two plays, *The Tempest* and *She Stoops to Conquer*. I was asked to play Antonio in the first, one of the servants in the second, and to assist with the stage management. I think I was offered seven pounds a week and I accepted with alacrity.

It was the hardest work I had ever done. At the end of those six months I vowed that I would never work as hard again and, although I have worked extremely hard since, I never have. The tour was hopelessly overbooked and generally mismanaged. We visited at least one different school every day, usually two and on two occasions three, some of them forty miles apart. We never knew when, or whether, we were going to eat or where we were going to lay our heads that night. I was the only member of the company who had had any professional experience, something I took no trouble to conceal. This may have given me a moment of gratification, but one of the consequences was that people expected me to know things of which I was in fact quite ignorant. No one in the company knew anything at all about electrical matters, for instance. Neither did I, but everyone stood back and waited for me to display my professional expertise. My first job on arrival was therefore to find the source and nature of whatever power was available and get the lighting plugged in. Then I would help unload and erect the scenery, set up the panatrope (the electrical sound effects), change and make up for the part I was going to play. In between entrances I would take charge of the prompt book.

Everything – actors, scenery, lighting, luggage – was packed some-how into one coach, which was driven by the company manager as inefficiently as he managed everything else. On one occasion when going down a steep hill he decided not to use the brakes but to go into reverse instead. The bus leaped into the air like a stag, the gearbox disintegrated and we arrived at the next date on tow.

One of our many embarrassments was the fact that most schools had evidently been led to expect the main Birmingham Rep company, not a motley crowd of novices, and added to the general awfulness was the feeling of our hosts that they had been had. The classics master at Marlborough College actually wrote an indignant protest to Sir Barry afterwards. Among the audience on that occasion was David Conville, future director of the Regent's Park Open Air Theatre and eventually best man at my wedding. He has not allowed me to forget it.

One morning – frequently the first performance took place in the morning – I was surprised to see a future star of *Emmerdale*, Toke Townley, jerking and grimacing during his first scene as Squire Hardcastle in *She Stoops to Conquer*. Presently Mrs Hardcastle was also jerking and grimacing. It turned out that the front row of our audience was armed with pea-shooters.

I think I was the only member of the cast to survive the tour without a disabling illness. One morning Hugh Manning, a future President of Actors' Equity, collapsed from what I suspect was exhaustion. He was playing Hastings in *She Stoops*. The finger pointed at me and, as we were lucky enough to have only one performance that day, I was able to spend most of it sitting in the coach learning his part. Unfortunately, as the girl playing Miss Neville and I were waiting in the wings to play a duologue scene vital to the plot, she too collapsed. There was no time for first aid so I laid her as carefully as possible on the floor and went on, playing the whole scene as a soliloquy.

After the tour had stumbled to its shameful end we were out of work again. Neither I nor anyone else had had a moment to wonder what we were going to do, and suddenly the immediate future became a matter of crucial importance. Sir Barry had been asked to take over the running of the Festival Theatre at Stratford-on-Avon (now the Royal Shakespeare Theatre) where I had done my first theatre-going. In his place at the Rep he had installed William Armstrong, and there was a rumour that Mr Armstrong might select one or two members of the Terrible Tour, as the survivors called it, to form the tail end of his new company. My luck held and I found myself part of the famous Birmingham Rep, a company of which almost every distinguished actor of those days except Gielgud had at one time or another been a member.

Sir Barry's 'Little Brown Playhouse' was a remarkable building. It seated only about five hundred, so its commercial viability was always precarious. The company had enormous prestige, having been in the forefront of the revolution in theatrical thinking early in the century, a revolution which popularised the plays of Ibsen, Shaw and others and enabled the theatre as a whole to take itself seriously once more and to serve again as a conduit for ideas. But one of the penalties for maintaining high intellectual standards in a small theatre is a constant worry about cash. A lot of front-of-house work at the Rep was done by volunteers, and actors are expected to work in such establishments for modest wages. I think my first weekly wage there was seven pounds, which was just about all right for me as I was still living at home in Edgbaston with my mother.

The Old Rep's small size did mean that it provided an intimacy and a rapport between audience and players which are hard to find elsewhere. This was much enhanced by the fact that there was no circle or gallery and that the auditorium was raked at an angle of forty-five degrees. For the spectator, every seat felt as though it was in the front row and actors made their entrances to find before them a wall of faces: a considerable extra worry for the nervous débutant but most interesting when one got used to it.

The design had its drawbacks; Sir Barry and his companion, Scott Sunderland, whom film fans will remember as Colonel Pickering in *Pygmalion*, would occupy gangway seats in the fifth row on a first night and Scott, a rather hectoring person with a very loud voice, would comment on the performances.

'He's good.'

'Yes.'

'Oh God, Barry, she's awful!'

'Ssh!'

'Well, she is.'

It would not be true to say that I had a part in the Christmas 1945 production, *1066 and All That*. I had eleven, and as the dressing room which I shared with several other actors was on the sixth floor and I had a change of costume for each part, I was kept pretty warm; on matinée days I ran up and down those stairs twenty-two times. It was probably as well, because that winter was one of the coldest on record and to compound matters it was a time of unprecedented austerity. Although the war was over, the economy was in ruins. Bread was rationed for the first time and power for domestic purposes was cut drastically. The dressing rooms were unheated – ours had a broken windowpane as well – and the electricity was not turned on until the half-hour, so if you had an elaborate make-up to put on you had to start by candlelight. In one of my few spare moments I looked out of the window, from which I could see the bomb site opposite that had been the theatre's costume store. It was deep in snow, with rats popping up, cruising along and then disappearing again.

Heading the cast of *1066 and All That* was the twenty-four-year-old Paul Scofield, whom I had already seen in three or four productions before I had joined the company. These had all been directed by the brilliant young Cambridge graduate Peter Brook, who was only twenty-one according to the press – for whom he remained twenty-one for several years. My first part in the season proper was as a butterfly in Karel Capek's *The Insect Play*. I have to say that I was rather pretty in those days and the more effete parts came my

My mother and grandmother, the
mistress of the workhouse

My mother entertaining the inmates
My father during the First
World War

As an altar boy with stout black boots and kirby grip

With my sister Shirley

Entirely unself-conscious on holiday in Cornwall, aged 7

Half-term at Sibford with my mother

Sketch done by Nora Ansell when I was seventeen

An early exercise in self-regard *(Lloyd Bates)*

Stage door, Birmingham Rep in 1945 (left: Toke Townley, far right: Alan MacNaughton)

Above: The one and only
Kate

Right: As Falkland in *The
Rivals* at Bath

Below: Off on honeymoon
with Tricia

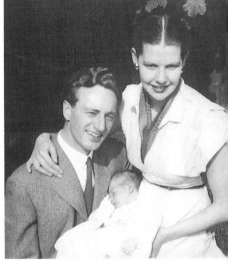

Left: A publicity shot taken during *Of Mice and Men* at the Bristol Old Vic *(Kevin MacDonnell)*

Above: With Tricia and our first son, Toby, 1954

Below: With Heather Chasen in *A Severed Head*, 1963 *(Iris Murdoch)*

Riding through the glen as . . .
Above: Will Scarlet
Below: The Lord of the Manor
(Dennis Edwards as the Clerk)
Above right: The Sheriff's Lieutenant (Alan Wheatley as the Sheriff)

Gemma, Toby and Hugo at
Albert Mansions

Tricia with Dominic

Would you buy a
second-hand car
from this man?
(*Brian Hawksley*)

As Jerry in *The Good Life (Anglia Press Agency)*

A candid camera moment with Richard Briers

A scene from *The Good Life* with Felicity Kendal, Penelope Keith and Richard Briers *(BBC Enterprises)*

way quite often. Luckily I was sufficiently self-regarding not to mind playing them.

William Armstrong was our chief and my mentor, which, my dictionary tells me, means 'experienced and trusted advisor'. A truly delightful man, he had spent the last thirty years as director of the Liverpool Rep where, amongst many others, he had 'discovered' Michael Redgrave. He seemed to me to be very old.

Willie or Billie, as he was known to everybody, was from Edinburgh and had retained its genteel tones. He was tall, thin, bronchial and took snuff, but he carried with him a unique aura of glamour. He had started his theatrical life in the last century as a member of Sir Herbert Beerbohm-Tree's company at the Lyceum Theatre, and he seemed to have known every great actor and actress in the intervening fifty years. He knew Shaw and Irving and had been a close friend of Mrs Patrick Campbell. He was undoubtedly gay, but he had a genuine love of young people which had no sexual overtones and he took infinite trouble to nurture such talent as we had.

Willie had a deep suspicion of overwork. When we were being directed by him we did not start very early in the day, broke soon afterwards for a long lunch, finished early in the afternoon and in between had frequent pauses for tea and coffee. Sometimes he would make an attempt to exert stern discipline. 'Oh, you naughty children!' he would cry. 'I'd beat you all if I didn't think you'd enjoy it.' The tea breaks were eagerly looked forward to, as they were often enlivened by his skills as a raconteur. He told us that, when he had played the messenger in Tree's *Macbeth*, he had reacted to Tree with looks and gestures which he felt to be appropriate. Tree took him aside later and said, 'Armstrong, during my scene, don't move a *muscle!*' He also talked of the last time he had met Mrs Campbell. It was in Paris, where, old and unwell, she was living in hostile retirement, as Shaw had said, 'Like a sinking ship, firing on her rescuers.' They spotted each other across the street and converged, arms outstretched.

'Billie!' she cried.

'Stella!' he exclaimed.

She stopped. 'No!' she said. 'Don't kiss me. The French are such gossips!'

After rehearsals and before the evening performance we would take tea in the foyer, the urn presided over by a lady named Geordie, forbidding in a white turban. One matinée, Laurence Olivier and Ralph Richardson had come talent-spotting and had lined up with everyone else for a cup of tea at the interval. As they reached the head of the queue she glanced up. 'Oh,' she said, recognising them. 'You two boys have got on!'

If a star was visiting Birmingham he or she would be sure to call on Willie. Nicky Bruce was a member of the company and I remember his mother, the great ballerina from the Ballets Russes, Tamara Karsarvina, coming to see us. Cameo brooches were in fashion then and the larger they were the more fashionable they were. Karsarvina's was the size of a dinner plate.

Willie was extremely kind and hated to disappoint people. Unfortunately his kindness sometimes led to misunderstandings, and promises he had made in order to make someone happy were not always kept. After the cast list for the next play had been put on the notice board, it was not unknown for rows to break out with demands made to see the director.

Willie managed to avoid this danger by waiting until all the company was on stage, taking the curtain call on the last night of the previous production. He would then creep down the stairs from his office with his hat, coat and muffler on and the cast list in his hand, a drawing pin already pushed through it. As the curtain rose and the applause rang out he would pin the list to the board, murmur, 'There, that's done!' and melt away into the night, to spend the weekend with the artist Laura Knight and Sir Barry at a house party in the safety of the Malvern Hills.

I came across him once having an asthmatic pause on a corner of the stairs. 'Oh, Paul,' he said with difficulty, 'I may see the daffodils, but I shan't see the roses.' The last time I saw him was two or three years later at the Malvern Festival. He was a delightful snob, and as we parted he told me mysteriously that he was 'staying with the aristocracy'.

I was crossing the foyer one day when I encountered Sir Barry himself.

'Ah, Eddington,' he said, removing from between his teeth the cigarette in one of the elegant paper holders he always used, 'saw the show last night. Very good, very good, very good.' He was evidently going to say something further. 'Have to get rid of those Birmingham vowels!'

I had had no idea. 'But Sir Barry,' I said, perhaps a little shrilly, 'I'm a Londoner!'

'Ha ha ha!' He replaced his cigarette and went on his way, leaving me, metaphorically speaking, sprawling on the cold marble.

The show that Sir Barry saw could not have been Eliot's *The Family Reunion*, because in that I was cast as a Eumenide and the Eumenides do not speak. Indeed they do not usually appear at all and E. Martin Browne, the doyen of verse-play directors at that time, said he thought it was a wonderful production except that the Eumenides should have been invisible. With his unvarying kindness, Willie had put on the cast list, 'Not many lines, but wonderful acting parts!'

I was, though, climbing steadily up those cast lists, and to my delight I finally found myself cast as George in Thornton Wilder's beautiful and under-rated *Our Town*. It is a play about very large subjects, like Life and Death, but told in such a deceptively simple way that sophisticated critics nowadays tend to get confused. Amongst other things it is a love story and cast opposite me was Miss Neville of the Terrible Tour, the one who had fainted in my arms just before our scene. Miss Neville – Jennifer – was an excellent actress, but at least as interesting to me was the fact that she had a mane of red hair, blue eyes, a creamy skin and a charming figure. She was not much more than sixteen and I fell heavily and, as it turned out, hopelessly in love.

My girlfriend of ENSA days from whom I had been separated when I fell ill at the end of the Shetland tour had since spent months trekking through the Malaysian jungle, and the rare letters I had received from her had hinted broadly (though not broadly enough for me) for a long time that All was Over. I got very tired of reading about the charming major who seemed to be escorting her everywhere and eventually I began to think of her as an ex-girlfriend. My goggle-eyed infatuation with her red-haired replacement was evidently difficult to disguise, and Willie was thrilled by the romance of it all. He took endless trouble over our scenes together. At one point in *Our Town* George is talking about his homework and, overcome by his feelings – feelings which, of course, I fervently shared – interrupts himself, saying, 'I love you!' Willie stopped us and told me that he was once playing a scene with Mrs Patrick Campbell and had had to utter those same words. 'Drop the octave, Billie!' she had said. 'Say what you have to say and then, dropping the octave, add, "I love you." It's an old trick, but it works.' Willie said that Mrs Campbell used to remind him to do it every night. After he had said the previous line she would whisper, 'Drop the octave!', and when he had done so she would add, 'Quite right. Very good.'

At Stratford, Sir Barry was planning to produce *Romeo and Juliet* and had asked Peter Brook to direct. Brook told him that he wanted a genuinely young pair of lovers and Willie suggested Jenny and myself. *Our Town* had been tremendously successful, Jenny and I were sixteen and nineteen respectively, and I at least was madly in love with her. The latter is by no means an advantage, of course, and could even be a major distraction, but I would be surprised if it had not influenced Willie.

In the event they decided to play safe and cast Laurence Payne, a mature, experienced actor, but rather unexciting I thought. I was there on the first night and, although filled with envy of the actors they had chosen, I was quite relieved in hindsight. Romeo is a fiendishly difficult part and, in that production at any rate, anyone would have been overshadowed by Paul Scofield's enthralling Mercutio. The play 'ended', as it so often does, with Mercutio's death. Sir Barry had taken Brook to see Bernard Shaw to ask his advice on the production. 'Get your fights right!' was all that Shaw had said. The fights were certainly thrilling. I tightened my belt and resumed my pursuit of stardom.

It is taken for granted nowadays that experiments in Shakespearian production began in the sixties and seventies and that until then everything was resolutely 'traditional', Shakespeare being played in some approximation of the original doublet and hose with occasional imaginative forays into jewelled boots and plumed head-dresses in Regency times. But this is not true, and between the two world wars Sir Barry Jackson had created something of a sensation in theatrical circles by presenting a series of Shakespeare plays in modern dress. Willie reminded Birmingham's theatre-going public of this remarkable innovation by presenting *Timon of Athens* in modern dress and I was lucky enough to be cast in the small part of the Painter, one of the artists being sponsored by Timon.

It coincided with one of my first attempts to give up smoking, a hopeless attempt because my friend Geoff Heaton, playing another artistic sponger, and I had to smoke in our scene. It was all the more hopeless because of the postwar shortage of commodities of every sort. Cigarettes were like gold dust, and the ones we smoked were only obtainable because they were a brand called Spanish Shawl, heavily scented and quite disgusting. Our scene was the first one, and when the curtain rose to reveal us inhaling deeply there was a gasp of envy. This quickly turned into a gasp of dismay as the smoke rolled into the auditorium.

I was asked to understudy Brian Oulton as Lord Trinket in *The*

Way of the World. The idiom of Restoration plays is notoriously elusive and learning them can be an ordeal. Brian was in excellent health and there seemed little likelihood of my having to go on for him and, cudgel my brains as I might, I just could not get the words in without incentive. Very unprofessional, but there it was.

Brian and his wife, Peggy Thorpe Bates, spent the weekend in London and that Monday the day hardly dawned at all as thick fog rolled over the Midlands and the southern half of England. I glanced out of my bedroom window with apprehension and over breakfast had yet another look at the play. As the day wore on my looks grew longer and more concentrated, but by the evening I still had only a very sketchy idea of the part. The half-hour found me sitting in Brian's dressing room, costumed, made up, bewigged and with my sword at my side. I had gone beyond panic and was coldly determined to play Lord Trinket or die in the attempt. At the quarter, twenty minutes before curtain-up, Brian put his head round the door. 'I thought I wouldn't phone,' he said. 'Easier to just press on.' I have never had the nerve to understudy since.

Brian's coolness had already deeply impressed me. On his first day, rehearsing Malvolio in *Twelfth Night*, he just did it, without so much as a glance at the book.

'How on earth did you learn it so quickly?' I asked.

'Oh, it's just one of those plays one knows,' he replied. 'Isn't it?'

Meanwhile my pursuit of Jenny was not going well. I was more or less accepted as her boyfriend, publicly at any rate, but that was as far as it went. As my ardour increased, so did her coolness. Her parents vigorously discouraged our association. Her father, a victim in his youth of polio, struck me as a bitter man and also quite outstandingly boring. Her mother felt, as so many mothers do, that any suitor of her daughter who was not also heir to the throne was really wasting his time. Now, of course, I am very grateful to them, but I went through agonies of unrequited love at the time.

I had been at the Rep for about two years when I received a long buff envelope marked 'Ministry of Labour and National Service'. I went cold.

I knew quite well what the letter contained. I had been directed by the judge to rejoin ENSA and I had not done so. This was my long-delayed summons to undergo a medical prior to being called up for National Service. I would, of course, fail to appear and eventually I should have to go to prison. As my thoughts raced on I turned the letter over and over, holding it up to the light and trying to see what was in it without actually opening it. At last I summoned up my courage. It said that, as I had now fulfilled the conditions of my exemption, I was free to find my own job.

My second year at Birmingham was coming to an end. I have never been very ambitiously forward-looking and have always been amused to read articles by actors who say things like, 'And then I decided to broaden my experience by making a few films in Hollywood', but I was galvanised into action when Jenny mentioned that she was going to do a season at the Connaught Theatre, Worthing. Anguished, I wrote to the director, Guy Verney, and begged him for an interview. He gave me one, and I managed to get a job at Worthing too. Jenny's heart must have sunk – and sunk further when I triumphantly announced that I had got digs in the same house.

Number 23 Alfred Place is a charming Regency cottage, just behind what was then Warne's Hotel. Kate Williamson was our hostess – 'landlady' was a description she did not accept – and it was clear from the start that number 23 was Liberty Hall. She took me to the top of the house to show me my room. It was at the back, overlooking the tiny, flint-walled yard. On the landing she removed her briar pipe and pointed to the other door: 'That's Jenny's room.' There was a pause. 'There are only two rooms on this landing.' She looked me in the eye. 'A double room would come cheaper,' she said.

At about five o'clock the next morning I rose from my (single) bed like a rocket. The most horrendous crash seemed to rock the house, and for the next hour similar crashes rebounded from wall to wall. When I staggered down to breakfast I asked what on earth had been going on. Kate was puzzled for a moment, but eventually she said it must have been the Co-op milk depot next door where they were loading empty bottles on to a metal-lined lorry. They did it every morning. Curiously, having been given a reasonable explanation I was never disturbed by it again.

My education at Alfred Place had only just begun. As I sat down, my foot encountered something very substantial. I looked under the table and found a large portion of what Kate told me was a horse. She had a friend at Smithfield who helped her to supply pet food for many of the local dogs, Kate's amongst them. Her dogs' names were Ace, King, Queen, Jack and Ten. 'Joker died,' she explained. Not that the dogs were the only consumers. 'You've heard of steak tartare, haven't you?' she said, as she carved off a slice and ate it.

It will be clear from all this that the Connaught Theatre was severely upstaged by life at Alfred Place, but the theatre was a pleasant place to be, despite being extremely hard work. Unlike Birmingham, which ran each play for four weeks, at Worthing we changed over weekly.

What this meant in practice was that on Tuesday morning, usually at ten o'clock, the company would begin rehearsing a new play, breaking, according to union rules, not later than two hours before the curtain was due to rise on the evening performance. If it was due to start at seven o'clock, therefore, rehearsals would finish at five. There was always a mid-week matinée, usually at two-thirty and usually on Wednesday, so the second day's rehearsals would be from ten-thirty until twelve-thirty. Thursday was the same as Tuesday and Friday the same again. Saturday was another short day's rehearsal because of the Saturday matinée, and then on the following Monday the rehearsal hours were the same. That evening, after a gruelling dress rehearsal, we would give the first performance. The following day, Tuesday, the cycle would start again.

Your spare time – that is, the time between rehearsal and performance and between the end of the performance and the following day's rehearsal, and of course Sundays – would be spent learning your lines. There were times when I would put the book down and turn out the light before going to bed, only to realise that for the last half-hour a light had not been necessary because dawn had broken. Casual acquaintances would sometimes ask, 'What is your work?'

'I work at the Rep,' you would say.

'Yes, I know that. But what do you do during the day?'

Despite all this we still found time to have a lot of fun and cards after supper were played with great concentration, late into the night. This was made easier by the fact that Kate herself was a keen player and never in all the years I knew her did she go to bed, sitting up instead in her large, comfortable armchair. One night, one of my former colleagues from Birmingham joined us; he was on tour at Brighton. We had a very merry time and a drop or two to drink. No one was as conscious then as we are now of the perils of drinking and driving, and when he left it was by car. Turning left at the end of Alfred Place, instead of right for the Brighton Road, he spent a puzzled night on the beach.

Alfred Place, though its dwellings were humble and discreet, is at the smart end of Worthing and at that time tended to attract the demi-monde – ourselves included, of course. All Kate's acquaintances, male or female, were divided into two groups: Camp and BM. BM stood for Bloody Manly, but it did not necessarily depend on sexual orientation. If you were Camp you could be admitted to her circle, but if you were unlucky enough to be BM (although people who were, were seldom aware of the fact) you had no chance. Dane, our stage manager, a large, craggy, black-haired man, all rough tweeds and curly pipe and a regular member of our nocturnal card school, was an honorary member of the Camp group, as was I. After the rest of us had eventually fallen into bed, Kate, who did not sleep, spent the rest of the night on the telephone, sometimes chatting to her friend in the CID and sometimes to her friend on the town switchboard. In consequence she was privy to all the gossip and scandal on the south coast.

Sexually Kate had, since her schooldays according to herself, played the field vigorously regardless of gender, but when I knew her her closest friend was Paddy, an elegant Irishman and a prominent member of the local gay community. The love that Kate and Paddy bore each other far transcended sex and each would have made any sacrifice for the other. Christmas was approaching and Kate saw in a local jeweller's shop a most beautiful intaglio ring, a classical head carved into its dull red stone. It would make a perfect present for Paddy. She enquired the price; it was considerable, but she started to save. Just before Christmas, to Kate's dismay it disappeared from the shop window. Of course it was Paddy who had bought it and it was his present to her. Inscribed inside was: 'Amor vincit omnia'.

Some years ago, long after Paddy's death, Kate had what I suppose must have been a stroke. Speechless and terrified she was loaded into the ambulance, her sister Alice at her side. Afterwards Alice told me that Kate was pointing to her ring and trying to say something. 'She had told me more than once how beautiful you thought it, and I am sure she was telling me that you were to have it.' And so I have.

Despite our both being at the Worthing Rep Jenny was further out of reach than ever, and as far as romance was concerned an air of stoicism settled over me. This grew to outright resignation when it became clear that she intended to marry someone else, and I was only marginally consoled by the thought that he was a much older man. I realised at last that what I had been suffering from was a severe bout of infatuation. I despised myself for being so helpless when I was in its toils and actually rather disliked her for making me conscious of my own weakness. The next time I met her was decades later; she was most satisfactorily matronly.

I thought that my taste of weekly rep had been as much as I wanted to have, and as the season at Worthing began to draw to a close I did what all actors in those circumstances do: I wrote dozens of letters to the two-and three-weekly reps, each with a CV and a photograph. My CV was not bad for someone of my age: a year in ENSA, a tour for Birmingham Rep, two years in its main company and five months at Worthing.

I received one or two replies – the profession was overcrowded even then – and one of them was from Geoffrey Ost, the director of the repertory theatre at Sheffield. Geoffrey was quite unlike anyone's idea of a theatre boss. He was then middle-aged and balding, with a ginger moustache and pale blue eyes which looked at one through thick-lensed glasses. It is my opinion, and that of many of my colleagues, that he was a great man of the theatre. After seeing me he engaged me for a year, and I was able to return to Worthing to complete the season there in the comfortable knowledge that I had a job to go to at the end of it.

I had been brought up to be aware of my social obligations – I had, for instance, held the thankless position of Equity deputy at Birmingham, collecting subscriptions, convening meetings and forwarding queries to the union headquarters. Amongst other things I had become a member of the Labour Party. It was while I was at Worthing that I was dismayed to learn that the party had decided to retain conscription. Politics, I discovered, is a matter of compromise. You may not agree with everything a party has to offer but you will not achieve anything unless you combine, sinking your differences with those with whom you differ in detail. It is a position with which I did not feel comfortable, and I have still not resolved the dilemma. I am not sure, looking back, why I felt so disillusioned – the Labour Party has never, after all, been pacifist – but nevertheless I was and I wrote a sharp letter of reproof to Barbara Castle, the minister concerned. Mrs Castle failed to take heed of my protest and one day I went to my room and locked the door to avoid interruption. I took out my party card, set light to it and held it out of the window until it was burnt. I watched the ashes fall into the yard below.

Most partings are poignant, and those in the theatrical profession are a fact of life. I bade farewell to my colleagues with regret, and to Kate with genuine sorrow. We swore we would stay friends for ever, and we did. When she died some of her many friends subscribed to a bench to be put in the municipal rose garden near her cottage, a place where every day she had been accustomed to exercise Ace, King, Queen, Jack and Ten. The inscription reads: 'Kate. From her friends in the theatre.'

5

The Pause Magnificent

I arrived in Sheffield on a cold day. There was a drizzle of rain and a bitter wind was blowing. Bombs had blown the middle of the city to pieces; they had not flattened it because it is built on a series of steep hills. A large granite-paved open space stretched before the Midland Station and over it rattled an occasional tram. Beyond the open space rose the ruins of Mappin and Webb, and beyond them, I assumed, lay the city centre and the Playhouse Theatre.

I had come from my home in Birmingham, a city for whose appearance I felt little affection, but I looked at Sheffield appalled and seriously thought of going straight back on the next train. Luckily, wiser counsels prevailed. I heaved up my large suitcase and, no money for a taxi of course, set off across the wasteland before me. I struggled up the hill through the soot-blackened streets. I had no map and no idea where Pinfold Street, the address of the theatre, might be, or Snig Hill, from which it led. I stopped a passer-by and asked. 'Oop t'street and round t'corner,' he told me. I have always been interested, and not just professionally, in accents and dialect and had seen such phrases written down, but I had never before heard Yorkshire spoken by a native. I was as pleased and excited as an anthropologist in the South Seas, and my reconciliation to my unlovely surroundings began at that moment.

Sheffield was a fortnightly rep, so as far as work was concerned there was an immediate relaxation. Geoffrey Ost's approach was not dissimilar to that of William Armstrong, and he kept his company on a loose rein. His faith in himself and his company was so well founded that, except for dress rehearsal days and matinées, we never worked in the afternoons – something I have not come across anywhere else. The usual session was ten o'clock until half-past one, after which we were free until the evening performance. At Birmingham, with only small parts to play, I had found the regime to be almost too leisurely; at Worthing it had been hectic. Sheffield seemed to me to be about right.

I once said to Violet Farebrother, an actress much my senior, 'I think you've got about as much as you can out of a part after about a couple of weeks, don't you?'

'Oh, my dear,' she replied in reproving tones, 'if a part is worth playing at all, it's worth playing for at least six months!'

Six months! I could not believe it.

She had played Regan to Sir Donald Wolfit's Lear, she told me, and had reacted to his speeches with speaking looks and gestures, very much in the old style. Wolfit had apparently found these as much a distraction as had Beerbohm-Tree before him. 'But of course,' she told me, 'he couldn't very well tick me off – I'd known him since he was in his cradle.' Wolfit had taken her aside. 'Fairy, dear,' he had said, 'Regan's much too clever a woman to show what she's thinking!'

Things nearly went wrong the day I first sat on a horse. With my friend Mike, an experienced rider, I took the train to Hathersage, where a farmer named Dungworth kept horses for hire. As we set off over one of the fields overhanging the beautiful Hope Valley, Mike said, 'Let's have a gallop!' and set off. It was not long before I lost my left stirrup and, like the novice I was, stood in my right one while hunting for the other with my toe. Soon after that I passed by my horse's ear, then its eye, then its nostril, after which I knew no more.

'I can't understand it – you fell so well!' Mike's anxious face bent over me as I lay there, puzzled. I knew that immediately after falling from a horse one should remount, or else one might Lose One's Nerve. I did so. 'That's Mike,' I thought, looking at his back as we rode along. I gazed at the hills and dales. 'How beautiful,' I thought. 'I wonder where we are.' I started an urgent question-and-answer session with myself. My surroundings looked very like Derbyshire, which was odd because I did not know Derbyshire. Where did I live, then? I thought it was in a large industrial city not far from here.

'Oh, yes. Birmingham. But hang on, Birmingham isn't near here and why on earth would I be living in Birmingham anyway?'

'Because you used to work there, in a theatre. You're an actor.'

What was I doing in Derbyshire then?

'Now you are working in a theatre in Sheffield.'

I paused, aghast. 'Tonight?' I asked myself.

'Probably.'

I gazed down, trying to work it out. A saddle! Good God, I was on a horse!

As we stared at one another in the train, Mike and I were clearly two worried men. I could not spare the time to question him; my mind was racing too fast. What was the play? Some sort of legal drama. My worst fears were realised as it gradually came back to me that I was playing a lawyer. It was the kind of play one used to see often. I rose at curtain-up, asked, 'Where were you on the night of the twelfth?' and continued to ask very similar questions for the next two and a half hours. I sat in my dressing room painfully recollecting the play, line by line, and it was not until the call for Beginners that I reached the end. No one was more thankful than I when that night's performance was successfully over.

Geoffrey Ost was a cunning manipulator of his audiences. Those were the days of the Recent West End Success, and he was not inclined to offend members of the public by confronting them with works of art which he thought they ought to like, unpalatable though the plays might be. He would put on, say, three popular comedies and, having lulled the audience into a sense of security, would then throw in a more controversial piece, or one of the great Russian classics. Over the years audiences came to trust his judgement.

This strategy was helped by the fact that people were encouraged to book seats on a regular basis: every other Tuesday or every other Friday, and so on. This gave each night a characteristic feel, which was interesting but had its drawbacks. Every other Tuesday a member of the audience who was a little hard of hearing brought a friend to amplify what we said.

Actor (fervently): 'I love you.'

Hard of hearing: 'What?'

Friend (in an undertone): 'I love you.'

Hard of hearing: 'What?'

Friend: '*I love you!*'

Every other Thursday there came someone who had evidently been released into the community prematurely. An actor on the stage might say something quite unremarkable like. 'May I help myself to a drink?' and it would strike this person as irresistibly humorous.

There would be a long, low 'Ha, haa, haaa . . .', starting quietly but with a rising intonation. A feeling of dread would seize the actors. The 'ha, ha's' would continue, increasing in pace and volume until they reached a lengthy crescendo which would last half a minute or so and then stop, abruptly, leaving the cast in a state of shock.

Sometimes, though, audiences were tested too far. Coming out after a performance of *A Month in the Country*, two playgoers were overheard in conversation. 'Well!' said one, 'I don't know what Geoffrey Ost is up to. The worst play since *The Cherry Orchard*!' I played Moses in Christopher Fry's *The Firstborn*. One of the cast overheard his landlady chatting to her neighbour about it. 'That's a lovely play at the Playhouse,' she said. 'Lovely. Mind you, it's all in Hebrew.'

The same kind of self-confidence was demonstrated by a passer-by who accosted one of our actresses, Eileen Essel. Eileen was looking into a shop window, her coat slung modishly over her shoulders. The passer-by tapped Eileen on the shoulder. 'Hey!' she said, 'We don't wear us coats like that up 'ere,' and passed on.

Geoffrey and his young company encountered each other at exactly the right moment; he allowed us to spread our wings and make our experiments and our mistakes just at the point in our careers when we needed to. But Patrick McGoohan, whom I remember as a fee-paying semi-student, was a difficult person to help. After rehearsals Geoffrey, as all directors do, would hold a 'notes' session. He would approach Patrick, nervously tapping his left forearm with his right hand. 'Ah, Patrick,' he would say. Patrick would glower. 'Er, very good, very good,' Geoffrey hastily added before passing on to the next actor. Unassisted though he appeared to be, Patrick nevertheless climbed swiftly up the cast lists; and people with a little more experience such as Peter Sallis, Peter Barkworth and myself benefited at least as much. All of us who were at Sheffield at that time are jealous guardians of Geoffrey's memory.

At the beginning of my second season I was standing in the darkened wings waiting for everyone to assemble for our first rehearsal. It was like the first day of term, greeting old friends and speculating about the newcomers, when up the steps from the green room and into the cramped space of the wings came the most enchanting girl. She had lively brown eyes, dark hair and that creamy complexion I always associate with the West Country. Her name was Patricia Scott. My memory is faulty about many things and that encounter took place forty-five years ago, but Fate evidently intended it to be a Significant

Moment because I can recall without difficulty the half-dark of the wings, the way she stepped up on to the stage and the sweet smile with which she introduced herself. It will have become clear in this context that it was indeed a significant moment. After a lot of water had passed under the bridge, Patricia became my wife and she still is.

For various reasons, partly professional and partly domestic, we were seldom able to appear on the same stage, but one of the first plays we were in together at Sheffield was *Macbeth*. I played Malcolm and Tricia was a very much more attractive witch than Shakespeare could have intended. Besides being a skilful director, Geoffrey Ost was also a more than competent designer. He had seen the play in traditional terms: Macbeth's castle was all stone steps and low Norman arches, and the men wore rough cloaks and horned helmets. I strode on to the stage one night as part of Duncan's entourage and caught a horn on the arch. I was thrown off balance and stumbled. To my indignation some members of the cast accused me of having done it deliberately to make them laugh; so to ensure that it did not happen again, the next night I held the helmet in the crook of my arm. It did happen again; the horn simply caught on a lower part of the arch. My colleagues' suspicions were apparently confirmed. Making people laugh, I was beginning to realise, was something I could do. I do not mean making my colleagues laugh on the stage when they should not – I mean comic acting.

It is the view of many actors, including myself, that for most of us comedy is a more difficult art than tragedy. The same rules apply: a devotion to that rather variable commodity, truth, but the heart of the matter is timing, and getting the timing right seems to be a matter of courage. Naturally it is not easy to speak of one's own courage, still less to congratulate oneself on possessing it; but it is a fact that comedy above all things requires one to dare, usually to dare to pause, and to pause long enough for one to judge precisely that the audience has had just long enough to say to itself, 'Oh, yes! I see!' before one delivers the line. Or, conversely, to take an audience by surprise, so that they laugh in the realisation that they have been led up the garden path.

Although, as I have said, the same rules apply to tragedy, it seems to me that in tragedy these rules can be applied with much greater elasticity. In other words, one can get away with more and cover up possible mistakes more easily. Of course at the highest level, in the finest production of a classical play performed by the best actors, comedy, drama and tragedy blend inextricably; but it is my view that a comic instinct, an instinct for timing, is something with which one is born and no amount of polishing and practice will take its place. A talent for playing comedy is rare. It was at this stage that I came to the conclusion that, if I were ever going to achieve fame and fortune, it would be through the vehicle of comedy. Clearly, I was right.

I nearly caused my career to be seriously interrupted when, one morning on my way to rehearsals, I encountered Marguerite. Marguerite was one of Tricia's fellow witches. She was an attractive woman but one could not fail to notice that she was of a nervous disposition and the idea of sex, particularly, seemed to worry her; if we had a love scene and had to embrace she used to go rigid with embarrassment. I am ashamed to say that this used to bring out the worst in me and when, one morning on my way to work, I saw her bending down looking into an antiques shop window I could only think what a jolly jape it would be to approach silently, bend over and give her a little bite on the back of the neck. I was poised over her, teeth bared, when I happened to glance at her reflection in the window. It was a total stranger.

Angst is built into the fibre of most actors: the precariousness of their calling, and indeed the precariousness of each performance, tends to diminish feelings of security. In large matters this gives us a considerable advantage over the rest of society: life is full of hazard anyway, and most people are disagreeably surprised by it; but hazard is part of our everyday lives and it is less likely to ambush us. Fortunately for me, on the occasion of this self-manufactured hazard there were no screaming headlines in the *Sheffield Telegraph* to blight my budding career.

Recent West End successes were our bread and butter. One of these, a play called *Miss Mabel* hinged on the rather elderly device of there being twin sisters, distinguishable only by the fact that one of them had a mole on her chin. The detective, played by Alan MacNaughtan, solved the mystery by looking at a photograph of them both and suddenly seeing the mole for the first time. I was not in it, so I had to make a special journey in from my digs one night in order to get hold of the photograph and decorate one of the sisters' chins with an obscene plasticine mole with a large pubic hair growing from its middle. My joke was wonderfully effective and totally disconcerted Alan, who disappointed me a little by not finding it quite as amusing as I did.

Alan gave a marvellous performance as Crocker-Harris in Terence

Rattigan's classic play *The Browning Version*. This has only one act and the play it is usually coupled with, *Harlequinade*, is not in the same class in my view. It is a lot of hard work for only a comparatively few 'in' jokes, and is about a very old-fashioned and tatty touring company dress-rehearsing *Romeo and Juliet*. I played the stage manager – on the stage almost all the time with every other line to speak and very nearly invisible. In fact someone came to see me after the show one night and was kind enough to say how good she thought I was in *The Browning Version* and she was sorry, she had not noticed, but was I in *Harlequinade*? The play was notable for me, though, because in it I got my come-uppance as a practical joker.

In the play someone falls ill and his one-line part is given to an otherwise wordless walk-on. The walk-on, played by John Rutland in an absurd medieval costume with a long peaked hat, is walking about the stage during a break trying out his one line in various different ways while I am attempting to have a quiet conversation with my girlfriend at one side. Exasperated by the walk-on's interruptions, I had to cross over to him and say, 'Look here, old chap, do you mind going and doing that somewhere else?' He was supposed to look up, say, 'Oh, sorry,' and exit.

One night I crossed to Johnny and said my line. Instead of saying, 'Oh, sorry,' and exiting he stared at me intensely from under his peaked hat. Then he put his tongue out and gave a little cough.

It may sound mild enough in the telling but the effect on me was like a blow to the solar plexus. Johnny made his exit leaving me simply doubled up, unable to speak.

In the next play, Johnny, from the other side of the stage, looked my way at one point, put his tongue out slightly and at the same time mimed a silent cough. Once more I was shamefully convulsed. By the end of the season he need do no more than simply glance at me meaningfully and I would have to leave the stage in order to recover. I wish I could say that he cured me, but I am afraid that would not be true.

Geoffrey Ost was asked to send a play to the Bath Assembly. The one he chose was, of course, Sheridan's *The Rivals*. Not only had Sheridan been a citizen of Bath, but the play itself is set there and contains many local references. I was delighted to be cast as Falkland, not only for the obvious reasons but for the fact that I was, and still am, a great admirer of Robin Bailey and I had seen him give a superb performance of the part in a modern-dress production at Birmingham Rep. I started rehearsals with Robin very much in mind.

Our production was in traditional costume, with silk coats, gilt-handled swords, lace jabots and powdered wigs. Perhaps because of the very different styles of the two productions or, more likely, because Robin's performance was simply inimitable, after two weeks' rehearsal my own was not working. Luckily we had four weeks, and I spent an agonising weekend deciding that I must do it entirely on my own terms and rethink the whole performance. It was an invaluable lesson in the approach to classic roles; inevitably, when asked to play Hamlet or Malvolio, one looks back and sees the daunting procession of great actors of the past who have enthralled audiences over the centuries. That vision has to be banished from one's mind – unless, that is, those players have left behind them something that one can steal.

It is said that before the Victorian actor Macready invented the device, no one had dared to pause in Shakespeare. Macready enumerated his pauses with precision: the Simple Pause, the Grand Pause and the Pause Magnificent. One night he was prompted in the middle of his Pause Magnificent. 'I strode from the stage,' he recorded in his diary, 'and felled him with one blow. God forgive me.' The line of people who have exploited the possibilities of the Pause stretches unbroken from Macready to Pinter. Albeit in a somewhat different manner, I was about to perform my own theatrical Pause.

I have said that I was not very ambitious, but on reflection it seems that that was not true either. A feeling of restlessness had been growing in me for some time. Why was I not a star? True, I had no more than my very meagre savings in the Post Office, but I was young, astonishingly good-looking and wonderfully talented. What could West End managements be thinking of? Agents and managers, I concluded, were too lazy and too well nourished to be bothered with young talent, and apart from anything else they were too far away. Despite the distinguished actors who regularly appeared there, very few agents had bothered to travel even as far as Birmingham. I thought how lucky Paul Scofield had been to have a sponsor in Sir Barry Jackson, who had been able to transport him directly to Stratford.

The likelihood of my being able to display my wares anywhere within range of the really influential talent-spotters in London seemed remote. One of my handicaps was clearly the fact that I had had no formal training and had therefore been deprived of the public show that all the theatre schools gave at the end of their courses. That was it! Apart from money, what was to prevent me from taking a year or so off, doing a course at a drama school and then knocking them all for six at the public show? The more I thought about it the sounder the scheme seemed to be, and I set about putting it into action.

Starting at what was generally reckoned to be the top, I sent off an application to the Royal Academy of Dramatic Art, RADA, and in due course I was summoned to London for an audition. I cannot now remember which pieces I chose to do, but clearly I started with a considerable, and of course grossly unfair, advantage over my fellow candidates. I ought to have performed them well, and I did, but although it would have seemed shameful not to have done so that was almost the last time I achieved anything through an audition. I appear to have persuaded myself that, unless an audience came at least halfway to meet me and had actually risked money on the chance of being entertained, I would find it extremely difficult, if not impossible, to give a convincing performance.

I am always impatient to get to grips with an audience and impatient with the longueurs of rehearsals, let alone auditions. There are some actors who can give clever auditions, but little else, and some who prefer rehearsals to an actual performance – something I have never been able to understand. Almost always the work I was offered in those early days was as a result of an interview across a desk.

After the RADA audition I was interviewed by Miss Browne, the bursar, very tall and copiously beaded. She raised the issue of fees. I wonder now why I had not gone into this matter beforehand, but I suppose I was hoping for some sort of scholarship. I told Miss Browne that I had very little money and after some consultation I was generously offered a bursary, which meant that I could have free tuition.

I would still not have enough to live on, though, and I did something which, most regrettably, would not be possible now; I applied to the Sheffield Education Committee for a grant. Amazingly, I was given one. I was a Londoner, only a Sheffield citizen by virtue of the fact that I was a member of the repertory company, but they gave me three hundred pounds. That may not seem a large sum now – indeed it was not a very large sum then – but you can multiply it three or four times over in today's terms. It made all the difference, and I shall never cease to be grateful for it.

With three other students I rented a maisonette in Ebury Street, SW1, consisting of ground floor and basement. I cannot now remember what rent we paid, but it must have been very low despite the grandeur of the address. We even employed a motherly body who, invaluably, taught me how to make cauliflower cheese. Our house possessed the unique cachet of being the one that Noël Coward had lived in as a boy. Or fairly unique, as one would say now. We discovered after a while that Coward had spent his boyhood in every house in Ebury Street.

I entered enthusiastically into student life, determined to make up for the years and the training I felt I had missed, and entered every course and class available. Everyone who knew anything at all about the subject strongly recommended Alice Gachet's French class – 'You know, the person who taught Charles Laughton!' Mme Gachet asked only one question at our introductory interview: '*Pouvez-vous lire?*' which I thought probably meant, could I read French? I cleverly replied, '*Mais oui, madame!*' adding, for safety, '*Un peu,*' and was enrolled. I was cast as the juvenile lead in Molière's *Le Malade Imaginaire* and given the job of ASM.

Mounting alarm is a mild description of what I felt at my first and, as it turned out, last rehearsal. I had what seemed like endless scenes in seventeenth-century French, all in rhyming couplets, some of them not quite rhyming and not all of them couplets. There was also the prospect of having to find a dozen or so fans, half a dozen fob watches, a gold-headed cane or two and no doubt the occasional parchment scroll. I racked my brains as to how I could get out of it without the humiliation of having to admit that *un peu* was not, after all, quite enough.

With relief I hit on an excuse which was plausible, and had the added merit of being true; small though it was, I could not afford the extra fee which was charged for the French class. There was a certain amount of wailing and gnashing of teeth in the front office, with Mme Gachet suggesting that I might 'borrow a little here, a little there', but I was adamant, and as Miss Browne was well aware of my poverty they let me go and I was able to return to the prescribed curriculum.

This kept me busy enough. There was Mr Froeschlein's fencing class – 'Ad-vance, ad-vance! Re-tire, re-tire!' – spoken with a marked cockney accent in spite of his impressively exotic name, but whose instruction in foil, épée and sabre fighting stood me in very good stead later on. There was Lydia Sokolova, another cockney, and Amy Boalth, who both taught ballet. Miss Boalth was a lady of a certain age who was inclined to demonstrate extravagant pliés in front of the class, displaying as she did a wealth of Directoire knicker from which even the randiest of the male students averted their gaze.

We were taught movement by a Greek god in an azure tracksuit, golden curls framing the face of an angry cherub. His friend Harry, cockney of course, accompanied matters on the piano. Harry was a small, bearded satyr whose dainty shoes concealed, I felt sure, shaggy hooves. In this class we sometimes ran across the room being cabbages. A running cabbage was something that few of us could manage, but now and then we had the easier task of being animals in a zoo. Sometimes at the end of a class the god would announce, 'Greek running. I think we've just time for Greek running, haven't we, Harry?' 'No,' Harry would say, and that would be that.

Hugh Miller taught us the core subject of acting. He had acted in the West End and on Broadway since time immemorial. LMS was Mr Miller's guiding dictum. This meant Look, Move and Speak. You looked at someone, you moved and then you spoke. Yes, well . . . He also instructed us in how to move across a stage if the play were a comedy. You pointed yourself in the direction you intended to go, then did a little jump into the air, stepping back with one foot and forward with the other. The effect is undeniably comic.

The Voice Department was where RADA really came into its own. Its head was a man called Clifford Turner who combined erudition with humour. He had published a book on his subject with, at the front, a quotation from the Old Testament: 'And they said to him, "Say Shibboleth" and he said "Sibboleth" and they took him and slew him.' Clifford had one of the most beautiful speaking voices I have ever heard – so beautiful, it was said, that he had failed as an actor because after a few minutes of listening to him audiences were simply lulled to sleep. When I knew him he was already a little old and tired, but advancing years happily coincided with the invention of the tape recorder and one of these machines would accompany him to his classes. He would place it on the table before him and record the first half of the lesson, using the second half in which to play it back, agreeing with himself and chuckling at his own jokes.

One of the first tasks he set us was to learn, and then one morning to speak for him, one of the prologues from *Henry V*. Now, I thought, was the moment when I would show them all what was what! I would give that speech My All and watch everyone's astonished faces as they were forced to realise that here was a genius. On the appointed morning I followed what I thought were some fairly weak efforts by my fellow students with a sensational account of my own piece. When I had finished there was a long silence. Clifford leaned back in his seat.

'Spoiling you, dear boy, spoiling you.'

'What is, sir?' I said faintly.

'Shushy S, shushy S. Next.'

That damned shushy S has pursued me throughout my career.

His assistant, Miss Scott, was as vital as he was relaxed. She kept on her desk a jumbo tin of glucose powder and we were convinced that she consumed several spoonsful between each class. Seated opposite her, it was an alarming experience to have to meet her fierce eye as she leaned forward and invited you to repeat after her: 'Take two tickets, ticket collector!' or, 'Mainalay, meenalay, minealay, moanalay, moonalay!' Her table was usually pushed a little way away from the wall, and some of her students would be seated behind her but facing the victim. The combined effort of speaking her tongue-twisters rapidly and accurately and keeping a straight face sometimes proved too much.

These two were not alone in attempting to teach us to speak our mother tongue clearly and, as they saw it, correctly. Tarva Penna (where did they get these names?) was an elderly and diminutive exquisite who taught us to pronounce medicine 'med-sin' and waistcoat 'wes-kit' and to polish our shoes extremely well, lessons not to be undervalued.

One morning early in my first term I was summoned to the principal's study for my introductory interview. Sir Kenneth Barnes greeted me warmly and reread my CV. I do not suppose he had often been able to welcome a student with quite so much professional experience, and he seemed pleased.

'What was your military service?'

Oh, dear. I told him and he rose from his chair. Brief as it had been, our interview was clearly at an end. It was obvious that Sir Kenneth was unhappy; as a student I must have been a bit of a catch and now I had, as it were, disqualified myself. But by great good fortune he was a notorious snob reputed to have few equals. I was in the act of opening the door when, clutching at a straw, he enquired, 'Oh, Eddington – any relation to the scientist?'

'A distant cousin, sir,' I replied.

Waves of relief swept over both of us.

'Well, good to have you with us!' He shook me by the hand and I returned to my class.

It was difficult for me to get to know my fellow students very well as my peculiar position meant that I tended to be shuffled from class to class, and in fact my two-year course was compressed into one.

Warren Mitchell was an impressive contemporary and for a time Joan Collins was a classmate. She was a devastatingly nubile teenager; not a girl one would be likely to overlook. It has always been difficult for me, and for most people I think, to see beyond her sensational good looks, and indeed we took it for granted then that she must be pretty stupid. I think we did her an injustice. She strikes me now as sensible and straightforward, as well as being a very good actress.

I daresay I deserved the disappointment of the public show to which I had looked forward so eagerly, and which had largely been the reason for my going to RADA in the first place. We did a rather limp American comedy called *Royal Family*, all about a very boring and self-centred theatrical dynasty camping around the stage being 'temperamental'. My rather jaundiced view of things was no doubt due to the fact that I had been cast as the patriarch of the family, with a beard and a grey wig. Hugh Miller was our director, and it was my impression that my ironic attitude to his antique style had not gone unremarked. My success in *Royal Family* was limited. I did receive one offer, to play a grey-haired sixty-year-old on a long provincial tour, but this was withdrawn when I met the producer and he realised that I was about forty years too young.

At the end of the year I went up on to the stage of RADA's little theatre to receive my certificate from Vivien Leigh's dainty, white-gloved hand. I turned from her to face a highly uncertain future. Once again I started writing letters. Tricia was doing secretarial work for some American friends who were trying without much success to start up as theatrical managers. One of her friends had given me a 'lucky' silver dollar. The friends themselves were unlucky, their house in a Mayfair mews was reputedly haunted, and I became convinced that the silver dollar was unlucky too. When it was in my pocket nothing seemed to go as it should, certainly not as far as my getting a job was concerned.

It was superstitious nonsense of course, but one day, on my way back to Ebury Street from yet another unsuccessful audition, I slipped furtively up to the bureau-de-change kiosk in Victoria Station and rather shyly offered the clerk my dollar. Without comment he handed me a couple of pounds or so and I slunk away again. On the doormat at home was a letter from Denis Carey offering three plays at the famous Bristol Old Vic.

*   *   *

The Theatre Royal, Bristol, is the loveliest theatre in the country, and when I first arrived it had hardly changed since it was put up in 1766. The original builders had used whatever materials came to hand. A vast tree trunk, originally a ship's keel, forms the main roof beam, and on my first trip underneath the stage I realised with astonishment that the wealth of stage machinery for raising and lowering the scenery, trap doors and so on was all counterweighted with cannon balls. The original dressing rooms were still in place – the principal actress's room known, accurately, as Mrs Siddons' room. Dusty and undecorated though they inevitably were, they retained an atmosphere that could be cut with a knife.

Situated in King Street, which runs straight down to the water, the theatre lies in the heart of the city's docks. Some mornings we would come to rehearsal and there would be a ship across the end of the street. One actor was so overcome by the romance of the scene that he was moved to hail a passing sand dredger, probably on its way to Cardiff.

'Ahoy there!' he called. 'Whither bound? To some spice-isle, no doubt?'

The deck-hand leaning on the rail spat his fag end into the water. 'Fuck off,' he said.

Tricia, by now my fiancée, had been trained at the drama school, which was then housed on the upper floor of a fruit warehouse opposite the stage door. She and some of her fellow students had appeared at the theatre in the chorus of the pantomime, as fairies in *A Midsummer Night's Dream* and in several other productions, so I already felt at home there.

The plays we did during my time at Bristol were *Love's Labour's Lost*, *Of Mice and Men* and *Venus Observed*. The Bristol Old Vic had enormous prestige and the company contained some distinguished actors: John Neville, Sheila Allen, Newton Blick, Laurence Payne and Michael Aldridge among them. Some of those names are familiar to theatregoers today, but they were all well known then and when Newton Blick's digs burnt down one night he was acutely embarrassed to read the headline in the *Evening Star*: 'Actor's Only Suit Lost in Blaze'.

There was a moving moment in *Of Mice and Men* when, playing one of the cowboys, I was required to unhitch the old dog from my bedpost and drag it outside to be shot. The dog had been lent to us by the landlord of the Old Duke's Head across the road. It was an excellent study, as we say, but not a very convincing actor. He soon learnt his cue and when unhitched used to leap into the wings and head for home, dragging me with him.

Tricia, meanwhile, had joined the weekly rep company which played on the end of the pier at Southport, and where, incidentally, they could see the sea between the cracks in the dressing room floorboards. At any rate it was up north, so at the end of my Bristol contract I asked Geoffrey Ost if I could rejoin the Sheffield company. He agreed and I more or less picked up where I had left off.

Every other weekend, when we both had a Sunday off, Tricia and I used to meet in Manchester, more or less halfway. Although we made a major discovery in Chinese food which was not only cheap and delicious but unusual in those days, we soon grew tired of the long journey and the brief meetings and decided to get married. I rented a flat in Fulwood, a hilly inner suburb, and, when Geoffrey found me a weekend when I would be free, Tricia left her job in Southport and we went down to her parents' home in Devon. Although 6 April is the beginning of the tax year, with a fine disregard for the Married Persons' Tax Allowance we were married on 28 April 1952, early on a Monday morning. It was a Monday morning because I had to be back at the theatre at ten o'clock on Tuesday morning – a true actors' wedding. Most of our honeymoon was spent on the journey.

Sheffield was a highly congenial place to work, and friends we made there became so for life. Two of our colleagues, Henry Beckett and Ella Atkinson, were happy to spend the rest of their careers at the Playhouse. But I hated the idea of getting trapped, and in due course felt it was time to move on.

Val May offered me a season at the rep in Ipswich, near the Suffolk coast. Like Sheffield it was fortnightly and Val maintained a high standard, attracting some good actors: Clive Revill, Elvi Hale, Nicholas Selby, Wendy Craig and Nancy Mansfield. Together with fellow actor Alan Nunn, his wife and children, we rented a house and I bought a bizarre kind of motorised bicycle, highly dangerous and now probably illegal, on which to go to and from the theatre. After a first night I could always tell whether I had done well or not. Tricia was usually warmly enthusiastic but if we trudged back up the hill in silence, me pushing the bike, I knew I had more work to do.

Our first son, Toby, was born in 1954. My motorised bike took me to the vast Ipswich hospital and from behind a glass screen he was held up for me to admire. I was appalled. The baby looked like an extremely unkind caricature of myself at about the age I am now. Happily the impression wore off and he is now quite the best-looking person that either of our families has known.

The following day was a matinée and I thought it would be a good idea to wet the baby's head with a bottle or two of hock between the shows. I was playing the Rev. Toop in the farce *See How They Run* and after a glass, or perhaps two, I thought it would be tremendous fun to amuse my fellow actors by wearing some orange-peel teeth for the evening show. The first act was indeed tremendous fun and the second was quite amusing. By the third my ludicrously projecting teeth, firmly established now with both the audience and the cast, had become a severe embarrassment. Not for the first time I did a round of apologies.

We did a rather dim comedy called *Life with Father*. I was the eponymous father and it was made memorable for me, though not at the time, by the fact that one of my sons was played by a local infant called Trevor Nunn – no relation to Alan.

After the first night I went to a party and got into conversation with a middle-aged man who asked me, in a markedly foreign accent, 'Vot is it like, being an actor?'

'Terrible,' I replied. 'Awful. You can have no idea of the endless work, the minuscule rewards, the agony of the creative artist.' I helped myself to another drink.

My companion became confidential. 'Vy not come to us?'

I looked at him again. He was clearly a colonel in the KGB. I was being recruited!

He revealed himself at length to be a Dutchman, the local representative of Shell who very much wanted salesmen to visit petrol stations in order, I suppose, to drum up trade. They wanted young gents who could speak the Queen's English and they would provide a car and a thousand pounds a year. Big money.

I have to say that I was tempted, and I consulted Tricia. I was now a family man with responsibilities; we had nowhere of our own to live and certainly no car. But Tricia said that she was unwilling to contemplate a lifetime of golf club dinners and Masonic ladies' nights.

'I think you have talent,' she said. 'I don't think you should leave the theatre. In fact if you do,' she looked me in the eye, 'I'll leave you', and I think she may have meant it.

One of the few times that Tricia and I were able to appear together was in Miles Malleson's adaptation of Molière's *School for Wives*. The heroine went down with a sore throat. My mother dashed down to Ipswich to look after the baby and, with only a day or two to prepare, Tricia took over, giving a most lovely and stylish performance which Malleson himself came to see. Instantly recognisable to film buffs, with his wig and his many receding chins, he was nevertheless a tireless ladies' man and he congratulated her very warmly indeed.

We had now moved to a small flat whose chief feature was a lavatory entirely lined with books by Angela Brazil. Surrounded by titles like *The Worst Girl in the Fifth* and *Come On St Hilda's!* it was easy to forget one's troubles. And life, despite the joys of a young family, was not at all easy. My father was dying of leukaemia and every other Sunday, when there was no dress rehearsal, I went to London to visit him at New End Hospital. One Sunday he just looked at me.

'How do you feel?' I asked, fatuously.

'Horrible,' he whispered. After a pause he raised his head and with a look of extreme anxiety enquired, 'Who am I?'

The question so shocked me that I did not know what to reply. Feebly playing for time, I pretended not to have heard him and said, 'I'm sorry, what did you say?'

He said, 'What is my name?'

I bent down to his pillow and recited his full baptismal name, 'Albert Clark Eddington.'

He sank back, relieved. That was the last time I saw him alive.

6

Riding through the Glen

∞

Although fortnightly rep was hard work I had settled into a comfortable routine and would no doubt have jogged along indefinitely. But Tricia, with immense faith and self-sacrifice, felt that it was now time we set our sights on London. Buying a house was out of the question and it seemed impossible to find a landlord who would accept children, so, reverting to my bachelor status, I found a large, scruffy room in the Old Brompton Road which I shared with my mother while Tricia had to take Toby and go to live temporarily with her parents in Devon. When I think now of the risks we ran – with our marriage, with our money, with our whole lives – my blood runs cold, but we simply had no alternative.

One day I visited the Television Centre to see Chloe Gibson who had been director at Chesterfield Rep when I was at Sheffield. She had nothing for me, but while I was sitting in her office she was rung by a colleague from BBC West. Holding the phone, she asked whether I could speak with a Devonshire accent. Although I would certainly have lied if necessary, thanks to my wife I could produce a tolerably convincing Devonshire and shortly afterwards I found myself back in Bristol playing a part in my first television production, Eden Philpot's *Yellow Sands*.

Live television is the most frightening of all the media; you are out there being watched, probably by millions, and in those days without any sort of lifeline. Noël Coward described it as being like a stage play without an audience, a radio play without a script and a film in one take. Actors will know what I mean. There was only BBC Television then, and if anyone in Britain was watching TV at all they were watching you. Just before transmission the studio manager, headphones on and script in hand, would warn the studio that the previous programme was coming to an end. 'Five minutes, studio!' he would shout. 'Absolute silence!' Then, 'Thirty seconds, studio.' And then he would count down, 'Ten, nine, eight,' and so on, silently counting the last four seconds on his fingers. Zero was an emphatic wave, which was the cue for the unfortunate with the first line to start speaking. If you forgot your lines, as Jack Warner did in an episode of *Dixon of Dock Green* that I was in, it was just too bad. On that occasion Jack struggled for minutes before he was rescued. For the rest of his life, whenever we met he used to say, 'Oh, my God, Paul, you were there the night I dried!'

When programmes began to be recorded it was not much better. The early tape was extremely difficult and expensive to edit, requiring laboratory conditions with microscopes and scalpels. Drying on an actor's part was not encouraged. The only reliable way to persuade a director to cut a scene and restart was to utter an obscenity, a technique which would probably be ineffective today. The next idea was to have someone sitting near the set with a script and what was known as a cut-key, a push-button instrument which the prompter pressed when you had a lapse of memory, thereby cutting the sound just long enough to shout the line at you. What the viewer got was wild looks and sudden silences. As soon as I could I watched a recording of myself – with severe embarrassment as I performed a repertoire of winsome little mannerisms designed, I can only suppose, to make me look attractive. It was a salutary lesson and I began a regime of austere reduction, a regime I am still pursuing.

I did my first day's filming on the farce *Sailor Beware*, unsurprisingly as a sailor. It was in fact a night shoot and took place on the banks of the Thames at Teddington on what must have been one of the coldest nights of the century. To me the phrase 'filming on location' immediately conjures up a vision of palm-fringed islands, a canvas chair with my name on the back and a luxury trailer. In fact it is usually the Balls Pond Road at six o'clock on a Sunday morning, but in this case it was the riverside at Teddington, sausage and mash in the small hours on the location bus and a lot of standing about in the freezing cold. It was actually too cold to snow, and the air sparkled with tiny ice crystals. During the occasional ten-minute breaks I fled to the generator van and stood under the Niagara of warm wind blowing out of the back.

My family and I were still having to live apart, and when I got back to the flat in Parliament Hill which my colleague Hugh Manning had generously lent me I took three aspirins and went shivering to bed wearing a vest, pyjamas and a sweater. I woke in the middle of the night sweating like a bull and realised that I had left the electric blanket on, treading a path between being burnt to a crisp and electrocuted.

When at last Tricia was able to rejoin me I resumed the search for work. It was not easy in spite of the fact that I had acquired an agent – one of the grandest, MCA. A young actor always thinks, as did I, that once he has persuaded one to put him on his books the agent will then take over and put lucrative contracts his way, and that his career will then simply move onward and upward. It takes some time to realise that this is not the case; until you reach a much later stage you still go on looking for your own work; the agent simply negotiates a fee for any you find. When the man who had recruited me left the agency I was inherited, as it were, by Philip Pearman, the doyen of London agents. Philip was then married to the actress Coral Browne, and there was a feeling amongst some of us that it was a marriage of strong affection rather than anything more carnal. During his brief acting career, when they were both about to appear in *Henry V*, it is said that they were lying in bed one night reading the play and looking for a suitable part for him. 'Here we are,' Coral is alleged to have said, "A camp near Dover".' He was a charming man but far too smart for the stage I had reached. When I demanded to see him one day to complain that I could not keep my family on a thousand a year, I am not sure that he knew who I was.

I had not lost my interest in political matters. One Sunday I read an article in the *Observer* by Father Trevor Huddleston, then a parish priest in South Africa, in which he said that white South Africans lived and breathed sport and that a boycott of their country by sportsmen and women throughout the world, in response to the Pretoria government's policy of apartheid, might have a considerable effect. I wrote to Father Huddleston to ask him whether an arts boycott might help too, and he replied that it certainly would. I spoke to some fellow members of Actors' Equity, principally a man called Hugh Forbes and his wife, and we devised a motion for the next annual general meeting which would have the effect of preventing members from appearing there.

This episode caused a most tremendous rumpus. Internecine warfare is meat and drink to Equity members and the pot boiled furiously.

When the meeting reached that point on the agenda, Sir Felix Aylmer left his presidential chair before the motion had even been moved and made a bitter attack on it. It was the most dangerous motion, he said, that had ever come before an Equity meeting, a deliberate conspiracy to undermine our whole profession and to wreck actors' livelihoods. It was clearly Communist-inspired and must be resisted at all costs. I had not to my knowlege ever met a Communist, but needless to say we were defeated. A few years later, however, it was passed in a modified form, and from then until the end of apartheid actors were advised by their union not to go to South Africa. If they did, they went without union support.

When visiting Hugh Forbes I had noticed that there was a flat to let in a nearby mansion block and I went to see the landlord. I asked him if any of his tenants had died in the recent cold snap – a ploy used sometimes in New York, I believe. He admitted that one of them had, so we came to live on top of Crouch Hill, with a commanding view over London including St Paul's in the middle distance.

Some time later Hugh came into some money and one morning I found, pushed through the letter box, a package containing fifty pounds. It was a wonderfully generous gesture and a godsend to us.

I was asked to be in a play at the Arts Theatre called *Komuso*, which had been done to great acclaim on the BBC's Third Programme not long before. It was about a group of English academics living in Japan in the twenties. Honor Blackman was the glamorous wife of one of them but was being courted by Michael Warre, a professor at the local university who, after the Japanese fashion, had brought her a singing cricket. Both the men being absent, who should enter but myself, devilishly attractive and quite ready to set my own cap at Honor. The original play ran to about six hours and, not wishing to subject an audience to an endurance test, we cut three of them. They may have been the wrong three.

In a tense scene Honor and I sat side by side on the chaise longue with the cricket singing in the background.

'Oh, that cricket!' she said.

I rose, moving into the shadows and murmuring, 'I'll deal with it.'

'Don't harm it!' said Honor. 'It's only . . . calling for its mate.'

'Yes,' I said, looming back into the light in a marked manner. 'Poor devil!'

Matters were not helped by the actor who played a Japanese professor. He had a drink problem and at every entrance he was drunker than the last, each time with his wig more askew.

Very few people came to see the play, but then the management had the bright idea of sending a few complimentary tickets to nearby London University. For the next five weeks we scarcely had an empty seat. The students loved it. Our singing-cricket scene they thought the funniest. 'Yes, poor devil!' brought the house down every night. I tried playing it with sincerity; they howled. I tried irony; they rolled about in the aisles. I actually played it for a laugh; they wept. We were reviewed in the *Financial Times* on pink paper, and copies were snatched up so eagerly that I was obliged to learn it from someone else's: 'Paul Eddington plays a howling cad in a toupé who gives his hostess an unaccustomed nip of gin, seduces her during an earthquake and appears in the last act in riding breeches and boots . . . or did one dream it?'

I was then invited to go to Dublin to appear at the Gate Theatre in a play by Eddie Lindsay-Hogg. 'We can't give you much money,' he said – fifteen pounds a week, in fact – 'but we can promise you a good time.' Eddie, tall and thin with a long pointed nose (he was known in Dublin as The Pointer) had been married to the film star Geraldine Fitzgerald. They had parted, but Eddie was grieving over her loss and the play was really about them. I was cast, amazingly, as an Irishman and just about got away with it without realising what a minefield I was treading. Geraldine's brother David, his wife Nancy and all the rest of their crowd – the racing set – were present on the first night. 'In the stalls,' as the *Irish Times* put it, 'snaffled and bridled.'

All I remember of the production is that the men shared a dressing room and that a number of them were gay – or homosexual, as we said then. I seemed to send them into spasms of great excitement. Many overtures were made to me and my lightest remark was turned and given a suggestive emphasis. I discovered later that some of them had had a bet on who should be the first to seduce me. As the weeks went by I became increasingly agitated by the oppressive atmosphere of the dressing room and made up my mind, contrary to my entire background and upbringing, that the next man who made an advance would receive a punch on the nose. My desperation must have been evident, and to my great relief the pressure was eased. It is a mistake to assume that sexual harassment occurs only amongst heterosexual people.

Every night I scuttled back to my digs in Rathmines, 'Ratmoyne' to Dubliners, and its reassuring Irishness: both taps in my room, I had noticed, were labelled 'Hot' but both produced only cold. I was having my hair cut one day in the Shelbourne Hotel and, finding myself alone with the barber, asked him if he remembered the Troubles and what it was like then. 'We was a very divided nation,' he said confidentially. 'Sure, I've seen houses with the thricolour flyin' out the one window and the Union flag out the other!'

I have never been out of work for very long, which in my profession is success of a sort, and at that time I had no choice. I had to grab at absolutely anything that was offered me. It was all television; fleeting glimpses here and there, minute 'guest' appearances, 'cameo' parts and, if I got a chance to speak at all, I was always a villain of some sort or an upper-crust smoothie. I even stooped to a week on a Danziger brothers' quickie (the brothers who made short films quickly and very cheaply) – or perhaps it was only half a week. Amongst many other things I played a tiny part in an episode of *Robin Hood*.

Some weeks later I received a summons to an interview with Hannah Weinstein, the producer of *Robin Hood*, as did about thirty other actors. They had found that they were spending a lot of money hiring people episode by episode on a casual basis and thought it would be a good idea to get one or two, put them under a yearly contract and use them for a variety of small parts.

I was not certain why, but to my delight I was one of two whom she chose.

Of course, when I was asked whether or not I could ride a horse, swim, shoot with a bow and arrow and fence I vigorously asserted that I was skilled at all those things, and I expect my fellow candidates said the same. What must have tipped the balance in my favour was the fact that they already had some footage of me in which I had worn my costume reasonably well, had remembered my one line and had failed to spoil any of the shots by tripping over a cable. Film people do like comfortable reassurance and if I had known at the time I might well have come dressed in Lincoln green; it is no good, for instance, turning up to be interviewed for the part of a coal miner wearing a clean shirt.

Robin Hood was filmed at the old Walton-on-Thames Studios, the oldest in the world. They had started life as the Dietrich Studios and I was assured that they had been making moving pictures there before the end of the nineteenth century. They were demolished some years ago to make room for a supermarket.

Walton is a long way from where we were living in North London and as a film make-up call seldom seems to be later than seven in the morning, at least for the small fry, I had to get up at the crack of dawn and take what was then called the workmen's train from Waterloo, filthy dirty and reeking of stale cigarette smoke. But I had no complaints; I had a year's contract and was earning the first real money we had ever had – fifteen pounds a day with one day's pay extra per episode in exchange for 'world rights for ever'. This was not in fact a very good deal; some time later I received a letter from a fan in Chicago who said she had been watching it on TV for the tenth time. At the time it was take-it-or-leave-it, though, and I took it gratefully.

The making of film differs radically from the making of television. For the actor this is most noticeable in that film is shot in brief 'takes', sometimes a minute or two long, sometimes only a few seconds, and that each shot is rehearsed and carefully lit, the lighting alone sometimes taking an hour or more. Television is rehearsed for days, perhaps about a week for each half-hour's screen time, and then shot in a day or two. Consequently, although in filming there is a lot of waiting about, the quality of the picture is much higher. On TV a single lighting session has to serve for quite lengthy takes, using up to five or six cameras at a time. In filming there is usually only one camera, so a 'master' shot of a scene is filmed and then all the close-ups are filmed separately, first in one direction and then in another. It was all most fascinating to me and I watched the process closely.

All our outdoor work was done on Wisley Common, off the Portsmouth Road. We were mostly well within earshot of the busy A3 and in consequence we had to dub all the sound, including voices, in the studio afterwards.

An experienced film actor always knows whether he is in close-up, medium or long shot, and I was taught a sharp lesson one day when, outside and therefore soundlessly, I was wrestling with a live eel in what I thought was a full-length shot. It was in fact a medium shot and as I was holding the eel at about crutch level, just out of sight, the effect was most unfortunate.

Richard Greene, as Robin, all glossy good looks, was having a struggle to rise above two things: his marriage to Patricia Medina, who had done better in Hollywood than he, and a series of poster advertisements for Brylcreem. Three, if you include the fact that at the time people felt that television was only for those who had failed in films, but the series, which I believe was the first of its kind in the world, was an enormous success and I did not hear him grumble. Alan Wheatly was the steely Sheriff of Nottingham, Archie Duncan a curiously Scottish Little John and Alexander Gage, Friar Tuck. Over the four years that I was in it there were three Maids Marian, all of them indisputably twentieth-century.

For the first year I was on horseback nearly every day and I realised one dawn, as a troop of us was lined up ready to ride in and set fire to a Saxon village, that I was the only actor who was present, the rest being stuntmen, ex-circus performers and even one retired cowboy. The fibs about my skills as a rider had been only too successful. The studios ran their own stables at Foxwarren, Hannah Weinstein's country house. My mount was a mettlesome little thing called Priscilla who was well used to filming, having been Laurence Olivier's horse in a film of *The Beggar's Opera*. I had not been on a horse for a long time and the first day it felt like an eleven-storey building with legs.

'You all right up there?' said Ivor, the riding master, as we prepared for a shot.

'Yes, I think so.'

'If she tries anything,' said Ivor, 'just hit her.'

'What's she likely to try?' I asked tentatively.

'Well,' Ivor drew a cautious breath, 'they're not riding school horses, these, you know.'

'I think we've got about five minutes' sun,' said the lighting cameraman, peering at the skies through a darkened lens. 'Stand by,' said the second assistant. Priscilla's ears twitched. 'Roll.'

'Running,' cried the distant sound man. Priscilla stirred uneasily and foamed a little at the mouth. 'Mark it.' She threw her head up with a rattle of harness.

'Shot twenty-three, take one,' said the clapper boy, clapping his board with a sound like a shotgun. Priscilla pawed the ground, trembling.

'*Action!*' yelled the director. She rose like a rocket, and, at an instant full gallop, headed for the trees. We stumbled back to the clearing some ten minutes later, my arms affectionately round her neck.

Another time Priscilla and I trotted into shot, I reined her in and, as she came to a halt, she put a front foot very gently into a hole. As she tilted forward, so did I, sliding slowly down her neck and between her ears, ending up with my Norman helmet resting on the ground and the toes of my boots on her nose. It may be that Priscilla was making a mild protest; I had begun to put on weight for the first and only time in my life. Made ravenous by all the fresh air and exercise, the cast would go to a nearby roadhouse for lunch and eat and drink extremely well. Over the weeks, our breaks steadily lengthened.

With no time to change costume, we had some surprising encounters. One day in the pub gents a well-oiled businessman, cigar in mouth, was having a quiet pee and I recall his look of alarm as he glanced up to see, standing in the next stall, Gaston, Champion Bowman of France, rouged and bejewelled, with a sword and a plumed cap. White in the face and wordless, he reeled out of the door.

Driving back to the studios one night the driver of the crowded location car suddenly said, 'Oh dear, he's had it!' as just ahead of us two cars collided. There was a loud metallic bang, silence, and then some screaming. I had only recently passed my driving test, and as the victims were clearly still conscious I thought it would be best to do what the handbook said: Control the Traffic. I sprang out of the car and brought the rush-hour traffic to a halt. After a very few moments the drivers – looking at me rather curiously, I thought – simply drove round me and carried on. I went over to the accident where a doctor was already on the scene.

'I think they're all right,' he said, 'but they all ought to go to the hospital for a check-up.'

I strolled to the grass verge where a couple of girls in long evening dresses were sitting dabbing their eyes, and repeated the message. Instead of the shy smiles of relief I had expected they both screamed and stuffed their handkerchiefs in their mouths. It was only then that I realised I was the Sheriff's Lieutenant: chain mail, gauntlets, sword and Norman helmet. I suppose I was the last straw; they must have thought they had died and were having an experience on The Other Side.

As I have said, there is a lot of hanging about in films and in the woods we became quite proficient archers, but one day my expertise seemed to have deserted me. We were in the studio doing some medium close shots of me with a bow and arrow and my arrows were going dangerously astray – a powerful bow can send an arrow with a warhead straight through an oak door. The camera was on a wheeled dolly, gliding from long shot to close-up, and the crew, fearful for their lives, eventually resorted to dustbin-lid shields.

I was baffled until next day, watching the rushes, I saw with horror
that I had been putting my arrows on the wrong side of the bow;
instead of shooting true, the cock feather was hitting it and swerving
to one side. In close-up this was almost unnoticeable, but the series
was extraordinarily popular all over the world and I knew that there
were hundreds of archery clubs in the USA alone. Had I confessed, the
whole day's work would have had to be rescheduled at vast expense.
Heads would undoubtedly roll – not mine, of course, since I was
needed but certainly that of the continuity girl and probably others.
I decided to keep mum.

I was a good boy on the whole and in time I was rewarded. I was
given the regular part of Will Scarlet, a bit more money and my name
above the titles. But it puzzled me that, in spite of this, I seemed to
have less and less to do. My words were reduced to not much more
than, 'Aye, Robin!', 'No, Robin!' or 'They went that way, Robin!'
Long afterwards I learnt the reason. There had been six principals,
if you include the occasional guest actor, which meant that their roles
were featured only once every six episodes. My joining them made it
once every seven and they were not pleased. We all got on very well,
and there was nothing personal about the matter, but a delegation of
them went to see the producers to protest and that was the compromise
reached. Elevation and emasculation, as is sometimes said of those
given peerages. The ironic result was that the others became so closely
identified with their parts that they found it hard to get other parts as
a result. A few years after the end of the series I believe I was the only
one still working.

One morning in the middle of January 1958, three weeks after *Robin
Hood* had come to an end, I was sitting on the edge of the kitchen
table swinging my legs and chatting to Tricia. We finished whatever
we were talking about and I jumped lightly down, perhaps three or
four inches. I fell the rest of the way to the floor uttering a cry of agony.
Pain is difficult to describe, or even to remember. What I told Tricia as
she helped me to a chair, both of us white and shaken, was that it was
as though a red-hot dagger had been thrust into my hip. The pain
was excruciating, and at every slightest move the dagger was thrust
in again. That night I hobbled slowly to bed, lying down with the
greatest care and staying as still as possible. When lying still became
intolerable I would turn over, taking about ten minutes to do so.

After two or three days the pain vanished as though it had never been and in a few days I had almost forgotten it. But two weeks later it struck again with devastating suddenness and I took myself to the doctor. By the time I got there it had gone again and I felt a little foolish. What can a doctor say, after all, when you tell him that you have been in pain but that it is now better? Only 'Jolly good', really. He humoured me by referring me to a specialist, but again I saw him between attacks and nothing untoward could be found. I retreated apprehensively to await the next blow.

A couple of months went by and every few weeks there was another attack, each lasting a few days. I almost began to get used to it. It was lucky in a way that I was not working – it was enough effort to hobble down to the Labour Exchange to draw the dole. The Inland Revenue, however, had not been idle and one morning I received one of those OHMS letters. It was a demand for just over double what we had in the bank. Missives from the Inland Revenue are rarely welcome but this one was particularly unreasonable, I felt, for later that year our second son, Hugo, would be arriving. I took the letter straight to the lavatory to reread it in greater comfort. I am usually pessimistic and I went backwards and forwards over the problem while my wife got on with registering an objection and talking to accountants. I was on the point of filing for bankruptcy when, providentially, one of my rare feature films came to the rescue.

It was called *Jetstream*. Before various technological developments had taken place, a significant part of a transatlantic flight was the Point of No Return, when if something nasty happened it was as far to go on as to turn back. A film about a crisis in mid-flight used to be made in those days about every six months. What made this one special, and is perhaps one of the reasons why no one has heard of it since, is that it was stuffed with British celebrities, including Sybil Thorndike and Stanley Baker. This is no reflection on British celebrities; it is a fact of life that to make any money you have to sell a film in America, and the average factory worker in Detroit has got to know who the actors are.

My wife was played by Lana Morris. As everything on board was going horribly wrong and the pilot was being sucked out of the window, I said to her, rather snappishly, 'I told you we should have gone by boat.' Unfortunately this aside was noted by several of the critics, who quoted it in their reviews. The general opinion was that we should all have gone by boat. However, the film served its purpose and with one bound I was free of the tax man, temporarily at any rate.

Not free, however, of the pain attacks which kept mysteriously coming and going.

Returning from the studio one evening, I was met by Tricia on the landing. 'I've got some bad news for you,' she said. 'Your mother died this afternoon.'

The devices nature uses to insulate one from shock are odd. My mother was very fond of nibbling Jacob's high-bake water biscuits, which no one else in our household cared for much; all I could think of at that moment was that we had several packets of them in the cupboard and what on earth were we going to do with them all?

She had been working at Simpson's in Piccadilly and a colleague told me he had seen her that morning, sitting in the lift waiting for the ambulance. She had been holding the rose she always wore, anxiously twisting it, this way and that; it is an image that has stayed with me. I went to see her in the hospital mortuary, but it was clear she was no longer present. As we had always been so close I was disconcerted to find that I was not as moved by the sight of her dead body as I felt I should have been. I wondered if corpses were as cold as people always said and touched her nose. Yes. Stone cold. Only gradually did I experience a full sense of loss.

My next venture was, I think, a long series for the BBC called *Kenilworth*, in which I played a dashing cavalier in the Civil War. My modest skills as a horseman were called for once again. As the opening titles rolled I could be seen, mounted on a glossy cavalry horse, cantering through a splendid park and scattering a herd of deer as I did so. Well, that was the idea. The park was, as I recall, Richmond and my horse, elderly, depressed and dusty, was absolutely determined to do as little as she could possibly get away with. Encourage her though I might, she remained indifferent to my commands, picking her way nervously round the deer. Some of them lay in her path while others merely stared, surprised and disapproving. The effect was less than heroic.

Patrick Dromgoole, who was then at the BBC in Bristol, asked me to be in a radio play he was producing – no danger of being embarrassed by an apathetic steed there. It was only a couple of days' work and poorly paid, but I went gladly; any actor will go almost anywhere to keep in work.

As the years pass, the profession grows friendlier; it is increasingly likely that a cast will contain at least one friend and probably several. In this cast were Nicholas Selby, whom I had worked with at Ipswich, and a young actor whom I had not known previously, David Baron. During a break we three were sitting in the canteen having a cup of coffee when David said, 'I've written a play. I think you'd be very good in it.'

I started like a gazelle but, alas, he was not addressing me.

'It's already been accepted,' David went on. 'It's going to be done at the Lyric, Hammersmith. It's called *The Birthday Party*.'

I learnt later that 'David Baron' was the stage name of Harold Pinter.

The piece opened to derisory reviews, played to empty houses and was withdrawn at the end of the week. Harold told me recently that he had gone in one evening and was making his way to the circle when he was stopped by an attendant who asked him where he was going. He told her.

'The circle's closed,' she said, but Harold made to go in nevertheless. She went on, 'Who do you think you are?'

'I'm the author,' replied Harold.

'Oh, you poor thing!' said the attendant.

The Sunday after the play had closed Harold Hobson, the most influential critic of his day, gave the play a rave review in which he said that Harold Pinter was the most important new writer in the country. The play had finished but Pinter, who had been on the point of giving up as a writer, was famous.

I was pleased, but a bit puzzled when Caspar Wrede offered me the chance to be in a TV production of Noël Coward's *Hay Fever* to play Sandy, the ex-Cambridge boxing Blue – highly unsuitable, given my rather wispy frame. The size of my nose alone would rule me out, I should have thought, as a boxer. The cast was headed by no less than Edith Evans and George Devine, with Maggie Smith and Richard Wattis, and I was certainly not going to say no.

We rehearsed somewhere in Chelsea. Edith was too mean, so it was said, and I was too poor to go to the pub at lunchtime, so we used to eat our sandwiches together and discuss world affairs. She was notoriously more comfortable in men's company than in that of women. It was the time of the U2 incident, when an American spy plane was shot down over the Soviet Union and Mr Khrushchev was seen banging his shoe on his desk at the United Nations. Actually I believe that a candid camera shot revealed that he had both his shoes on at the time, so perhaps it was someone else's.

'The trouble with Mr Khrushchev,' said Dame Edith, 'is that he's not a gentleman.'

I thought about this. 'Don't you think, Dame Edith, that it's rather a lot to expect a Russian peasant to behave like an English gentleman?'

She looked at me for a long moment and then patted me on the head. 'I like talking to you, dear boy,' she said. 'You have the other point of view.'

At one point in the play we all play an after-dinner game. Maggie Smith's character was very dense and was unable to grasp the principle. 'But it's so simple!' Dame Edith's character had to say. At a late run-through she forgot to say it. Sitting next to her on a piano stool I nudged her sharply in the ribs and heard myself speaking the line for her, in a fairly accurate imitation of the fruity tones she had made so famous. I wished the floor would open beneath me but she only said, 'But it's so simple! Thank you, dear boy.'

She was elderly and plain but still possessed the magic ability to convince you otherwise. In the play she used to lie back on the sofa at one point and in seductive tones say, 'Oh, Sandy!' I really thought I could quite fancy her.

The day we recorded gave me my first inkling of what it was like to be a star. I had always thought that it was the most highly desirable objective for an actor; one could choose whatever part one wished to play, whichever colleagues one wished to work with, more or less dictate one's own salary and generally bask in public regard. The reality, I discovered, was rather different.

Edith was clearly in a blue funk. She depended heavily on what she called her 'anchors' and her 'bridges'. Her anchors were pieces of furniture that she could, if she wished, touch, presumably to remind herself that she was really awake and still attached to the stage, whilst her bridges were verbal hints from her fellow actors of what she had to say next – for instance, hearing someone say 'garden' might remind her that her next speech contained the word 'flower'. She locked her dressing room door and forbade anyone to wish her good luck, and I could see what a strain she must feel her celebrity to be, especially in a play where not only her reputation but the investors' money and all her colleagues' livelihoods depended on her being a success.

Coward himself directed a later production at the National Theatre, with almost the same cast. I was very sensibly replaced by a rather more robust actor.

The West End is the goal to which all actors aspired then, and I was thrilled, after all those years and all that hard work, to reach it when I was cast in *The Tenth Man* by Paddy Chayefsky presented by the most important of the West End producers, Michael Codron.

The Tenth Man is the reworking of an old story about a girl who is possessed by a devil. It takes place in a Brooklyn synagogue and has an all-Jewish cast. People were not then so sensitive about cross-racial casting as they are now. Political Correctness was a concept whose time had not yet come, so when Michael asked me to read the part of the young rabbi for him I did not hesitate and soon I was setting out on a long pre-London tour.

There were eleven characters in the cast, all Jews. We actors consisted of five Jews and six Gentiles and we were directed by Donald Macwhinnie, who had his hands full. I discovered that being a Jew is like being a member of a huge family. As in all families, however, internal feuds could become bitter, and there was no shortage of them. Explosive rows were a regular occurrence and one would meet mild, gentle people hurrying along the corridors bearing make-up boxes and piles of clothing and muttering, 'Never, never again will I share a dressing room with that man!'

The mood was lightened somewhat when I made my first acquaintance with The Woman in White. She was a familiar figure in the West End at that time, always dressed entirely in white: white dress, white hat, white gloves, white stockings, white shoes, white handbag, white mackintosh and white umbrella. A striking sight, even more so when she appeared in the middle of the front row.

Towards the end of the play there is an impressive exorcism scene. The entire cast assembles enveloped in their prayer shawls, lighted black candles in hand, whilst prayers are intoned. Overcome, The Woman in White rose from her seat at this point, raised her umbrella and paraded slowly back and forth across the space between the stalls and the front of the stage. As one of the few members of the cast with normal sight I was transfixed, and it was not long before she was hurried out. She was deeply affronted. She had believed, she said, that ours was the cleanest show in town. She now felt that it was the dirtiest and for the next few days she picketed the theatre, warning passers-by of the unclean goings-on inside. Business improved noticeably.

If acting with a lot of Jewish colleagues and enjoying their shoulder-shrugging, self-deprecating, ironic brand of humour (as well as their tantrums) had made me feel part of one large family, I was not doing too badly on that front myself. It was during the run of *The Third Man* that our third son, Dominic, was born.

While matters were healthy enough as regards work and family, the pains in my spine and hips still came thundering back every two or three weeks. Whenever they did so I had to arrive at the theatre on two sticks. Any movement was accompanied by the sort of pain that left me ashen-faced, and when I sat down I was never sure whether I would be able to get up again. I made yet another visit to a specialist at Charing Cross Hospital, and luckily this one took place during an attack.

I was invited down to the lecture theatre, where I sat amongst the students as another consultant discussed my X-rays. He explained that they were not normal and pointed to some small cloudy areas in the joints. He said I was suffering from something called ankylosing spondylitis, a form of arthritis. I was invited back upstairs where I was told that the proposed treatment was a course of radiotherapy: twenty minutes a day for two weeks. It sounded rather alarming and I asked whether it was really necessary.

'Well,' said the specialist, 'you've seen those old men bent double, unable to look up? That's what it is,' and he explained that ankylosing spondylitis progressively fuses the joints. 'When it reaches the ribs and the whole frame becomes rigid, the lungs collapse and you die. You have a thirty per cent chance of surviving,' he added. 'Do you want the treatment?'

I came out and stood at the top of the steps. The hospital has moved to the suburbs and the street is now one-way, but I can still see all the cars and the way they were parked. What on earth was I going to say to my wife, my agent, the producer?

Every day for two weeks I lay in the radiotherapy room, my back covered with sheets of lead to prevent the radiation spreading while the therapists lowered the ceiling on to me and retreated behind a plate-glass porthole, keeping watch while I cooked.

Every evening I arrived at the theatre, feeling a little sick. The pain continued.

7

The Great White Way

⫘

Val May, now the artistic director of the Bristol Old Vic, had asked me in 1961 to come and lead his company. For some reason I had declined, but I said, 'Ask me next year.' Somewhat to my surprise, he did.

The BOV was going through one of its crises. A poorly led season had culminated in a disastrous *Macbeth* which did not just do badly at the box office but led to some patrons cancelling their regular bookings. I was the distinguished West End actor who was going to ride to the rescue. Not surprisingly, many members of the company had only a sketchy idea of who I was, and people would peer curiously at me from behind pieces of scenery.

The place certainly was in a mess and morale was low. Some people were having unsuitable love affairs, and I would pass distraught couples gazing at each other in the rain beneath the lamplight in King Street. Dressing room doors would slam and women would burst into tears behind them. Men would arrive late for rehearsal – unusually, for those days, unshaven and tieless.

Leading a company is not simply a matter of playing the plum parts, and I decided I would have to set an example. I arrived at least five minutes before time, in a clean shirt, tie and polished shoes, and I had always shaved. Apart from mere appearances, personal enmities and jealousies had begun to arise. In one instance I was told by one of the actors that another was 'a troublemaker'. This obviously had to be nipped in the bud, so I asked the stage manager to make sure that I shared a dressing room with the alleged troublemaker. The matter turned out to be trivial enough, but it could easily have got out of hand. I hoped that my attitude would be seen as simple professionalism, and gradually it did seem to take effect.

As a *bonne bouche* we started the 1962 season with *War and Peace*, with myself as Prince Andrei, to be followed by Shaw's *The Apple Cart* in which I would play King Magnus. I had not done any learning of lines for well over a year and felt very uncertain and insecure. *War and Peace* was a four-hour marathon, while Magnus had what was then the longest speech in the history of the British theatre. I sat on the edge of my bed and read that speech with one eye on the clock. Nine minutes. It actually played at eleven. I put the light out and went to sleep. I had heard the expression 'having cold feet', meaning being afraid, but I had not realised that it had a basis in physical fact. I woke at five o'clock and my feet were like stone.

I lay and stared at the thin curtains behind which the dawn was beginning to break. I thought, 'We open *War and Peace* in a week. Three weeks after that we do *The Apple Cart*. There are posters round the city announcing this, as a fact. Not even "God Willing".' Should I get up and walk about a bit, I wondered, and have a cigarette to calm my nerves? I lay there with my heart thumping.

'No!' Suddenly I knew that if I got up I would have to stay up, pack my bags and catch the first train to London, resigning myself in future to playing supporting roles in television and walk-on parts in films. It felt like a huge turning-point. I lay down again and went back to sleep.

War and Peace was the kind of huge epic drama to which Val May's talents were particularly well suited. The domestic scenes were played down-stage centre; the Men of Destiny, Napoleon and Kutuzof, appeared on platforms thrust out over the heads of those in the stalls; and the battles were illustrated on a sloping rostrum, with wooden soldiers about a foot high and points of light representing explosions. The audience was guided through the play by a dinner-suited master of ceremonies, played with great panache, by John Franklyn-Robbins, and the whole thing was intensely moving and dramatic. Rumours began to circulate immediately that it would eventually transfer to the West End.

The Apple Cart was terrifying. Shaw wrote exactly what he meant to write and it is simply not possible to take liberties with him. Stray from the text by so much as a comma and you are in trouble. The very size of the notoriously long speech was inhibiting, and the more I worried about it the more uncertain I became. Yuri Gagarin had only recently made man's first journey in space and as I sat on my throne, up-stage centre with my cabinet ministers ranged on either side gazing up at me, I knew exactly how he must have felt hundreds of miles above the surface of the earth and totally isolated. As I neared the end of the speech the weight of words above me felt like a house of cards. One more word, I felt, and the whole edifice would collapse. And, night after night, it did.

I remembered a friend of mine, Jerome Willis, telling me that he was in a season at Stratford-on-Avon when Ralph Richardson was appearing in a production of *Macbeth* which had been savaged by the critics. As he passed Richardson's open door one night Sir Ralph had stopped him. 'Oh, Jerry, my boy,' Richardson had said. 'Sooner than do this play tonight I would willingly clean the boots of the entire company!' So I put a notice on the company notice-board: 'If I do not get through that speech tonight without fluffing or drying I shall clean the boots of the entire company.' My courtiers and cabinet looked at me with eager expectation that night. 'Yes, you buggers,' I thought. 'You're not listening to a word I'm saying about kingship and democracy. You're lining up your boots!' I was damned if I would clean them. It broke the jinx, and I did not have to.

I only had a few minutes off the stage in that play. It was a great strain and the moment I was in the wings I would light a cigarette and drain it like a tumbler of water, going back on with a red mist before me. I had made many attempts to give up smoking, but never for long; being crossed in love or struck down with arthritis seemed a good excuse to resume. Then I received a letter from Toby, who had evidently been got at at school. 'Dear Dad,' it began. 'If you don't stop smoking your lungs will look like this' and there was a very worrying multi-coloured drawing. 'Don't be a clot, Dad,' it went on. 'Give it up now.' He had signed it with his full name.

It was a message I could hardly ignore. I remembered that I had been about his age when I had first realised, with a horrible feeling of insecurity, that my parents were mortal. I felt I had to spare my own children that, so I stopped, and I have always been grateful to him.

The Sitting Duck, by a French author whose name escapes me, was a farce about the Paris Communes and had no doubt lost something in the translation. We thoroughly mangled what remained in an unsuccessful attempt to make it understandable and/or funny. Algeria was at that time still a French colony and for some reason the play had offended the French settlers there, the Pieds Noirs, who had threatened to shoot the author on the streets of Bristol should it go ahead. I met him backstage and he positively wrung his hands, declaring in broken English that he did not recognise his play. As it indeed bore no resemblance to the one he had written and he was still going to be assassinated for it I had every sympathy. Luckily he survived – better than we did.

Ross, the Terence Rattigan play about Lawrence of Arabia, fared better, with John Franklyn-Robbins giving a deeply committed interpretation of the title role much influenced by Stanislavsky's Method. In one scene Lawrence, who has been captured in the desert, enters on his knees having been severely assaulted in every way by the licentious Turkish soldiery. One night an excited ASM warned me that, in preparation for the scene, Lawrence was being assaulted in the wings. I hastened down. Sure enough, there was John being lightly caned by a highly embarrassed Turk. I crept away.

Well aware of the value of a star performance, John had arranged with the electrician for the lighting to be put up a point every time he entered. 'I think Mr Franklyn-Robbins is wonderful,' one of the usherettes was heard to say. 'Every time he comes on the lights seem to grow a little brighter.'

My next challenge was Ibsen's great play *Brand*. I had seen Patrick McGoohan giving the first English performance of it at the Lyric Theatre, Hammersmith some years before. Michael Meyer, the poet and Ibsen authority, had made a rugged and thrilling new adaptation in rhyming couplets and, like most people who saw it then, I was overwhelmed by its grandeur. Patrick had asked me afterwards what I had thought of it and I had said, sincerely, that it was a performance of genius. (His wife, Joan, told me a few days later that Patrick, ever reluctant to accept praise, thought I had disliked it!) Now it was my turn.

Brand is something of a problem. Ibsen said it was not for the theatre but for the study, to be read. Brand himself is a young clergyman who takes his religious morality to what proves to be insane lengths. During the play he climbs a mountain, spiritually and physically, and is finally engulfed by an avalanche near the summit. As if this did not pose sufficient difficulties, Ibsen included a great deal of contemporary Norwegian political argument which Michael had sensibly expunged.

I did not see the National Theatre's revival some years later but they managed to extinguish it for another generation or so by commissioning another new translation, no doubt wishing to have their very own. This extended the already long running time and restored the polemics. I understand that audiences walked out in droves.

This was not the case in Bristol and the play was a sensational success, symbolised by an extraordinary event at the end of one performance when a woman, quite unknown to me, found the pass door from the auditorium, burst through it and flung herself at my feet. It was difficult to know quite what to do with her.

On 28 October 1962 Tricia had come to Paddington with me to see me off to Bristol. Anyone who remembers that day will recall the stunned feeling that this might really be the beginning of mankind's last days on Earth. Soviet nuclear missiles had been identified on ships bound for Cuba, and Kennedy had told Khrushchev that unless they were ordered back that day he would unleash a nuclear war.

Tricia and I were active anti-nuclear campaigners. Tricia had been on the first Aldermaston march and I had sat in Trafalgar Square, against police orders, with a toothbrush in my pocket in case I was arrested. We knew enough to know that the effects would be devastating. When we said goodbye on the platform there had seemed a real possibility that we might never see each other again.

On the way to Bristol I had thought long and hard. If there were a war and it lasted long enough, I would be called up to do armed service. Presumably, having once been admitted to the roll of genuine conscientious objectors, I would have little difficulty in avoiding conscription. But would the grounds still be valid? For years I had not thought about anything other than how to get by from day to day, and could not truly – conscientiously, in fact – call myself a religious person.

By the time I reached Temple Meads Station I had decided that if called I should have to go. At that moment it was difficult to know exactly where moral courage lay.

Early in 1963, Val May sent me a play adapted by J. B. Priestley from Iris Murdoch's novel *A Severed Head*, asking me to look at the part of the psychiatrist, Palmer Anderson. Like much of Iris Murdoch's fiction it is a tangled web of unconventional, and usually improper, interlocking relationships set amongst a group of very Hampstead professional people. When Val rang I told him I thought it was extremely funny.

'Funny?'

'Yes, a sort of intellectual French farce.'

'Oh.' There was a pause. 'We thought it was about Spheres of Influence.'

Whatever misgivings Val may have felt, that April I was back on stage at the Bristol Old Vic, taking my place in the semi-circle of chairs facing the lowered iron curtain with, ranged before it, the costume designer, designer, stage manager, ASM, Val, Iris Murdoch and Priestley. The cast was a formidable one with Robert Hardy playing the lead, Heather Chasen, Sheila Burrell, Monica Evans, Christopher Benjamin and Barbara Leigh-Hunt.

Val stood. 'You've all read the play,' he said. Then he turned to the ASM, 'Take a timing, darling . . . Right,' he said, 'off we go.' And he resumed his seat.

I was surprised. A director usually feels obliged at this point to give a little dissertation – on the period, perhaps, or the intellectual milieu. I certainly expected at least a mention of Spheres of Influence, but no.

What none of the cast knew was that Priestley had only just returned from a Greek cruise with his future wife, the prelude to a sensationally undignified divorce, to find that in his absence Val and Iris had been tinkering with his script. His rage, I learnt, was being expressed in threats to take his name off the credits, suits for damages and so on, and our reading was taking place in the wake of a placatory champagne buffet in the manager's office. The atmosphere could have been cut with a knife, but I am notoriously insensitive to such things.

Palmer's first entrance comes about twenty minutes after the rise of the curtain (in those days curtains used to rise after the audience were seated and the lights had dimmed). During those ambiguous twenty minutes Martin, the hero, has learnt that Palmer is having an affair with his wife and has gone round to Palmer's place to punch him on the nose. Soundlessly on the deep carpet, Palmer enters, taps Martin on the shoulder and, after an electric moment says, 'You found a parking space?'

There was an explosion of laughter from all but Val and Iris, who looked at each other with a wild surmise. Could it be funny after all? I am not sure whether Priestley was surprised; I discovered that the line was his own and I suspect that he knew what he was doing. We played to full houses in Bristol and collected some excellent reviews. Alan

Brien in the *Sunday Telegraph* said, 'It must transfer to the West End with its faultless cast intact,' and, courtesy of Donald Albery, it did.

Sitting over supper one night while still in Bristol, Robert Hardy said, 'I wonder if it will run.'

'Well, I hope so, darling,' drawled Heather Chasen. 'We've come an awfully long way to do it.'

Between the Bristol run and the play transferring to the West End the Eddingtons had a private success of their own. After our three boys Tricia produced our only daughter, Gemma.

In the middle of Piccadilly Circus, the Criterion Theatre occupies one of the best sites in London. Most of it is underground and I am convinced that some of the audience think it is the Underground itself as they make their way downstairs, confident that they are on their way to Cockfosters. It has an extremely pretty auditorium but the dressing rooms, at least before their recent refurbishment, left something to be desired. Airless cells, they were surrounded by restaurant kitchens and one seldom dressed entirely alone. Mice that had taken poisoned bait lost their inhibitions and leapt about like grasshoppers; a colleague found one in his overcoat pocket one night. Twice I put my foot into a shoe only to find it already occupied by cockroaches. The number one dressing room, once occupied by Robert Donat who suffered from severe asthma, had an air extractor but that was its only concession to glamour.

There is no tonic like success, though, and we bore our privations stoically. Priestley and Iris Murdoch gave a hundredth performance party. I overheard him on the telephone saying, 'I'm giving a party at my chambers in Albany. Iris is providing the drinks.' One night Iris brought the novelist Elizabeth Bowen to see the play. Unversed in theatrical ways and ignorant of pass or stage doors, the two ladies were seen scrambling on to the stage at the end of the performance.

Yes, I know where I was when I heard the news of Kennedy's assassination in 1963; I was on my way to the theatre, driving round Piccadilly Circus (which one could do then) listening to the car radio. I thought that when I arrived at the stage door I would be told that the performance had been cancelled, for laughter seemed totally inappropriate that night. But no, it would have been too complicated, not to say too expensive, to do that, so we compromised by playing the American National Anthem as well as our own at the end of the performance. 'Why are they playing that?' an American woman in the audience asked her neighbour. She fainted when told.

With the Bristol run and a brief tour we had been doing *A Severed Head* for about eleven months when I had a most unpleasant experience. For some reason I had decided that my performance had to be perfect; every word, every gesture exactly right; anything not absolutely necessary eliminated; my suit perfectly pressed, my shirts perfectly laundered, my nails clean, my hair in place. Subconsciously I think I had been influenced by hearing Iris say one day that a line about Palmer flying to New York by BOAC must be rewritten. 'Gods,' she had said, 'don't fly by anything so specific.' A god! Quite apart from speaking the same words and making the same movements night after night I was, without realising it, placing myself under an enormous and increasing strain.

One night, rested, relaxed and refreshed, I went on stage. Halfway through the scene I felt as though I had been struck by a bolt of lightning. I had absolutely no idea who I was, where I was, what I was supposed to be doing or why I was wearing these unfamiliar clothes. I was baffled as to what the audience were expecting to see. Although it seemed endless, this blackout only lasted a moment – not long enough in fact for anyone to notice anything amiss. Nevertheless it left me sweating and trembling. I was tense for the rest of the evening, and enormously relieved when it came to an end.

The next night it happened again, and the following night twice. I would finish every evening exhausted with relief and wake every morning filled with apprehension. Who had died? Had I got to appear in court? What awful thing had happened, for God's sake? And then I would remember and the tension would begin to build towards the evening performance. I was ashamed, and the shame seemed to be increased by the fact that it was secret; I was unable to tell anyone about it, even my wife.

I was sitting one morning, staring moodily at the cornflakes, when she said, 'What's the matter?'

It was a brave question. It could have been anything – a financial scandal, a mistress or worse. I burst into tears. 'I can't remember my lines!'

Confession should have purged me, but it did not seem to help. Night after night I went to the theatre with the greatest reluctance, holding on to my sanity, I felt, by a shred. No doubt I was over dramatising the situation absurdly, but that is how it seemed. I remember going to a party after the show one night and passing a group of workmen digging a hole in the road. I thought what a wonderful job that must be. No worries, just digging; and tomorrrow, just digging again.

I met my friend Alan MacNaughtan in the street and told him about it. 'Yes,' he said. 'It happens after about eleven months. The brain rejects repetition.'

I had to do something to bring matters to a head. I decided that I must say my lines clearly, accurately and without faltering by, say, next Friday – the day was chosen quite arbitrarily – or I should have to run away and perhaps seek professional advice.

Friday was a day of horrible nervousness. When I got to the theatre I dressed immediately and then paced up and down, unable to relax. Yes, I knew the first line. Should I look at the first scene? Should I read the other scenes again? No, no, there was no point; I knew the words. That was the trouble – I was too familiar with the words, I could almost have spoken them backwards but I knew that if the blow fell I should be paralysed and speechless.

Minutes before I was called I was in the wings, waiting. I got through the scene, just, and fled back to my room. I had several changes of costume and fairly long waits between scenes; but that night, the moment I had changed I ran straight back into the wings, pacing up and down until my next entrance.

The curtain fell just before the monster got me and I did not have to consult a psychiatrist after all or run away, but it took many months and three more productions before I was able to regain my confidence.

After a year each of the principals in the cast was offered, in turn, a fortnight's holiday and Tricia, completely selfless as she has always been, pressed me to accept an invitation from two of our oldest friends, Garry and Patty Thorne, to spend a week at the villa they had rented in the South of France before taking the family for a week at the seaside in England.

I had dreamt about the Villa Terre de Sienne (so called because of its colour, like artists' burnt sienna) about seven times over the years. Although I had never been to that part of France, it was unmistakably Mediterranean. Standing on a slight rise before a navy blue sky, with peeling green shutters and flanked by pine trees, it was a landscape by Dufy. I recognised it immediately, principally because it had no front door. This detail had always puzzled me in my dreams but I found when we got there that, unusually, the house stood sideways on to the drive and the front door faced the long garden. I never dreamt of it again.

Early on the Thursday morning I was lying in bed contemplating our dinner, which was to be at the famous Colombes d'Or in St Paul de Vence, when the telephone rang. 'Oh, Paul,' called Patty. 'You've got a message.'

I leaped from my bed as though there were a charge of gunpowder under me. In those days an international call was an unusual event, and in the five minutes it took me to get dressed I decided that one of the children must have been run over. Then I read the message. Could I please ring the office after ten? Whoever it was evidently thought, quite rightly, that I might be unreachable after then. So, not one of the children. It must have been my understudy who had been killed.

My mind went into overdrive. Today was a matinée day. It was probably already too late to get to London for that, but I should be in time for the evening show if we drove over to Nice airport immediately and got to work booking a plane and cancelling the Colombe d'Or. I could phone from the airport. There was a single first-class seat left on the two o'clock plane. While Garry saw to that I went to telephone. When I got through I snapped, 'What's the matter? What's wrong?'

'Calm down,' said Anne Rawsthorne. 'It's just that Donald doesn't think that the man who's playing Palmer out of town in America is quite right. Would you be prepared to open on Broadway in a few weeks' time?'

I breathed hard for a few moments. 'Let me ring Tricia and find out what she feels and I'll call you back.'

For over forty years Tricia has worked tirelessly to promote my career, sacrificing her own in the process. We had less than a thousand pounds in the bank and four children, the youngest only a few months old, but she never once mentioned the hardship or the loneliness she would have to bear. She enthusiastically said that of course I must go.

I walked out of the phone booth on air and told Garry he could cancel the plane. Then we went up and sat on the terrace to drink cold white wine, contemplating our dinner in St Paul de Vence and watching the planes leaving for London.

The four of us from Bristol who were going to join the Broadway production scrambled somehow to New York, packing up after the show on the Saturday night and flying the next day. I sat next to Heather Chasen on the plane. Not long after take-off the pilot announced that we were thirty-five thousand feet above Bristol. 'Do you remember,' I said pointing down, 'that night when you said you hoped the play would succeed because we'd come an awfully long way to do it?'

We discovered that J.B. Priestley and his wife Jacquetta Hawkes were on the same flight and confidently expected a cheery message or even a bottle of champagne sent from first class, but no contact was made.

Many people I know love New York, and now and again when the bright October sun was shining, the nipping air gripping your ankles, the flags flying on Fifth Avenue and I caught a whiff of that authentic urban odour which used to excite me when I came back to London for the school holidays, I knew what they meant. But you have to be rich and successful really to enjoy New York, and I was neither. Three hundred dollars a week I had imagined to be a fortune; it was in fact a pittance. State tax, Federal tax and union dues mopped up over half of that at source, and I had to send a hundred dollars a week home. I was looking for dollar lunches. 'David Merrick loves English actors,' someone in the front office said to me one night. I thought she was going to say something nice about us. 'They're cheap,' she added.

It was about now that I noticed a red patch on my left hip, in one of the places where I had had radiotherapy. It was small, about the size of a walnut. It did not hurt or irritate, but no matter what ointment or unguent I applied it did not go away. I am aware that the tone in which this is written is somewhat ominous, but at the time it would have been invisible to all but my nearest and dearest and I put it at the back of my mind.

At intervals, too, the arthritis continued to pay me crippling visits and my spine began to twist a little, giving me a slight but, I felt, rather distinguished stoop. During these bouts it was not easy to move, but a stage is not usually very big and if one avoids, as I did, the heroically athletic parts, one does not have to move far in any one direction. I think I have always been able to manage things so as to disguise the awkwardness.

Robin Bailey was now playing the lead in *A Severed Head*, and was, as always, superb. 'You'll find the food in New York very samey,' he had said before we left. I was surprised; so far as I could see there were Italian, Jewish, French, Mexican and Japanese restaurants on every block. I even found an Indian restaurant one day, with the authentic red flock wallpaper and curry-stained tablecloths. One night he suggested that we had supper after the show and took me to Gilhooley's Irish Pub on Tenth Avenue where we had ham and eggs. I discovered that he only liked the plainest English food and went to Gilhooley's every night.

The show was under a heavy financial burden. Joan Fontaine, whom Heather had been brought over to replace, was substantially compensated – both her wounded pride and her orange groves in Florida were in need of irrigation – but the real reason for the play's short run was that the very English, straight-faced irony of Iris Murdoch's play escaped the curiously unsophisticated Americans and they were scandalised by its sexual excesses. When I was discovered in bed with my sister a horrified sussuration swept the audience: 'His sister! His sister!' And when I explained that she was only my half-sister there was a shocked silence, broken one night by a woman saying, 'As if that made any difference!' This apparent prudishness struck me as strange since, to get to us, our genteel audiences had to pick their way between the numerous porn shops of the theatre district.

Perhaps a kind of prudishness affected me too; the sleaze began to depress me. I had moved from my grand hotel on the Park to a much cheaper one within walking distance of the theatre, and one day I noticed a pin-sized hole in my bedroom door. I told Heather that night. 'Oh, yeah,' chuckled Billie, her black maid. 'My husband used to work there. He's seen some horrible things!'

Our Health Service in Britain was young then, the envy of the world. I used to look at the old men playing chess in Washington Square and think that to be old and ill in New York must be like Hell. There always seemed to be rubbish blowing about the streets and beggars rattling tin cans on every corner. Like the weather, all that has now drifted east to our shores.

I was accosted one morning on Macdougal Street in Greenwich Village by two black men, one of them short and malevolent, the other tall and malevolent with an ugly scar down one cheek. Scarface's opening was, 'You look like a businessman.'

I was deeply affronted: a businessman was the last thing I wanted to look like. 'Certainly not!' I said firmly.

There was some hesitation. 'Well, anyway,' he resumed, 'you can afford to give me fifty cents.'

'Oh, no, no, no, no,' I said in tones Lady Bracknell would have approved. 'I'm sorry.' I nearly added, 'my man.'

'You're sorry!' said Scarface, putting a fist under my nose. 'You won't live to be sorry!'

'I'm being mugged,' I thought. 'How utterly disgraceful. I shall complain to the British Consul first thing in the morning.'

I was only slightly surprised when the pair slunk off down the street.

Some time later I read a US Marines study on courage. Their finding was that everyone has some: some people have more, some less, and it gets used up. My tank was evidently still full.

British shows were very much in fashion on Broadway then. Barbara Windsor was appearing next door to us and there was a good deal of inter-dressing room visiting. It seemed to me that admiration for Miss Windsor's figure was based on firm foundations.

One day all the shows on Broadway were entertained to tea in the ballroom of the Hotel Pierre by the New York Guild of Lady Theatregoers, or a name very like it. It is always a pleasure to cock a snook at our tyrannical audiences and Victor Spinetti gave a speech entirely in cod Welsh, very rude but very funny.

Most of my friends, as I have said, are thrilled by New York. My comparative poverty undoubtedly put a damper on things for me, and when a prominent Broadway producer bounced into my room one night in our last week and said he wanted me to be in his new musical, I astounded him by politely declining. My flight was booked and the children's Christmas presents bought. After a last night when all the horrors of stage fright returned, and which was rounded off by my having an actual tug of war with the wardrobe mistress who claimed that my suit belonged to the producer, I climbed gratefully aboard the plane and fled home.

My association with Priestley continued briefly, and perhaps appropriately since he had told me in New York that he had been the one to 'discover' me – a distinction, in fact, claimed by several people. This was a TV adaptation of his play *Johnson over Jordan* with Ralph Richardson, who sometimes came to rehearsals in a chauffeur-driven Rolls Royce and sometimes on his motorbike.

We did all Richardson's scenes first to enable him to return to Spain where he was filming *Dr Zhivago*, and when we had finished them we said a collective farewell to the great man. A characteristic incident took place; Scott Finch came forward and said, with I think a slight genuflection, 'Bon voyage, Sir Ralph!' Richardson looked astounded, took two paces backwards, saluted and said, 'Hey, hey, hey. Captain!' No one was quite sure what to say.

The demon stagefright pursued me still, and did so into the next play, *Portrait of a Queen*, produced by Val May, which we did first at Bristol and then at the Vaudeville Theatre in the Strand. The play is a compilation of letters, diary entries and speeches by or about Queen Victoria, played beautifully by Dorothy Tutin with her husband Derek Waring a handsome Albert and Peter Vaughan an impressive Gladstone. I was Disraeli. If you act Disraeli in a play about the Queen you inevitably come on late, and in an act of absurd bravado I used to have a light supper at home in North London, after the curtain had in fact risen, and then drive in. Covent Garden was in those days still a fruit and vegetable market and by the time I arrived the streets were crowded with huge lorries. On two occasions I must have got the last parking spot in the West End.

Most of the speeches were distributed evenly between the Queen, Gladstone and myself, and to keep stagefright at bay I used to go over each of my own speeches while the other two were saying theirs. 'Thinking ahead' like this is not generally to be recommended, but it did reassure me and if I stuck on a word it gave me time to think of a substitute. While everyone else was giving eight performances a week, however, I was in effect giving sixteen.

Eventually I decided that this was a silly way of going on; I was inevitably going to forget my lines at least once in every play and life was too short to agonise over the fact, so I stopped worrying about it. I have appeared in many long and arduous pieces since then and have in fact had less trouble over them, in that sense, than I had anticipated.

Billing is of the utmost importance to actors and can cause difficulties even between the best and oldest of friends. I remarked jokingly to Peter Vaughan one day that I had the edge over him in the billing outside the theatre. 'What do you mean?' he asked with evident alarm. I replied that, as he knew, our names were hanging under the awning over the pavement. Mine, I reminded him, was at the Trafalgar Square end, his at the Kingsway end. 'How many people are going to come to the theatre from Kingsway?' I asked. 'They're all going to surge up the Strand.' He hurried away, and next day I noticed that they had been changed round.

One night Peter said to me, 'You know who's in front tonight?' I did not. 'The Greek princesses! You know who they are, don't you?' he demanded. 'Only the great-granddaughters of the Kaiser!' The girls must have gone back to Claridge's and told their parents that they had enjoyed the show, because a few nights later the King and Queen themselves came. A note came from the front-of-house manager asking us to stay on-stage after the final curtain as Their Majesties wanted to meet us. I confidently expected a diplomatic incident; at the very least, I thought, Peter would simply go back to his room. So I was not very reassured when he lined up beside me. There was some pleasant chat as the King and Queen passed along the line, but when they reached Peter I was aware of a slight commotion at my side. A nervous glance revealed that he was bowing deeply, rather like Winnie the Pooh on meeting the King of France. I like and admire Peter very much, but he is a big and formidable man and I did not feel like causing offence by laughing.

Charlie Girl with Anna Neagle and Derek Nimmo opened next door at the Adelphi, to most ghastly reviews. 'Well,' I thought, 'at least we'll run longer than they will!' *Charlie Girl* seemed to be at the Adelphi for most of the next decade.

After playing Disraeli I went back to Bristol again, this time to do my first musical, *Jorrocks*, an adaptation of R. S. Surtees' comic novels about fox-hunting. These appeal strongly to what turned out to be a comparatively small group of fans, but it was a jolly play and work is work. The eponymous hero was played by Joss Ackland, with Willoughby Goddard, Thelma Ruby, the beautiful tenor Bernard Lloyd and the young Richard Stilgoe. I played Captain Doleful, a lugubrious social climber. It went as merrily as a marriage bell and soon transferred to the Albery Theatre, then called the New, where the number of admirers, like those of the book, remained small but devoted.

Amongst some, though, it achieved cult status: one group of young men occupied a stage box on thirty-six occasions. They were accompanied one night, much to the management's chagrin, by an enormous Pyrenean mountain dog which sat shoulder to shoulder with them and appeared thoroughly to enjoy the show. The young men, who turned out to be a kind of harem kept by a millionaire businessman, threw a party for us in their handsome apartment.

'How lovely!' I said to one of them. 'What's it like living in Wilton Crescent?'

'Piss elegant,' was the reply.

For my Captain Doleful I was given the Derwent Award, a particularly pleasant thing to have as it is given by a committee of colleagues convened by our union, the British Actors' Equity Association.

At this time the BBC had just shown a highly successful series of Shakespeare histories. They now proposed to follow this up with the Roman plays, giving them the overall title of *The Fall of Eagles*. I had already done *Julius Caesar* at Bristol, playing Brutus to Keith Barron's rather well-fed Cassius in a production by Toby Robertson. When Val May had first asked me to do it and enquired what part I wanted to play, I had hesitated. I had not done a stage play for some time and felt very rusty; neither was I very familiar with this one. Memory told me it was a political play about a liberal revolt against tyranny that goes horribly wrong. Brutus I had remembered as a long and rather dull part. Mark Antony is the showy, starry part but I decided to play Brutus, which I knew would be hard work but would nevertheless be a good exercise. My virtue was rewarded; it is one of Shakespeare's most exciting plays, with so many modern parallels that one's hair stands on end.

When Peter Dews asked me to play the same part for the BBC I jumped at it. Keith Michell would be Mark Antony, Peter Cushing Cassius and Barry Jones Caesar. It was all done in the studios at the Television Centre in West London – even the scenes on horseback before the battle, for which the dead-level, rubberised studio flooring was covered with peat, making it very slippery. During the Brutus/Cassius farewell I saw, behind the camera shooting us, Mark Antony's horse at the head of the opposing army slip on the peat and fall. There was a crash of armour and a jangle of harness, and Keith Michell's scarlet cloak spread out beneath him.

'Forever and forever farewell, Cassius,' I said aloud, and to myself, 'There's a horse rolling on the star!' There was no stopping: it was live television.

The quarrel scene was thrilling – Brutus cool and ironic, Cassius trembling with anger and dismay. I think it was one of the best things Peter ever did. Sadly, I doubt if it was recorded. Peter's character, child-like and sweet-natured, was absurdly far from the horror movies for which he became so well known. He told his producer once that, although it was very kind of them, he really could not allow the film company to insure his life for such an enormous sum. It had to be explained to Peter that if he dropped dead the whole film would have to be recast and shot again. The insurance was not for him but for the producer. I took my children to see him once and we were entranced to find him lying on his back in the study with a ping-pong gun, shooting at a squadron of model planes suspended from the ceiling on threads. The death of his wife, Helen, was an enormous blow to him. He survived her with the greatest reluctance and retreated from almost everyone until his own death fifteen years later.

8

A Good Life

By 1968 I had many years' experience in most branches of the media, I had toured the whole country, worked abroad and appeared in several plays in the West End with some of the country's most distinguished actors, but Alan Bennett's *Forty Years On* was about to move my career into a subtly different dimension. To begin with it was a new play, which one does not come across all that often. A West End run was more or less guaranteed, and the actors already cast were Nora Nicholson, Dorothy Reynolds, Alan Bennett himself and above all John Gielgud, the actor I had always most admired.

When I was sent the play to read I fell for it immediately. The text is littered with some of the funniest jokes and scenes I had ever read and yet the cumulative effect is an Elgarian sadness – in fact a passage from Elgar's Violin Concerto is played in one scene – but any danger of sentimentality is avoided by Alan's use of ironic self- mockery. I longed to be in it, and I am sure that my enthusiasm was an enormous help to me when I was interviewed by the producer, Toby Rowland, the director, Patrick Garland, and Alan Bennett himself.

I realised much later that, by the time the producers are interviewing candidates for the supporting roles, they have lived with the play so long and so intimately that they have only a vague memory of the excitement they felt when they first read it. My bursting in as I did and telling them how marvellous it was must have been a great encouragement to them. Producers must feel at such times that, even though the chap might turn out to be an indifferent actor they had better keep him around if only for moral support. For whatever reason, they kept me around and we began our highly pleasurable rehearsals.

Gielgud was a constant source of instruction; his lyricism, the clarity and, crucially, the simplicity with which he conveyed his thoughts were lessons which I absorbed as diligently as I could. His vulnerability – one of the secrets of his appeal, of course – nevertheless surprised me, and I understood another aspect of the strain of being in such an exalted position. For years no one, except perhaps his long-term companion Martin had criticised him and he sometimes seemed unsure of himself. In the first scene the headmaster of the school in which the play within the play is set addresses the parents and old boys, in other words the audience. 'I think this talking-to-the-audience idea is so old hat, Patrick,' he said one day. 'Couldn't I just turn round and talk to the boys on the stage? Luckily he was dissuaded. In another scene he had to sit by the proscenium arch, speaking across the stage.

'I don't really care for this profile acting, you know,' he said.

'Where would you prefer to be?' enquired Patrick incautiously.

'Well, I really think I ought to be a little nearer the centre, don't you? And up a bit. And on something,' he added.

He eventually played the scene up-stage centre, seated on a tennis umpire's step-ladder and revealing so much gold bridgework when he spoke that Alan said it was like a glimpse into Fort Knox. I repeated this at home and my daughter wrote in a school essay, 'My daddy has a friend with a very precious mouth.'

For the first couple of weeks I was careful to call him 'Sir John'. He became increasingly restive. 'Oh, do call me John, please,' he said at last. Dame Edith certainly remained so during our brief acquaintance.

He could also be a wonderful teacher. There is a scene in which the master I was playing stands before a huge montage of photographs of young men of brilliant promise who did not return from the First World War. All I had to do was recite their names and go off. Sad passages had never been my forte. Faced with a sad speech I invariably fell for the temptation to speak it sadly; in other words, instructing the audience as to how they should receive it. Just as invariably this would go down like a lead balloon. It was the one bit of the play I did not feel happy with, and I was always glad to get it over. I came off one night to find Sir John standing waiting for his next entrance. He whispered to me, 'Why don't you say those names as though they were old friends you are glad to remember?' It was a most wonderful piece of advice. If the audience found the passage sad, well and good. If not, bad luck. I stopped patronising them. It opened up a whole new field of theatre for me.

When we took the play to the huge Opera House in Manchester, we had a disastrous week with sometimes no more than thirty people in the audience; evidently it baffled the Mancunians. This response did little for John's feelings of angst. The head is supposed to be rather seedy and unkempt. 'Martin feels I should have my hair nicely brushed,' John would say. 'He says I look a little farouche,' or 'Martin says my gown is very shabby. Do you think I should have a new one?' I suggested that we had a whip-round to send Martin to the Bahamas until after the London opening.

The only hint we had that week that we might after all be on the right lines was the night when we had a group of submariners in. They were on an electronics course and were guests of Messrs Exide. They laughed appreciatively, and at all the right moments.

The next week we were in Brighton and the whole thing was transformed; packed houses and a wonderfully warm reception. But John was still anxious. I met him wandering round the Lanes and we fell into step. 'I wish Alan would pull his finger out and write a funny scene,' he said at last.

Nora Nicholson was a delight. About eighty, she had avoided one of the major perils of old age, that of one's friends dying and leaving one alone, by preserving a talent for constantly making new friends amongst younger people. This is a piece of luck that surprisingly often comes an actor's way; most casts cover a wide age range and a feeling of camaraderie is the norm. She and I shared a love of *Twelfth Night* and knew it well. We were not in one scene of Alan's play but had to stay on the darkened half of the stage, so we used to play a game of cues. She would whisper, 'He has broke my head across,' and I would whisper back, 'And he has given Sir Toby a bloody coxcomb, too.'

The traumas and shared anxieties of rehearsing and touring a show reach a climax on an opening night in London, but this one was a triumph and thoroughly renewed the audiences' obvious affection for Sir John. Not that the play was entirely without critics. There was a hilarious scene in which Alan, as the divinity teacher, instructs a boy in the facts of life. He is evasive and inexplicit and is too embarrassed actually to tell the boy anything at all, but the scene aroused a fury in some reviewers that was surprising even then.

Alan's sharply critical view of Chamberlain's Munich meeting with Hitler and his appeasement policy in general enraged many older

Tories, and R. A. Butler's ex-Parliamentary Private Secretary wrote a letter of complaint to Sir John. ('Not to me, I notice!' Alan remarked.) During the Chamberlain scene one night a very large and, I suspect, drunken man, started to boo. 'Rubbish!' he shouted, and later, 'Not like that at all. Boo!' In due course he clambered out of his seat and stood in the aisle, ignoring his neighbours' appeals to shut up and sit down and booing from time to time. For the last ten minutes or so he edged his way nearer and nearer to the front of the stage and I began to wonder if he were going to leap up and physically assault us. I had been impersonating Chamberlain. The final curtain just beat him to it. As it was falling I saw the ever-volatile actor David Buck leap from his seat on the front row and crash his head into the heckler's midriff, bearing him out through the emergency exit.

The next night Alan appeared to be in a rather sombre mood. We shared a cup of tea in the interval. 'I didn't sleep very well,' he said. 'I was thinking about that man.' He took a sip. 'He didn't like the play, did he?'

'No, he didn't,' I replied.

'There we were,' Alan went on unhappily, 'all bowing and smiling, and the audience all cheering and clapping, and I suddenly thought – we're in the majority.'

The presence of the boys drew the adults together, and we cemented this feeling by supping together at least once a week. One night in Kettner's, at that time still a rather grand restaurant, Dorothy Reynolds' husband said in his rather affected voice, 'John, I've just been reading Edith Sitwell's letters. Loved hers to you!'

'Really?' said John vaguely. 'I don't think I've read them yet.'

'Did you really know Vita Sackville-West?' I asked one day.

'Oh, yes,' he replied mistily.

'Gosh!' I said. 'What was she like?'

'Oh . . .,' he hesitated. 'Tiresome old dyke.'

He seemed to have known all the people Alan had written about. One evening he observed, 'I can't think why Ottoline Morrell had an affair with Bertie Russell. Terribly bad breath, you know.'

I think I was present at the birth of an idea one night. Alan and Nora and I were standing in the darkened wings during a scene about a small boy and his nanny. 'I had a nanny,' whispered Nora. 'A strange woman – she didn't like to be touched. She used to say, "No, don't touch me; something might form."' Alan was thrilled and reached for the notebook he always carries. He was writing *Habeas Corpus* at the time, and when eventually I saw it I heard Lady Rumpers say, 'No, don't touch me. There's far too much touching nowadays. If I want to be touched there are people at home who can touch me.'

When you go to the theatre you see the posters outside advertising, say, Joseph Bloggs and Ethel Strange, in such and such a play by J. B. Murdoch and then there is a list of the other actors ending perhaps 'And John Dull'. In smaller letters, unless he is Peter Brook, will be the director's name. The placing of these names and the size of the lettering will have been a matter of sharp dispute and bargaining between the actors, their agents and the management, of a nature that would make the average oriental souk seem like Marks and Spencer's.

The manager's aim is to get as many people into the theatre as possible and if one or two of the names will help, they go to the top. The aim of most of the stars is to go just there and thus demonstrate to the world that the manager regards them as having huge drawing power. The rest of the cast will want to be as near to the top as possible, for the same reason. John Dull may have accepted 'And John Dull' with bad grace, feeling that he really ought to be up there with Joseph and Ethel above the titles. As one reads from left to right the name on the left is regarded as more significant. Joseph and Ethel are equally important stars, so the manager's solution is to put Ethel's name in slightly larger letters than Joseph's.

Money is naturally also of vital importance. A star with Sir John's dizzy status will probably have received a basic weekly sum and ten per cent of the profits. Not necessarily – it could have been more – but all actors tend to be very cagey about their incomes and this, of course, plays into a manager's hands.

The bargaining can even extend to dressing rooms. I heard a malicious story (true, nevertheless) that two very well-known actors were unable to agree over this and swapped dressing rooms, and billing, every night. When my dear friend Richard Briers and I were in *Home* at Wyndham's Theatre, he allowed my name to appear on the bills to the left of his in exchange for his having the number one dressing room. The bargain was made entirely amicably, but we both noticed quite a hard look in each other's eyes.

The length of a contract is another bargaining factor. The manager naturally wants to keep a star as long as possible and it has become a bit of a feather in an actor's cap to negotiate not, as you might expect, as long but as short a contract as the manager can afford. Sir John's in *Forty Years On* was short, and the search began for his successor. Naturally I was not privy to these matters, but a theatre grapevine is a lively vegetable and I learnt that, amongst others, Robert Morley had been to see the play – twice. Interestingly he was reported as saying no – he was a funny man and the play was too sad. Emlyn Williams was the eventual choice.

When this was announced I saw one of the small boys – probably Freddie Foot, who had put the theatre's ten-pin bowling team on the notice board with Sir John Gielgud as captain ('How absurd, I know nothing of bowling,' he had said, delighted) – jumping up and down in front of him. 'Sir John, Sir John!' he was saying. 'Has Emlyn Williams got a bigger name than yours?'

John looked surprised. 'Well,' he said, 'it's longer.'

It quickly became apparent that it was not as good a choice as it looked on paper. There was a ghoulish quality about Emlyn that did not suit the headmaster at all. At one point he summons one of the boys: 'Come here, boy!' Gielgud said it with a lofty impatience. The way Williams said it sent shivers down one's spine.

'Emlyn,' said Patrick Garland tentatively, 'could you say that line a little more benevolently?'

'Oh, "benevolently". You're not trying to teach me how to play comedy, are you Patrick?' replied Emlyn menacingly.

Emlyn's benevolence closely resembled Count Dracula's and the boys thoroughly enjoyed it. Twice Emlyn caught them behind the scenes imitating him and, as audiences declined, the atmosphere grew steadily more uneasy. The bubble burst one night halfway through the headmaster's long opening speech. He stumbled over his words, recovered, then stumbled again. There was a pause. At last he said to the audience, 'I'm sorry, I'm so sorry', backing out of the line of 'staff' and disappearing into the wings.

We were paralysed. After what seemed a lengthy pause there was a heavy thud as of a body collapsing and the boys, being boys, burst into giggles. Emlyn was carried to his roon, his understudy crammed on the costume and about five minutes later we started again.

Emlyn never rejoined us. I went to see him, propped up in bed in his bijou residence in Dovehouse Street in Chelsea, all pink ribbon and Dresden shepherdesses, and later he asked me to go and see his one-man Dickens reading, which he had done all over the world and which was wonderful. Perhaps he had done the one-man show for so long and with such success that he felt uneasy in an ensemble.

SO FAR, SO GOOD

* * *

Forty years On may have been more intellectually demanding but television had always been good to me. In 1968 Thames Television made its last series in black and white. Called *Frontier*, it was set at the end of the nineteenth century on the North-West Frontier of India, where the tectonic plates, as it were, of the British and Russian Empires constantly ground together in dispute over the buffer, Afghanistan. It was one of those rare occasions when everything worked exactly as it should. The scripts were good, the direction and camera work excellent, the cast could not have been bettered and the whole enterprise seemed to draw out everyone's best. My old friend John Phillips played the Colonel, James Maxwell the political officer and Patrick O'Connell the sergeant major.

The stories were about a young officer (Gary Bond) serving in an élite cavalry group, and the first episode contained scenes of a passing-out parade at Sandhurst. The general taking the parade was played by an actor called Geoffrey Lumsden, and he gave us a strong hint that the gods were on our side. The stories were based on fact, and it turned out that a great-uncle of Geoffrey's had raised just such a group in India, called 'Lumsden's Horse'. At the top of the steps before which we filmed the parade stood a neo-classical building containing Sandhurst's India Museum, on the walls of which hangs a portrait of General Lumsden.

When I was discussing my appearance with the designer I said I thought that the character I played, a journalist from *The Illustrated London News*, one of the earliest war correspondents, would probably have romantic military aspirations himself, dressing and behaving as much as possible like the officers he was messing with. I wore breeches and boots, a military-looking coat, a Sam Browne belt and a bush hat – an officer, but for badges of rank. The centenary of *The Illustrated London News* fell while we were filming and a special edition was published. It included a photograph of their correspondent in the Afghan Wars. Apart from a moustache and pince-nez his appearance was identical to mine. The coincidence was almost uncanny.

Meticulous attention was paid to historical detail. The Lee Enfield, the Army's standard rifle for generations, had not yet been introduced at the time the series was set. A less conscientious producer would not have bothered, but we had the authentic Martini Henrys. The outside work was done in North Wales, near Beddgellert. It was certainly a long way from Afghanistan but my father-in-law, who had served on the Frontier in the twenties, was astonished by its similarity.

One plot had three of us disguised as Afghan warriors with head-dresses, silver-bound rifles and flowing robes. We stood shivering on a mountaintop for a long time, as one can easily do when filming. Looking at the catering wagons far below, it began to feel very like lunchtime. 'I'll bet they've forgotten all about us,' we agreed, and set off. Halfway down we met a party of climbers on the way up: backpacks, spiked boots and bobble hats. It was a scene that could only have taken place in Britain. They looked at us, dumb with embarrassment. Clearly they had slipped into a nightmare – something to do with the altitude, perhaps. Each party remained silent and, after a last appalled glance, the climbers bent once more to their task.

Earl Mountbatten paid us a visit at the studios in Teddington and we were paraded to meet him. As he walked along the line he came to Cyril Shaps dressed as a mufti, with a beard and a large leather-bound book. 'What's that – the Koran, I suppose?' said Mountbatten and Cyril was alarmed to hear himself saying, 'Solly, no spik English.' The Earl passed on his way.

Colour suddenly took us – the actors, anyway – by surprise, and with much anguish the series was axed. There was a brief period of optimism when we heard that we might go on filming it in Malta but, just as his pen was poised over the very large cheque that would have been needed, Lew Grade's hand faltered and we bade the series a sad farewell. I think it might well have continued very successfully and sales abroad would almost have been guaranteed. It would certainly have looked wonderful with the scarlet coats, white pipeclay, colourful robes, Pathan tribesmen and wild scenery. Ah well!

The need to earn a living has led many times to my having to suspend my critical faculties. Not for me the luxury of deciding to steer my career in a particular direction. Which is how, in the mid-seventies, I came to be appearing in a dim little thriller called *Hine* for Thames TV.

Barrie Ingham, who was playing the eponymous hero, came into rehearsals one morning and said that he had been at a dinner party the previous evening. He had told his fellow guests what he was doing and had mentioned the fact that I was in the cast. On hearing my name, one of them had exclaimed, 'My God!' When Barrie had asked him what he meant, he said, 'My God. He is my God.' Apparently his home town was Ipswich and he used to see me there at the Rep.

He had actually played my son in one of the plays, and went on to say that it was seeing my performance as Petruchio in *The Taming of the Shrew* that had made him decide to make the stage his career.

Naturally I was eager to know who had made this declaration, and was told it was Trevor Nunn. It crossed my mind to wonder why I was not playing leading roles in the Royal Shakespeare Company. So I wrote to Trevor and mentioned casually how long it seemed since we had met. Was it not time we had lunch?

We met at the Waldorf Hotel – the RSC was then still at the nearby Aldwych Theatre – and I was comprehensively 'Trevved'. A 'Trev' is a smothering embrace, often in a fur coat, and is sometimes the prelude to a deal.

I wasted no time. I said the two great repertory companies had always made me feel rather nervous. They were such large organisations, I had the feeling that one might get swamped. I had seen it happen; fine actors had gone into such companies, done lots of good work but had gradually dropped out of the public consciousness. Also there seemed to me to be a danger of allowing the comparative security of such a position to encourage one to play safe and perhaps fall into a routine. None of this was Trevor's concern, of course; I was really clearing my own mind. I did go on to say, though, in a heavily hinting way, that were I to be asked to join one of these companies I would feel that I ought to take up the challenge.

Before Trevor had time to issue one I told him that I did, however, have one or two worries. I said that I suffered from a painful arthritic condition and was anxious about the daily exercises in which, I had heard, everyone in the company was expected to take part.

'Yes, I'm afraid so.'

'Even Peggy Ashcroft?'

'Well, no. Not Peggy.'

I have never been able to give a convincing performance at an audition. Was it true, I asked, that all candidates for the RSC had to do one?

'Oh, yes. Everyone.'

'Everyone?'

'Oh, yes.'

'Peggy?'

'No no, not Peggy.'

He said that I need not worry; they were not really auditions – they were, he said, 'workouts'. He explained that at a workout a director would 'work' with an actor, they would examine a scene together, explore its possibilities and find out how the actor responded to them. I said I thought that sounded a much better idea than an audition where you just stood on the stage and recited some pieces to a darkened auditorium.

A few weeks later I got a call from the office to make an appointment for my workout. The young woman asked me to learn one of the longer speeches from *Henry IV*.

That was fine, I said, but I was in the middle of recording a TV series and I doubted whether I would have the time to learn that as well. But she said that as it would be for John Barton and Buzz Goodbody she thought they really would like me to learn it. I tried not to let Miss Goodbody's first name worry me and replied that I did not think my ability to learn lines was in question.

'It is only a workout, after all,' I told her.

'Yes,' she said, doubtfully.

On the appointed day I arrived at the Aldwych stage door and told the doorkeeper my name. I said that I had come for the workout.

'The what?' he said.

'The workout.'

He looked baffled.

'With Mr Barton and Miss Goodbody.'

His brow cleared. 'Oh, the audition!' And he directed me to the stage.

I gave a rather dull reading of the Shakespeare and was thanked warmly for my trouble. Perhaps I should not have been all that surprised to get a letter from Trevor a few days later. He said that some members of the company whom he had been expecting to leave at the end of the season were not, after all, going to do so. To his great regret, therefore, he would not be able to offer me the place he had been hoping to. Perhaps another time.

The various kinds of entertainment media seem to fall into watertight compartments, and people who work in one are often ignorant of what is going on in the others. I had often felt the frustrations to which this gives rise. Having once successfully played a Jew on TV, it was quite difficult for some months to persuade producers that I could be anything else. Then a particularly courageous producer offered me the part of an SS officer, but having played that I was rejected by the next because I 'didn't look Jewish enough'.

For years now I had played nothing but comic roles in the theatre, and on TV nothing but serious ones. I felt sure that I would not get very far with the vast audiences that TV provided until I was allowed to play a comic part and suggested this to several producers. I was met with patronising smiles and the implied request not to try and teach them their business. At her suggestion, I did once get to read for a part in a new series starring my friend Wendy Craig, opposite whom I had played many such roles at Ipswich Rep; but I was rejected, on the grounds that the series would be recorded before a live audience. I was clearly very clever, the producer told my agent, but he was worried that I might not be able to act in front of a live audience.

John Howard Davies who, as a fair-haired waif, played Oliver in the film of *Oliver Twist*, was now a producer at the BBC. Unusually amongst his colleagues he and his PA and floor manager, Brian Jones, went frequently to the theatre and, moreover, allowed what they saw there to influence John's casting. What he was casting in the autumn of 1975 was *The Good Life*. It so happened that the series, written by Bob Larbey and John Esmonde, and very different in character from anything written by Alan Ayckbourn, nevertheless explored the same social territory. There had already been several West End productions of Ayckbourn plays which John and Brian had seen; Felicity Kendal and Penelope Keith had recently been in *The Norman Conquests* and Richard and I had both, at different times, been in *Absurd Person Singular*. Richard, of course, had long been a TV star. I had done other series, playing subsidiary roles; I was the sinister Mr Strand in *Special Branch*, as nasty as I could make him, with George Sewell and Patrick Mower, and I had 'featured' – I think that is the word – in that distinctly unthrilling thriller, *Hine*, but now I jumped at the chance to play a comic role in *The Good Life*.

We all met, long before one freezing dawn, in someone's garage in suburban Northwood. We were in the garage because the lady of the house was unwilling, understandably enough, to allow actors into the house. She had already agreed, for a fee, to let the BBC plough up her lawn, plant (plastic) vegetables in her borders and erect pigsties and chicken-coops on the rest. By the time the series was finished the garden had been dug up and relandscaped four times. In other respects our hostess was not unlike Penelope Keith in the series. As soon as the sun was up she was on the telephone to the neighbours, inviting them round to sit in the lounge and drink sherry whilst watching the actors filming in the garden. On recording days it was a pleasure to see her and her husband take their seats on the front row of the studio audience.

The BBC was grateful to her; finding the location had not been all that easy. Surbiton, which sounds so right, consists mostly of large Victorian mansions divided into flats, and Brian, having discovered what he thought to be the ideal house in another suburb, had been sharply rebuffed by the owner who had said that her TV aerial was seriously out of order and she wanted nothing further to do with the BBC.

The cast was immediately a team. I had acted with Felicity some time before in a highly implausible science fiction play, and Richard and I had sat together as Equity councillors. Penny I knew only from a very funny advertisement for Benson & Hedges which she did on television. Our friendships were genuine and have held fast ever since. Such relationships not only make one's working life infinitely happier but are an invaluable ingredient in a successful show. Many people remarked on the comradely feelings we appeared to share.

Not that we knew that it was going to be a success. It seemed to all of us, I think, a little pedestrian. The only slightly unusual thing about it was the fact that the Goods – Richard and Felicity – decide to get out of the rat-race and try to be self-sufficient. Otherwise it was a simple tale about a very ordinary couple, over the garden fence from another very ordinary couple.

It quickly became clear that its ordinariness was one of the magic ingredients that made it a fairy-tale hit. The other was that the authors had anticipated by no more than a couple of days, it seemed, the sudden public awareness of The Environment. Instantly, everyone was talking about open spaces, animal welfare, pollution and the rat-race.

There was a third factor which was quite accidental. The first few scripts we read were peppered with some racily fashionable four-letter words. None of us, as actors, has any objection to saying them if the context is right, but for those people in those surroundings it did not seem so. We could not imagine Margo allowing Jerry to utter a rude word even behind a closed bedroom door. We spoke to the authors, who thanked us warmly. They explained that it was the first posh script they had written. They removed the offending words and this proved an enormous bonus; we lost count of the number of letters we received and the number of people who stopped us in the street, congratulating us on doing something they could watch with their children. I have no doubt that the little beasts knew at least as much as their parents and perhaps we should, as 'artists', have despised such an attitude, but we were purveying family entertainment and we did not.

Writing stories about mankind's relationship with vegetables is, I expect, limiting and attention inevitably turned to the relationship between the two couples. Although the Goods' efforts to wrest a living from their garden (quite impracticable, incidentally) were always centre stage, Margo's snobbery and social climbing and Jerry's gross materialism seized the public fancy. There was even a piece in the *Evening Standard* one day which said that we, the neighbours, had stolen the series.

I think the friendly spirit in which we worked is illustrated by the awkwardness that Penny and I felt at the next day's rehearsal. She and I arrived first and decided to pretend that we had not read the script. A moment later Richard and Felicity came in laughing. 'Oh, isn't it marvellous!' Richard shouted. 'We do all the work and you two get all the credit! Never mind,' he went on, 'I get the money.'

As well as editing out the rude words the authors made another change, just for me. Aware of the enormous power of television and of the fact that to most viewers the life that Jerry and Margo lived – two cars, a yacht, restaurants, theatres and so on – represented what for most people would be The Good Life indeed, I was worried that Jerry was written as a smoker. I asked the authors to write that out if they could, and very kindly they did. In the same spirit I always used a seat-belt in the car, even though wearing one was not yet the law.

Before long the series was being sold to thirty, forty, sixty countries and sub-titled or dubbed into many languages. It was *It's a Green World* in Denmark, I remember, and *Good Neighbors* in America, and as many countries again pirated it across borders. The series was not sold to France, although they later bought, astonishingly, *'Allo 'Allo*. Sales to South Africa were banned at the time but someone told me I was 'very big in Johannesburg', and Donald Albery in Monte Carlo told me that all the episodes could be had from the video shop round the corner.

Understandably, most people think that all this must have made us millionaires, and in America perhaps it would have done. Penny's success was exceptional and it was a great pleasure to watch her graduation from public bus to chauffeur-driven limousine. A tax inspector once put his head above the parapet to observe sarcastically, 'You seem to take a lot of taxis, Miss Keith.'

'Mr Smith,' she replied, point-blank, 'a woman in my position is simply unable to use public transport.'

He dissolved.

The BBC has many ingenious ways of keeping costs down, and one of them was the payment of royalties on the basis of the number of TV sets owned by the population in a particular country. Commercial television based on that criterion naturally paid handsomely in the USA, but sales there were as rare as hens' teeth. In less sophisticated regions of the world the usual arrangement seems to have been that a set would be slung from a tree in the rainforest and tribes from miles round would gather to watch the goings-on in suburbia. I once had a cheque for royalties from half a dozen Central African states – for £1.25, plus VAT. Even some royalties from US sales would, I suspect, bring a smile to the face of an American actor. I have a notification of one before me now for a part I played in an episode of *A Bit of Fry and Laurie* which was sold to the USA. It is dated 9 December 1994 and is for £11.34.

There are many advantages in doing a series, apart from the obvious one of simply being in work and not having to rely on meagre royalty payments to keep body and soul together. If it is successful you can reasonably expect a certain amount of continuity, and usually there is plenty of time in the year to do other things. Most series are organised to be put out each week for half a year and they are rehearsed and recorded in batches of six, seven or eight – one episode per week.

Those few weeks are hectic. Tuesdays you read the script, make any necessary adjustments to it and start rehearsing. By the next morning you have more or less learnt it. Saturday morning you do a couple of final runs, and on Sunday you are in the studio for an all-day dress rehearsal with the cameras. The director disappears into the control gallery, his instructions transmitted via the floor manager.

Few things are more disquieting than to find yourself surrounded by four or five cameras with the cameramen all chuckling at something they have heard over their headphones. I instinctively check my zip. I was once standing near a discarded pair of headphones and heard, 'Tell that stupid cow to get out of the shot!' 'Darling, could you move a couple of inches to your left?' was the floor manager's tactful translation.

Technical wizardry can be a hindrance. At one dress rehearsal I was enjoying a scene that I was watching on the monitor when suddenly the action ground to a halt. 'Hullo,' I thought, 'someone's off who should be on!' It was me. Big Brother lurks all round the studio. You only have to mutter a disparaging word about the producer to realise that there is a microphone hovering six inches above your head and that the entire control gallery is listening.

One day we were told that the Queen had said she would like to see an episode of *The Good Life* recorded. This was something that royalty had never done before, and the Television Centre was plunged into a frenzy of excitement and preparation. There were sniffer dogs, marksmen on the roof, security checks here, there and everywhere, and fierce competition for seats – internal competition, of course; the public was rigorously excluded. On our monitor we watched the royal Daimler's stately arrival. Once in our costumes, made up and having crossed the corridor dividing the dressing rooms from the stage, we were only allowed back under escort.

The highlights of that episode, so far as Her Majesty was concerned, were clearly the occasions when we forgot our lines. She laughed heartily, but we were so infected by the hysteria that had taken hold of the entire BBC that night that we did not make many mistakes and raced through the piece in record time. This had mildly unfortunate consequences, as the drive back to the Palace had been minutely programmed to sweep through all the traffic lights and bottlenecks without interruption. No matter how much amusing conversation the royal party made with us they still left earlier than planned, and the Daimler home was apparently brought to a halt two or three times under the startled gaze of various rush-hour taxi drivers and bus passengers.

We had not long completed the first series when, early in 1976, Pietro Garinei and Alessandro Giovannini, the foremost comedy producers in Rome, decided to present *Absurd Person Singular* in Italian (*Assurdo Singulari*) at the Teatro Parioli. They needed, they said, an English person who was very familiar with the text to advise them. Alan Ayckbourn's formidable literary agent, Peggy Ramsey, suggested me. I would be needed for less than two weeks and the money, 300,000 lire, although it sounded princely to me, was little more than a tip. They would give me B and B at the tiny Hotel Sistina, near the top of the Spanish Steps. Presumably my job would be to come in at a late stage of rehearsals, say, 'No, no, in London we did it like so and so,' show them how to do the funny business with the light fitting and generally sit back and . . . well, advise. The idea of a few days in the early spring sunshine in Italy was by no means unattractive, either. I said yes.

At about the same time Michael Codron asked me to direct the UK tour of *Absurd Person Singular*, with a cast headed by the then relatively unknown John Thaw. Michael offered me the sort of fee I would get for two weeks in the West End. I suppose he wanted me for the same reason they wanted me in Rome, and not because he saw in me a brilliant new director. Again I threw him into a rictus of anxiety by saying that I did not want a fee at all; I asked him for a royalty – there was no agreed minimum then – of one half of one per cent of the gross. It turned out to be a reasonable deal, and I eventually made about double what I would have done otherwise. The only snag was that rehearsals were due to begin two days before my return from Rome. Well, they would have to start without me.

In the weeks before I was due to fly out to Italy, Garinei rang me several times and asked me to 'bring something for the show'.

'What sort of thing?'

'Anything. Anything that would help.'

I was baffled. Then I thought that perhaps I could act as a sort of assistant stage manager and gather some props. I knew that they wanted the production to look as English as possible and that it might be difficult to get Gordon's gin in Rome, so I got a couple of empty bottles of Gordon's. A light bulb has to be changed in the play and I thought that British bayonet fittings would be a nice touch. The bulb had to be incapable of lighting up, and although light bulbs always 'go' by the half dozen, finding a dud is not easy: the local shopkeepers in North London were beginning to look at me a little strangely. The pet shop came up with a good assortment of budgerigar toys, little mirrors and ladders and so on, and though I discovered that taking clothes pegs to Rome is something of a wasted effort I was right in thinking that a plastic tea-cosy would be welcome; I think mine was the only one in the Eternal City.

Three yards of clothes line was a problem. The assistant brought me some in dazzling white nylon.

'It's a bit clean,' I said doubtfully.

'Well, yes,' he agreed.

He showed me some in electric blue.

'No, no,' I said. 'Far too blue.' Eventually I settled for some sash cord.

'Excuse me, sir,' enquired the assistant. 'May I ask what you want this for?'

'Yes, of course,' I replied. 'I should have told you. It's for a woman who is trying to hang herself in a very dirty kitchen.'

'I see.' He glanced round uneasily.

I could read his mind. He had seen my face somewhere before. Clearly we were on *Candid Camera*, and he was not going to make a fool of himself.

The same communications problem that I had experienced with the shopkeepers of Hornsey arose when a customs officer at Rome Airport asked to see my baggage. There were the contents of a budgerigar cage, a bag of clothes pegs, a washing line, two empty gin bottles, a plastic tea-cosy and some dud light bulbs. I daresay a kilo or so of cocaine would have gone unnoticed. I was glad that Giovannini had come to meet me.

Rehearsals in Rome never start before 3p.m., and as he drove me to work the next day – the wrong way down a one-way street – I asked him how long they had been rehearsing.

'We have read it,' he said, ignoring two policemen who were waving ping-pong bats at us.

'But how long have you been rehearsing?'

'We have read it.'

Curious.

The Rome Tennis Club, where we were to rehearse, is a very grand marble hall on the banks of the Tiber opposite the Foro Italica (known to all as the Foro Mussolini). Actors are actors the world over, and that afternoon the hall rang to reassuring cries of, 'Darling! *Caro mio!*' and the rattle of coffee cups. Dubbing foreign films into Italian is big business amongst actors there, and their English is good. I was introduced to Luigi la Monica, my voice in the Italian *Good Life*. A marquis, no less.

After a few minutes Pietro clapped his hands and shouted. '*Silenzio!*' He smiled at me. 'My darling,' he said. 'Start!'

Everyone turned expectantly. To say that I was dumbfounded would be an understatement. There had obviously been a serious misunderstanding. Most directors spend several months preparing a production. I was given less than ten seconds. There was Alessandra Massaini, the foremost comedienne in Rome, standing at the side of the set waiting for my instructions. The three acts of the play are set in three different kitchens. In the rehearsal room a series of trestle tables stood in for the furniture, and for the convenience of the actors these were labelled '*lavatrice*', '*lavandino*' and so on, and the light fitting '*porte lampa*'. For my convenience, too, as it happened. I had not appeared in the first scene, I had not even seen it for several months and I had quite forgotten the layout, let alone the moves. I took a deep breath.

'*Signorina!*' I croaked. '*Al lavandino!*' She went to the sink. I breathed again.

I was surprised that the actors were not holding their scripts. Not that they had learnt their lines; they had not. Nor did they ever, in the sense of swotting them up at home. The ASM, a sturdy young woman in black riding boots and a light moustache – a Neapolitan and therefore for some reason deeply unpopular with the rest of the company – stood in front of the actors and loudly dictated their lines which they shouted back, learning as they went. Or so they said. We were in a marble hall, the walls of which shouted the lines all over again amongst themselves. A three-way argument was sheer Bedlam.

By the middle of the week, though, I was getting bold and inserting little bits of half-remembered musical directions. '*Gino*,' I would say. '*Alla lavatrice. Presto, ma non troppo!*' or '*Largo*,' or '*Molto vivace*,' as the fancy took me, and by the end of the week I was becoming quite inventive. '*Enrico*,' I said, explaining how I wanted him to go stiff on receiving an electric shock. '*Elettrico! Tutto rigido!*' They were deeply impressed.

Giovannini took me aside. 'How you speak Italian?' he demanded. 'You have lived in Roma?'

I shrugged modestly.

'You have learn in Londra?'

I shook my head.

'*Singulare!*'

I had set myself a punishing routine. In spite of not rehearsing in the mornings we worked as many hours as we would have done in London. We did not have tea breaks; a tray of sandwiches and flasks of coffee stood on a table and we helped ourselves as we could, finishing rehearsals at about nine. Then it was back to the hotel for a shower and out foraging for supper. Sometimes I was courteously offered a menu in English. 'Shepherd-meat pads' I remember avoiding.

I could not stay for the first night but the play did not run very long. The moment I was out of sight the cast were, I was told, at each other's throats.

They gave me a delightful send-off lunch in a smart restaurant which was already full to bursting when we arrived. The problem was dealt with like the parking problem outside; you just pushed and shoved until there was room.

'Alessandro,' I said to my host. 'I should be at the airport, you know.'

'How you fly? British Air?'

'Alitalia.'

'Oh,' he said, relieved. 'You arrive half an hour late, you all right!'

And so it proved. I arrived at an apparently deserted airport, clutching my suitcase, half of it packed with my pyjamas and toothbrush and the rest with crisp Italian banknotes. I was waved through empty passport and customs halls and out on to the tarmac, still running. I little knew, as I scrambled into a taxi at Heathrow and sped on my way to the English rehearsals of *Absurd Person Singular*, that, while I was still in the air, the lira had been devalued. My little store of banknotes had dwindled to half the already modest sum it had been when it started the journey.

The English job was a bit more disciplined than the Italian one; it looked good and sounded good, and I very much enjoyed the opportunity to help people to give of their best. John Thaw did not need my help, of course, and seemed a little wary of me anyway, but it was an interesting experience; it filled theatres, made money for everyone and generally served its purpose.

Meanwhile the popularity of *The Good Life* continued to grow. Turn by turn we used to give end-of-shoot parties after the last recording of each series. At one of them Penny gave us all a very delicious chilli con carne. At about three the following morning Tricia and I rose from our bed like rockets and fought each other for the bathroom. At midday I struggled up from the floor and telephoned Richard.

'Are you ill, too?' he said, relief in every syllable. 'Thank God, I thought alcohol poisoning had got me at last!'

Penny had not been called the next time we met and we nervously discussed who would be the one to tell her. John Howard Davies got the short straw, but never had the courage to confront her. So one day I suggested to Penny that she should tell everyone she was having another chilli con carne supper, as the last one had been such a success. 'Why? Were you ill?' she said, understanding immediately. It seems that dried kidney beans have arsenic in them and they have to be soaked overnight to leach it out. This Penny had not known, and as a result had nearly wiped out the entire cast and crew. I have never seen her laugh so heartily.

I joined Penelope Keith again on stage when I took over from Peter Barkworth in Michael Frayn's comedy *Donkey's Years*. Michael Rudman directed and Michael Codron was the producer (why were they all called Michael?). As in *Absurd Person Singular*, the first cast had been together for the best part of a year; now there was to be a clean sweep, and Anna Massey and I headed an entirely new one. Michael Rudman was a stern taskmaster and, despite being a Jew, is the possessor of a keen Protestant work ethic. He has little sympathy for sybarites like myself who just yearn for a quiet life, but he was good for me and rehearsals rattled along. We were due to open on a Monday.

The previous Wednesday morning, the stage manager telephoned. Peter Barkworth, Tricia told me while I was in the shower, had got a horribly sore throat and would not be doing that day's matinée. As I already knew the part pretty well, sooner than frighten the understudy and go through all the hassle that putting him on would entail, might it not be a good idea for me to do it instead? Just for the one performance? I asked her to say that we would talk about it and call him back in five minutes.

We thought that starting that afternoon might have several advantages. It would, partly at any rate, neutralise the trauma of the first night; the afternoon cast would not be suffering from nerves, and anyway it was a mid-week matinée. Only a few elderly ladies would be there, up from the suburbs for a look round Harrod's, a light lunch with a friend, a show and home for a late tea. I could see them clearly. Tricia said she would come with me to act as my dresser and generally hold my hand. I rang the stage manager and left for the morning rehearsal.

What none of us had taken into account was that Penny had had a very considerable success in *Donkey's Years* and that, in the eyes of the television public, each of us was a star. It seemed as though the whole of theatrical London had come to the Globe to see her last mid-week matinée; it was packed. I doubt if you could have got standing room in a box. It seemed to have little to do with the play. When Penny and I had our first encounter, from all over the house you could hear whispers of, 'Jerry and Margo! It's Jerry and Margo!'

The play itself seemed quite unfamiliar to me. With twelve months' performances behind them the cast raced through it, leaving me standing but kindly helping me out when I was caught open-mouthed. Some of them I had met before, while others were strangers whose identity I had to guess when they came on to the stage. I have seldom felt less at ease. Tricia gave me a comforting hug afterwards and I gratefully prepared to go home. It was not to be. Peter never reappeared, and I played opposite Penny for all her final performances that week.

It all reaped a dividend on the following Monday, the opening night of the replacement cast. By that time I had already given six performances and was able to observe the first-night nerves of the rest of the cast with some complacency. Unfortunately we have no record of what the critics thought of our performances; Anna Massey, who had taken over from Penelope, had a sudden rush of self-doubt and they were not invited.

There were, of course, other things going on in my life at this time. Charing Cross Hospital did a fourteen-year follow-up of patients with ankylosing spondylitis. About twenty of us turned up and Dr O'Connell, who had made the original diagnosis, said that although my blood tests showed it to be still active – a fact of which I was painfully aware every three or four weeks – I was the only one of the group who was still upright and relatively mobile. He put it down to willpower, although I have to say that I was never aware of any great struggle; it is simply taken for granted in our profession that, if humanly possible, an actor turns up for work. Dr Greasepaint is a very remarkable physician.

The mysterious red patches on my trunk were still there. The skin remained unbroken, it was not painful, it did not itch. Year by year it grew a little more extensive. No one could tell me what it was.

9

Very Droll, Minister

∽∾∽

The first play I did in the West End which was both new and in which I had top billing, shared with Julia McKenzie, was another Alan Ayckbourn piece *Ten Times Table*. It had already been tried out in Ayckbourn's home theatre in Scarborough, and Ayckbourn himself decided to direct it in the West End.

A small-town committee is making a doomed attempt to organise a historical pageant. Without stretching the imagination too far, it could be taken for a political allegory: there is a fierce left-winger, a radical right-winger (Julia, not a million miles from Mrs Thatcher) and myself, a dithering liberal, failing to hold the ring between them. But in spite of Alan's usual juxtaposition of hilarious comedy with ominous darkness, and a wonderful cast, the play was only a moderate success.

Soon after we opened he took us all out for supper one night, a pleasant surprise as we had heard that, like many very rich people, he was rather careful with his money. As coffee approached he began telling us about his income tax problems. It looked very much to me as though we were about to have a whip-round for the bill, so I made my excuses and left – staying just long enough to hear him say that he was going to set an example to his West End directors and come and check the show every two weeks. That was the last we saw of him.

While we were still doing *Ten Times Table*, John Howard Davies, the producer of *The Good Life*, sent me the script of the 'pilot' – the trial episode – of a new series called *Yes, Minister* by Jonathan Lynn and Anthony Jay. I had been interested in politics, as I have mentioned, almost since infancy, but I knew as little about administration as Jim Hacker, the 'hero' of the series, the principal theme of which was the interaction between the politician Jim and his senior civil servant adviser. I was immediately intrigued.

Nevertheless, I approached it with caution. The script broke entirely new ground in that, for the first that I could remember, viewers of a situation comedy were being invited not only to laugh but at the same time to think about matters of vital concern to them – in this case, the way they were being governed. Despite the originality I wondered, however much I myself enjoyed it, how many viewers would feel the same? *The Good Life* had been one of the most successful series of its kind; could one about the relationship between politics (British politics at that) and administration ever achieve the same sort of popularity? It seemed unlikely. If it were to bump along the bottom for a while and then be withdrawn, how professionally damaging would that be? Playing for time, I told John that I would like to see another script.

The patient authors wrote two more while I dithered. I was assured that the domestic relationships would not dominate the plot, as they inevitably did in every other sit-com. There seemed, too, to be a lot of verbal jokes which, though funny enough in themselves, could distract from the main theme. The relationship between the two main characters was essentially that of Bertie Wooster and Jeeves and I said I preferred the Jeeves part of Sir Humphrey, who, I had cannily noticed, always had the last line, 'Yes, Minister.' But Johnny Lynn said that they had had me in mind from the start for Jim Hacker, and anyway Humphrey was always the same; Hacker was the only one who had a chance to develop his character.

I read an interview recently in which Johnny was quoted as saying that at this point he and Tony Jay had given me an ultimatum: they had done enough work on the series, and I must now say yes or no. This may well have been the case, but our exchanges were tactfully filtered through John Howard Davies and my impression was that I finally agreed because I did not want to disappoint him; he was by now an old friend and I was, moreover, godfather to his beautiful daughter Georgina. I took the plunge.

When I think now how nearly I came to rejecting *Yes, Minister*, my blood runs cold. I had not yet learnt the golden rule that no considerations, especially financial ones, should be placed above the quality of the work. I was delighted to discover that Sir Humphrey would be Nigel Hawthorne and Bernard Woolley, Hacker's private secretary, would be played by Derek Fowlds. Although we had never worked together, I liked and admired them both; I saw that we were going to have fun.

The fun, however, was not immediately apparent. I was still doing eight performances a week of *Ten Times Table* when we started the outside filming. We spent most of the daylight hours of Sunday, 21 January in Whitehall and Downing Street, alternately sweating and shivering. Our caravans and the make-up bus were stiflingly hot; outside it was bitterly cold. I spent most of Monday, until it was time to go to the theatre, on top of the portico of the old Chiswick Town Hall, representing that of my Birmingham constituency, being presented as the new Member. The temperature had risen just sufficiently for it to begin snowing.

It snowed hard all Tuesday and there was a rail strike but on Wednesday we were at it again, this time at Euston Station.

Thursday morning found me, unbelievably, recording an advert. I spent most of Friday in bed, struggling in to the theatre that night trying to convince myself that I had not got bronchitis.

I had, needless to say, and my gallant understudy, Doug Nottage, played Saturday's two performances for me.

On Monday we assembled in a vast room in the BBC's multi-storey, purpose-built rehearsal block, known to actors as 'The Acton Hilton' for the first rehearsal of *Yes, Minister*. During the script's gestation Mrs Thatcher had become the leader of the Conservative Party, and for the first time in British history it became possible for there to be a female Prime Minister. Since we were anxious at all times to avoid being identified with any particular party we had to avoid any hint as to the sex of the Premier, who was always referred to ambiguously as 'The Prime Minister', 'The PM', 'No. 10', 'Downing Street' or even just a finger pointing significantly upwards. Something that few people noticed was that much later, when Jim Hacker himself became Prime Minister, the episode in which this metamorphosis took place restored the PM's sex and it emerged that he had been a man all the time. By then both the series and the Tory administration had become so firmly established that viewers were in danger of assuming that the series was a lampoon on the Tories – whereas it was, of course, directed at any administration of whatever colour.

The pace was hectic: we rehearsed all that week, mornings only on the days when I had a matinée, and were all day in the studio on Sunday, recording before an invited audience in the evening. I had managed to place an extra burden on everyone by pleading, successfully, that if we could not be spared the audience, perhaps we could be spared the ghastly 'warm-up' man with his racist and honeymoon jokes and his invitations to the audience to shake hands with each other and shout out where they came from: 'Anyone here from Potters Bar?' With several generations of show business in his veins Brian Jones, our floor manager, cheerfully put on a black tie and added MC to his other duties. In the event the recording went remarkably well with so much laughter that I thought we might over-run.

Both Nigel and I were, however, uneasy about the director. He had made a big hit with *On the Buses*, a TV series designed to appeal to the most popular taste and which had had a long run. The sophistications of our show did not, I suspect, appeal to him very strongly and he was inclined to fall back on well-tried visual gags. One which particularly jarred was a scene in which Diana Hoddinott, absolutely right as the Minister's wife, was scrabbling on the floor for her tranquillisers. Large close-up of her behind. Wrong!

In the fullness of time the bigwigs at the BBC decided that, yes, they would like to make a series of *Yes, Minister*, using the pilot we had made as the first episode. But it was not to be – at least, not then. Before long, Callaghan's Labour government had collapsed and the nation was girding its loins for a general election. In what was surely a quite unwarranted fit of political delicacy the BBC decided that somehow, somewhere, it could be accused of party bias and decided to withdraw the whole project until calmer waters prevailed. Many months passed before we made our next rendezvous in the Acton Hilton, this time with a new director Sidney Lotterby.

I have a 'snapshot' memory of myself some years previously, standing outside Alan Bennett's house in Camden Town, chatting to Jonathan Miller and telling him that I had always wanted to do a Restoration play but had never had the opportunity. He had evidently not forgotten this conversation, because he now asked if I would like to be directed by him in Sir George Etherege's 'seminal' (how I hate that word!) Restoration play, *She Would if She Could*. My part would be that of Sir Oliver Cockwood.

There was little I would have liked more. Not only was it true that I had always wanted to do a Restoration play, but as a director Jonathan's name carried almost as much prestige then as it does now. Apart from that there was the social aspect; Jonathan is without doubt the most entertaining conversationalist I have ever met. He can talk about almost anything, it seems, with erudition and wit and is a natural advocate, taking the opposite stand to almost anything proposed. He could argue the case for black being really white with eloquence and conviction.

None of us is perfect. Jonathan's mercurial mind takes a lot of keeping up with, and for an actor trying to learn the lines in conjunction with the moves life can be difficult, especially when those moves are changed at least twice a day and a fresh interpretation of them is offered at the same time. Like everyone in demand, Jonathan was tempted to take on more than was practicable; it was said that he was not always present, or at any rate not able to give his full attention to the job in hand, being distracted by preparations for the next. The job itself had its drawbacks, too. It was to be produced at the little theatre at Greenwich, with only token salaries for the actors, to be followed by a ten-week tour. This would be for a little more money and would make the whole thing just possible especially if, as promised, Margaret Courtenay were to play the female lead.

I agreed to do the play, therefore, on condition that Jonathan would be there the whole time to direct it and that Margaret Courtenay would definitely be playing Lady Cockwood. It would be extremely hard work with little financial return, but the rewards, artistic and professional, might well be considerable.

Colloquial speech of the kind found in plays of the seventeenth and early eighteenth centuries is fiendishly difficult to learn. The metre, the syntax, often the words themselves seem only vaguely familiar to the modern ear and eye, and one needs to know the words very well indeed to be able to convey their sense. Sir Oliver has a long speech early in the play which I realised I should have to get on top of straightaway or I would be struggling and wasting everybody's time, so I decided to have ten days of luxurious starvation at Shrubland Hall, a 'health farm' in Suffolk. I had, as usual, to explain to my fellow guests in the sauna that the, by now, huge red patches on my trunk were neither infectious nor contagious.

Jonathan's introductory talk to the cast gave us to understand that we would be 'playing the text'. This puzzled me as I thought that was what one always did, but it emerged that what he meant was that we would be doing without the bowing and scraping, the swords and the plumed hats, all the Restoration flummery that some people find so tedious (and which I, actually, had always felt to be part of the fun!).

The first few pages took quite a long time as everything was changed several times. 'How would it be if you said this next speech lying on the floor? No, perhaps not.' We puzzled over the technicalities of meetings and partings. Mid-seventeenth-century men wore hats all the time, indoors and out, and much was said about 'making a leg', that is, bowing in a certain way. In what manner should we greet each other if we were to be without hats and bowing was going to get in the way of the text? We came to a scene in which two irate gentlemen draw their swords on each other. How was that to be managed if we were not going to wear them? 'Oh, well, wear them just for this scene then,' said Jonathan. I began to suspect that he had not actually read the play in much detail before deciding to direct it.

I kept a very sketchy diary at this time, mainly for appointments. At moments of crisis it sometimes expanded. 'Friday, 30.3.79. Maggie C in fragments. Managerial conference over lunch. Continued in stalls afterwards with MC who left eventually to see doctor recommended by JM. Would it were day and all well.' The last sentence is from *Henry IV* – misquoted, I think, but it expressed what I felt.

Margaret Courtenay is one of the finest actresses on the English stage, which is why I was doubtful whether she would be willing to do such a low-profile job and why I made her presence in the cast a condition of my being in it. To a lay person it might seem odd but she, like most of us, finds it difficult to learn lines until she knows just where she is going to stand to speak them. Added to the difficulties of Restoration dialogue that I have already mentioned, we had to cope with a relatively brief rehearsal period and, above all, Jonathan's extreme fluidity of method. If, day by day, you are all going to 'find out about the play together' you need, in my view, a good six months in which to do it. The next day, Saturday, Maggie's confidence seemed entirely restored until about halfway through, when it went again. My own was shaken by a rumour that one of the other actresses was contemplating breaking her contract, having had a tempting TV offer. Our opening night was the following Tuesday, and I desperately prayed that Dr Greasepaint and the flow of adrenaline would come to our rescue.

While all this was going on the Bristol Old Vic, of which I was now a governor, was in crisis over the projected closure of its studio theatre and its subsidiary, the Little Theatre in the Colston Hall. A meeting was called for the Monday, for which I gratefully sent my apologies. I was also involved in organising a Quaker-inspired symposium at Friends' House with Equity's Afro-Asian committee, of which I was a member. I confess I was not able to give either matter much attention.

At our last 'ordinary' rehearsal Maggie did not attempt to remember the words and simply read them. The wardrobe master, who had been working non-stop for thirty-six hours and was in the process of being evicted from his flat, collapsed with bronchitis and moved into his boyfriend's room at the hospital where he was a nurse. His place was taken temporarily by the designer, Bernard Culshaw. Brilliant though he was, there would be no costumes for the dress rehearsal.

Dress rehearsals are never the happiest times and this one lived well down to expectations. We donned the bits of costume that were ready (no hats) and had the usual problems with lighting, moves, entrances and exits. The set was the one unqualified success: a huge marquetry cabinet which opened up to reveal all sorts of ingenious doors and compartments, out of which the characters stepped on to a beautiful parquet floor. Unfortunately we had to play the play and not the set. We struggled through much of the day, with Maggie still reading from the book. Suddenly it was clear that something had snapped. She put the book down and left never to return.

An emergency meeting was convened in the stalls. After lengthy discussions, from which I was grateful to be excluded, it was decided that the production would be postponed for seven days and a search begun immediately to find an actress who could learn Lady Cockwood in one week rather than three. I saw Michael Billington arriving at the head of a posse of critics and being turned away. I wondered whether they would be furious at having had to toil all the way out to Greenwich for nothing, or pleased to have an unexpected night off. I was exhausted, in the way one might feel if the whole night had been spent in tears.

Miraculously, in Ursula Jones they did find an actress who learnt her part in a week. She did not have Margaret Courtenay's comic timing nor her ability to look like a giant, rabid Pekingese, but she was extremely good and we quickly became friends. Ursula bore the additional burden of having to do without a director; Jonathan's contract expired the day Maggie left the cast. He had to be in New York to publicise his new book, *The Body in Question*. Regrettably he would not be able to attend the first night, nor could he return to the production as he was contracted to direct *A Midsummer Night's Dream* in Vienna. His parting advice to us was not to worry too much about the reviews: 'To get a bad notice from Nicholas de Jongh,' he said, 'is like being savaged by an earwig.' A young and frightened stage manager took over and seemed glad to do as he was told. Our designer disappeared halfway through the week to supervise a production at Pitlochry, so we opened at last minus the leading lady, the director, the designer and the wardrobe master; so much for my contractual stipulations. Jonathan rang, from Hollywood of all places, for reassurance. I am not sure I gave it to him. I told him the costumes looked as though the POWs' Drama Committee had done wonders with their old army blankets and Red Cross parcels.

The first night audience responded well enough and in the circumstances the reviews were not too bad, although I recall one, in the *Observer*, which said something like: 'The actors strolled through the play with a nonchalance which was quite inappropriate.' Had they known, our 'nonchalance' was something approaching a catatonic trance. Michael Frayn came to see us one night and said that he had enjoyed it. He told me that he was a great fan of mine and added, in answer to my unspoken query, that although there was nothing suitable for me in his next two plays he would bear me in mind.

We did our ten-week limp round the country, learning the hard way that, if a play has been neglected for three and a half centuries, there is probably an excellent reason for it. The architect of the grim Forum Theatre in Billingham on Teesside had decided that windows in the dressing rooms would have spoilt the look of the building, and he may well have been right. The view out of them, though, would have been dramatic: burnished steel chimneys belching violet and emerald smoke. The walls were of bare breeze-block and the mirror, screwed precariously to the back of the plywood door, reflected Sir Oliver Cockwood. Plumed hat (at last!), skirt breeches, sword, lace jabot. It reminded me of something. What could it be? Ah, yes. A double-page spread in one of the Sunday tabloids: HOW WE PAMPER OUR PRISONERS.

Only five weeks after the end of the tour I started rehearsals for a play called *Middle Age Spread* by a New Zealand author, Roger Hall. John Gale was the producer, and we had a combined party and first reading at his house in North London one hot August night. It was a jolly reunion for me and Richard Briers, and the story – marital infidelities among a quartet of suburban teachers – had a distinctly *Good Life* flavour, though with a rather sharper bite. Robert Kidd, the director, was a dapper little Glaswegian who had married an heiress and whose rocket-like social rise was symbolised by his crocodile shoes and Gucci ties. Although we did not know it, he also had a massively enlarged heart and this proved to be his last production.

It was wonderful middlebrow entertainment and hit the bullseye from its opening in Brighton, with cheers and cries of 'Bravo!', which was followed by a splendid opening at the Lyric in Shaftesbury Avenue. John Gale rang the next morning to ask me what it felt like to be in a hit. Very pleasant!

Towards the end of 1979 I was plunged into further episodes of *Yes, Minister*, preceded as usual by all the filmed bits. One sequence was for an episode in which Jim Hacker got drunk at a reception at the French Embassy. This had to be night-shooting, after the play, and involved a lot of falling down in copious bursts of artificial rain and scrabbling in the gutter for my car keys. On New Year's Day we started rehearsals for episode two and the going got really rough. The weekly calendar went like this:

Monday: Evening performance of *Middle Age Spread*.

Tuesday: Cast of *YM* meet and read the episode, then start rehearsing it. In the early days this was when Nigel and I spent a lot of the time fighting to get rid of the 'gags'. We both felt that it was a genuine situation comedy – the comedy lying in the situation rather than the jokes, verbal or visual, which could tend, we thought, to be a distraction. Evening performance.

Wednesday: Having roughly learnt the lines (never fewer than sixty pages), half a day's rehearsal and into the theatre for two performances.

Thursday: Having polished up the lines, a full day's rehearsal. Evening performance.

Friday: Full day's rehearsal. Evening performance.

Saturday: We do a run while the director has a meeting with his technicians. Another run for the lighting and sound people. To the theatre for the last two performances of the week.

Sunday: 10 a.m. call at the TV Centre to start work with the cameras and other technicians. At 6.30 we cram in a second dress rehearsal if there is time, the audience is let in and at 8 p.m. we start to record. Quick drink at 10 and home.

Monday: Most of the day in bed, answering letters, paying bills, telephoning, reading and marking the next script, then what is known in Yorkshire as a 'knife-and-fork tea' and in to the theatre to do the play.

We made six exhausting episodes in a row that time and I thanked Providence frequently for my dresser, Cliff, who looked after us so well (I was sharing him on that occasion with Richard Briers), bringing me tea and biscuits and defending me from the outside world.

I used rather to enjoy the Sunday technical rehearsal. In all plays one tries to keep to the text as accurately as possible – to keep faith with the author, if nothing else – but in television it is especially important because the technician in the gallery, with her or his finger on the button which will signal a change of camera angle, is following the text and waiting to hear the actor speak the cue word before doing so. If the actor says, for example, 'committee' instead of 'commission' there is a moment's confusion, everything is brought to a halt and the scene has to be started again. In *Yes, Minister* accuracy was supremely important because amongst the viewers were hundreds of thousands of people with a keen professional interest in both politics and administration, and who all knew perfectly well the difference between a committee and a commission.

But at a technical rehearsal much of that sort of pressure is off the actors and you have time to think of other things, such as how the telephones work, changing your clothes, is the doorknob on the left or the right, taking care not to speak under an archway where the microphone has difficulty in reaching you, or simply standing around drinking in the atmosphere.

I was doing that one day when Brian Jones, the floor manager, showed me a photograph. 'That's the Cabinet Room at No. 10,' he said.

'Yes, I know,' I replied. 'I'm standing in it!'

'No, no,' said Brian. 'This is a picture of the real one.'

It was astonishingly accurate. I went round examining the ornaments, the design of the chairs, the moulding round the fireplace and so on. It was hardly distinguishable from the original, and this was true of all the interiors: the Permanent Secretary's office, the Cabinet Secretary's, the Whips' and so on. Only two things were deliberately inaccurate: the views out of the windows and the labels on the doors. In the unlikely event of a gunman getting into No. 10 he might well burst into the room marked 'Prime Minister' and shoot an innocent secretary, but he would not reach the PM. In the slightly more likely event of a rocket launcher being driven past Horseguards Parade, the terrorists who had made a careful study of our pictures would have missed the Cabinet Room.

At the outset we had all had misgivings, as I have described, about the prospects of *Yes, Minister* and our first viewing figures were not encouraging. The first episode of a new series is generally expected to attract about five or six million viewers, and if it is going to be a success this number will increase gradually and settle at about eight or ten. The first episode of *Yes, Minister* attracted only about two million, but the second immediately hit the top, so everyone must have said to everyone they met, 'Don't miss the next episode of *Yes, Minister!*' Before long it was transferred from BBC 2 to BBC 1. And before long again the series was being seen all over the world. It was bought by at least fifty different countries, and those who did not buy it I suspect stole it. It was told that restaurateurs in both Washington and Canberra complained that on *Yes, Minister* nights their establishments were empty. Soon a steady stream of awards began to come our way.

Meanwhile *Middle Age Spread* was continuing triumphantly and reaping its own awards. We all trooped along to the Café Royal on the night of the SWET Awards, now more happily renamed the Olivier Awards, knowing that we had been nominated for one but hoping for little. The author had even brought his family over from New Zealand.

Award ceremonies are always trying affairs, full of artificially pumped up glitz and glamour. When Penny Keith was winning everything in the wake of *The Good Life* and was expected to have a male escort – this was before her marriage – I could usually count on a free lunch at least once a month. They are often held at the Grosvenor House Hotel and consist of salmon mousse, chicken Kiev, cassata ice cream and coffee. The odds against one's winning are naturally long and, when the cameras and spotlights have glanced briefly at those who have won, they swoop like birds of prey on to those who have not, hoping for grimaces of anguish and chagrin. I have to confess that it is sometimes difficult to maintain an air of selfless generosity in the circumstances.

The speeches, which go on until four in the afternoon, normally fail the buttock test by a long way. They are mostly everyone thanking everyone else for everything. Television viewers may think they already know this – but all they see are the edited highlights. By the time it is all over and the cloakroom queues have dried up, the rush hour is already under way and it is impossible to get a cab. I only go to such junkets now after one of the organisers has nudged me heavily, looked me meaningfully in the eye and hinted that my presence would be very, very welcome.

Middle Age Spread, though, was lucky and won the Best Comedy of the Year award at the culmination of a triumphant evening. Flushed with success, John Gale asked me if there was anything – *anything*, he emphasised – that I would like to do. I suppose a serious-minded artist would have asked him to revive a neglected early nineteenth-century masterpiece from eastern Europe but the regrettable truth is that I do like a bit of fun. I suggested a revival of *Present Laughter*.

At that period it was fashionable to curl one's lip at Noël Coward's plays for being trivial ephemera, but the theatre is a catholic institution and it is no longer necessary to apologise for the opinion, which I have always held, that they fit firmly into the great tradition of English (mostly Irish, of course) comedy. I had done several of Coward's masterpieces in my twenties – far too young. I had thought then that by the time I was the appropriate age he would be ripe for revival. I was now in my early fifties, with years of experience of playing comedy; *The Good Life* and *Yes, Minister* had brought me not only a domestic audience but a worldwide one as well. My hour had clearly struck. John was delighted with my suggestion, and said he would buy the rights straightaway.

There followed a hectic series of battles of which I caught occasional glimpses of troop movements and the sound of distant gunfire, but remained otherwise pretty ignorant. Another producer told me that he, not John, had the rights: would I do it with him? In what I thought in my innocence was a rather surprising change of mind, John poured scorn on the idea of anyone wanting to do *Present Laughter* and the next day sent me the script of a play called *Illuminations* by the well-known political columnist Peter Jenkins; it was a fascinating piece about his political hero, Anthony Crosland.

The medical tempo was increasing, too. Both my skin and the arthritis were giving me problems and I made full use of the NHS as well as running up and down Harley Street in search of help – to little avail, I am afraid. One doctor said that, in addition to the arthritis, I was suffering from radiation sickness as a result of the original treatment and would probably succumb to leukaemia in time. He also vouchsafed that, following wartime undernourishment in childhood, I was suffering from incipient TB. I had apparently cured myself – being unaware of it. The tubercles are now encysted and therefore dormant. The doctor told me that fifty per cent of people of my age were in a similar position. All this was told me in the brief intervals between phone calls to his broker. He did, however, give me one piece of invaluable advice. I had been taking some painkillers for a couple of years and he told me to stop doing so. They were extremely powerful, he said, and had unpleasant side-effects. As their painkilling properties had long since waned, I did, and the black fits of depression which had been becoming more and more frequent vanished within twenty-four hours.

Another doctor triumphantly diagnosed the by now substantial red patches on my trunk as something with a very long name. But a third medical 'expert' said this was nonsense as that was a geriatric disease and had never been seen on anyone younger than seventy. He did not know what it was either but was confident that it would never appear on my face.

Since no one seemed able to agree with anyone else I was only too glad to immerse myself in work and do my best to forget about my ailments. My agent Michael Anderson, by now an old family friend, said he thought I ought to do *Illuminations*, and I agreed. Good new plays are rare enough, but this one was interesting in many ways – not least politically. Set in Blackpool during a Labour Conference, it uncannily anticipated the break-up of the Labour leadership and the formation of the Social Democrats, then still a year away. It was Jenkins' first play, I believe, and although it was not perfect it was well worth doing. It was due for a short run at the Lyric, Hammersmith, and I thought that if I were very lucky I might be able to do that and follow it with *Present Laughter*. I wrote to the producer and said I hoped that he could wait until then. Peter Barkworth told me he had been asked to direct it, which seemed a delightful idea to me. *Middle Age Spread* finished in the middle of June and Tricia sent me off for a few days' elevated rigour to Shrubland. I sat in the sauna and sweated, dreaming of the ideal cast for both plays.

Those of us who are lucky enough to be able to, mark time between jobs doing 'voice-overs'. These are the voices heard over the pictures on a TV advertisement. Radio adverts are usually called the same. Doing voice-overs requires a great deal of skill, and the advertising agencies feel comfortable with only a relatively few actors. A fair income can be made from them and some actors do little else. In consequence there is sharp competition to be admitted to the charmed circle.

I owe my entrée to it to Penelope Keith. At the time when we were sharing so many award lunches, advertising agencies' creative directors saw in her the ideal voice of snooty middle-class England and, like the organisers of the award lunches, wanted her to be accompanied by the man already coupled with her in the public mind. Penelope was by then an old hand and I learnt from her quickly – as you have to when you must sound enthralled by the product, have twice as much to say as the time allows, be funny and bring it all in to within a tenth of a second. A creative director once said to me that, although the recording I had just made was perfect and could hardly be bettered in any respect, could I do it just once more, speaking it a tiny bit quicker, but making it sound slower! Yet after a while we actually found we could do that sort of thing. When I was with Richard Briers, an acknowledged expert, we found we could be in and out of one of the little recording studios in Soho in twenty minutes – forty minutes under the allotted time.

At the height of my desirability with the advertisers I was doing three or even four a week, but some of my colleagues did that number every day. Many carried bleepers so that they could be summoned instantly, and one group I heard of actually rented a little rest room where they could sit and have a cup of tea between jobs. No doubt they all have their mobile phones now.

A week or two after I had returned from Shrubland Hall my agent telephoned me to say that John Gale had at last managed to buy the rights of *Present Laughter*. His original enthusiasm for the play had returned, but as he had the rights for only a limited period he could not wait for me and would do it with Donald Sinden instead. I have had such wonderful luck throughout my professional life and I had been greedy, I suppose, in wanting to do both plays. It was time I suffered a setback, but I must confess that, after waiting more than twenty years, I was bitterly disappointed.

When we started rehearsals for *Illuminations* that autumn then, with John Gale producing, it might be supposed that the atmosphere was tense; but if it was I do not remember it. Theatrical feuds and setbacks are quickly put behind one or life would be impossible. I heard of a Hollywood producer who quarrelled violently with an actor and told him that he would never, ever, employ the actor again. 'Until I need to!' he concluded.

Politicians of all colours packed into the stalls on the opening night and excitement was so high that someone fainted in the interval and had to be attended by Dr David Owen. Well received though it was,

John Gale decided not to risk bringing it in to the West End – wisely I suspect. That Peter Jenkins was a political commentator, and thus by definition a political forecaster, was significant: only a few months after we had produced *Illuminations* the so-called 'Gang of Four' broke away from the Labour Party. Was our play a bit of pre-publicity for them?

10

The Corridors of Power

Curiously, such setbacks as I have had always seem to have paved the way to something better. Had things worked out exactly as I had wanted with regard to *Illuminations* and *Present Laughter*, I should not have been able to contemplate going to the National Theatre.

I was having a cup of coffee with a friend in the canteen there when I ran into Michael Rudman, who had directed me in *Donkey's Years*. Michael, under Peter Hall, was then director of productions at the National's Lyttleton Theatre. How would I like, he asked me, to play George opposite Joan Plowright's Martha in Edward Albee's *Who's Afraid of Virginia Woolf?* I immediately told him I should be thrilled.

I think it may be characteristic of me to leap before looking. Paradoxically I am a reluctant theatregoer, and the shameful truth is that I had neither seen nor read the play. However, I had read many reviews and knew a great deal about it. I knew that it was extremely funny as well as being extremely cruel and exciting, and generally regarded as one of the century's finest works. An immense challenge, no doubt, but mine is not a business in which challenges can be ducked. I knew it was something I simply had to do.

The director was to be Nancy Meckler, the first woman director of the National. She was a slim, dark, American ex-academic of whom my agent said he had heard only good things.

Rehearsals started in May. We were in the smallest of the National's rehearsal rooms: windowless, neon-lit and not very clean. A glance outside the door showed a breathtaking view across the river to Somerset House, with St Paul's majestic dome a little further downstream, but I suppose they would have been distractions. There must have been at least thirty people there to launch the production, and I realised what a big event this was seen to be. Olivier had left his position as artistic director of the National in acrimonious circumstances some years previously, and his wife's appearance was to be the great reconciliation. We looked at the model of the set, chatted and had coffee. Eventually the room was cleared and we started.

'Right!' said Nancy Meckler. 'We've all met, we've read the play and seen the set, let's get on and start blocking the moves.'

'Oh, surely,' said Joan, who I noticed was chewing gum, 'we ought to read it, you know.'

There was a long pause. I think that even then I had a premonition that the production hung on a thread.

'Oh, OK. Let's put some chairs around and we'll read it.' The thread snapped.

Of course, Joan was quite right. It is enormously helpful to read a play together, to get a bird's eye view of the piece, its length and some idea of what it all sounds like aloud. But Nancy's authority had received a blow from which it never recovered and from then on the confidence and security which to an actor are almost as necessary as air were seldom present. Matters were not helped by the fact that the National's rehearsal rooms are imperfectly, if at all, soundproofed. On one side of us was a Passion Play, with a jazz band, and on the other what sounded like a troupe of Bulgarian clog dancers.

Nancy is of the empirical school, and we struggled to find out about the play together. Although I know this method appeals to many of my colleagues, it is not one with which I feel comfortable. In my view it gives enormous responsibility to the actors without very much power. Moves and interpretations were changed more or less arbitrarily, and the ground was constantly shifting beneath one's feet.

In the play, Martha has several coarse bellows from off stage. 'George!' she shouts, 'George for Chrissakes!', several times, and one of Joan's early worries was that she could not possibly do those herself: the vocal strain would be too much, so her understudy must do them. Diana Boddington was our superb stage director who had worked for, and been a devoted follower of, Sir Laurence's for many years and had adored Vivien Leigh. She was a fervent royalist and a devout Catholic and had a vocabulary that would make a navvy wince. The latter she used on this occasion, freely and, luckily, privately. Joan was persuaded that only her own voice would do, so it was recorded and played over a speaker in the wings. Apart from the fact that the person with her finger on the button never quite got it right, it sounded as though Joan's head was in a biscuit box.

The production was set in its own period – that is, twenty years previously – and no expense was spared to get it right. I noticed that my shabby knitted tie was by Dior. I told Nancy that my own wardrobe was full of twenty-year-old clothes.

'We're in the pursuit of excellence,' she replied.

'It's been budgeted,' said the wardrobe mistress.

Who's Afraid of Virginia Woolf? is three and a half hours of intense black tragi-comedy. And it takes place in 'real time', intervals included. The dialogue is not easy, and included in my case a recitation in Latin of the Dies Irae. I grew more and more tense, and as I said goodbye to Tricia every morning I used to say 'HATE HATE HATE' to myself. I was still keeping a sketchy diary in those days, but I was too stressed to do so then. Written over all the rehearsal period in capital letters is the word TORTURE.

One day Joan said to me about our planned tour, 'We must protest to our agents. We can't possibly go to Dublin.' I said that was disappointing, I liked Dublin. 'No, no, there's the IRA and all those hunger strikes and we are, after all, the British National Theatre.' I said I thought it unlikely that the IRA would target artists, and if they did, I added stoutly, we surely should not give in to that sort of intimidation.

'It's all very well for you, dear,' she replied, 'but I am a Peeress of the Realm. I have a coronet.'

I am sure it was a joke.

One Friday, with one week's rehearsal to go, as the jazz band on one side of us was going full blast and the clog dancers on the other had reached a crescendo, Joan, very sensibly, refused to work there any more. So we upped sticks and went in search of another room. But as soon as we had got started there, what sounded like a school outing came whistling and shouting down the corridor and off we went again. We rehearsed in four different rooms that day, ending up in the boardroom at the top of the building. I said that we had already been on tour without having yet left the building. No one laughed. The one young ASM who always laughed at my jokes had been sacked the week before.

We managed to cope for most of that day, just, with the jack-hammers at work on the IBM building next door. But when workmen started hammering on the roof above us we packed up for the week and I fled with Tricia down to the cottage we had bought in Suffolk. First thing on Saturday morning Laurence Evans, the distinguished head of my agency, telephoned. What, he asked, was going on? I had no idea. Joan was one of his clients. 'Joanie wants to withdraw from the production,' he said.

She had said, apparently, that rehearsal conditions were intolerable. Quite true, of course, but to walk out of a show on those grounds, or practically any grounds for that matter, was something that was wholly alien to my entire upbringing in the theatre. I could not believe that that was the real reason. The insecurity I felt at that time made me suspect immediately that, as she had not confided in me, I must be the cause.

Panic gripped me. I was her leading man. The entire profession would know that I was impossible to act with. They would remember the fiasco of the Greenwich non-opening of *She Would if She Could* and draw the obvious conclusion. I spent the rest of the day telephoning everyone: my son Hugo, Mike Rudman, Nancy Meckler, Laurence Evans again. Mike said she must play, Laurie said the National Theatre would sue, Nancy said she thought she herself was the cause, which was some comfort. I lost seven pounds that weekend.

On Monday we did our best to rehearse without Joan, but Tuesday found us in a boys' club in Battersea, reunited, by what means of persuasion I do not know, and joined by the general manager of the National bearing a tray of propitiatory salad rolls from Harrods and a couple of bottles of warmish white wine. We ground into gear again.

The gracious Theatre Royal, Bath, was the scene of our first night. Nerves left me only just this side of paralysis, but as the hours went by the gigantic horror of the play took its inevitable hold. At the climax, when I was reciting the Dies Irae at Martha with, as it were, bell, book and candle, I was riveted by the sight of Joan taking a series of pills – nothing to do with the play – and washing each of them down with a gulp from her glass.

Albee asked me afterwards why in this production George *recited* the Dies Irae. 'How come he knows it? He's just a teacher.' It was I who had suggested reciting it because I thought it would lose a lot of its power if I had to keep glancing down at a book – quite apart from the fact that I had spent a fortnight at my cottage learning it. I told Michael Rudman. 'Albee's a cunt,' he said.

Bath was our only out-of-town date so we all heaved ourselves back to London for another dress rehearsal, a couple more previews and the opening proper. As the play starts George enters, followed immediately by Martha. On the first preview I entered, surveyed the room and turned to face Martha. Nothing. After a few moments I turned away again and did something trivial to fill in. No Joan. I did something else – poured a drink or suchlike. I sensed that the audience's feelings of anticipation were beginning to match my own. In the silence all I could hear from the wings was some passionate muttering and an occasional obscenity. After perhaps a minute – it seemed like fifteen – Joan appeared, hobbling slightly, and we got going. I could not leave the stage myself until the first interval, so I was unable to discover the trouble for over an hour. It seemed that one of Joan's high heels had slipped between two slats of wood on the steps. The muttered expletives had come from Diana Boddington as she tried to extract her.

Olivier came round afterwards looking thin and old but not actually ill. He told me how awkward it was for him to go to the theatre nowadays, especially the Olivier: 'Everyone nudging and pointing.'

I said, 'Why not wear a big hat and dark glasses?'

'I've tried that,' he said, 'and nobody recognised me.'

I wondered who had chosen his clothes. He was wearing a coat and an open-necked shirt in two different tartans, with a maroon tie. Olivier gripped my hand and gazed at me with inexpressible warmth. 'I'm so glad,' he said, 'to have seen that performance.'

The ambiguity was disturbing. However, Nancy came to my room the next night and told me that when she had bumped into him he had said, 'That leading actor – what's his name? Yes, Paul! Oh, he's a great actor!' I drove home in a dream, playing Bach at full volume and stopping at every crossing to invite startled pedestrians to make their way over the road.

The eve of press night produced its quota of incident. As Beginners was being called for Act 2 there was a power failure and the entire theatre was plunged into darkness. *Man and Superman* in the Olivier Theatre packed up and went home, but we started again as soon as we were able. Joan, however, seemed only to have half a voice, and in the second interval she too decided to go home. Michael Rudman happened to be in the theatre and he managed to persuade her that that would not be a good idea – how, I do not know – and so we tiptoed through to the end of the play and I hastened gratefully to my bed to prepare for press night.

Our tribulations were far from over. At 11.30 the next morning Diana rang to say that Joan was suffering from a sore throat. Press night would have to be postponed, and could I come straight in to rehearse with the understudy?

Well, no, I could not; I was just leaving the house to have lunch with Roy Plomley and record *Desert Island Discs*. The soundproofing in the recording studio was tested to its utmost when a thunderstorm of Wagnerian proportions broke overhead. As we emerged from the BBC Roy Plomley said that he too was on his way to the South Bank and proposed sharing a cab. Unhappily the storm had put all the traffic lights out of action so we ran a sort of three-legged race, with his raincoat over our heads, to Charing Cross Station where we boarded an overground train to Waterloo.

I arrived at the theatre, my pale grey suit now rain-blackened, stumped dripping round the stage with the understudy for half an hour, then retired to my room. In Ralph Mills I was lucky indeed to have a dresser who was notoriously one of the best in London. He ran me a hot bath, took all my clothes away to be laundered and pressed, and had me ready in time for the show.

The understudy, Pam Butchner, was extremely good and, as far as I could tell, word perfect. She performed a miracle in the circumstances and richly deserved the ovation she received at the end. At 10 a.m. the next day I was in a recording studio being a cucumber sandwich in a butter advertisement.

Joan's sore throat persisted and she sent a doctor's note. Some say that Olivier had forbidden her to reappear. Peter Hall, the director of the National, decided that, good as Pam Butchner was, the part demanded a star whom the public would recognise as such and told me that he favoured Gloria Grahame, a fading ex-Hollywood icon. She was not all that well known, to me at any rate, and I understood that she was considerably older than myself. By now I was beginning to feel that it was time my wishes were consulted. I proposed my old friend Margaret Tyzack. Although I had known Maggie for many years and shared a host of friends, we had never acted together. I knew her, though, to be an extremely fine actress, and the freedom supplied by a good working relationship was what I was yearning for just then.

As if things were not already complicated enough, another enormous spanner was now thrown into the works. Some time previously I had been flattered into signing a contract for Thames Television to do a series called *Let There Be Love*. It was a piece as light as thistledown about a footloose bachelor, his funny friend and, of course, an enchanting woman. Nanette Newman had no difficulty being the latter and Henry McGee was the funny friend – none funnier. I had thought it would be fun to do something undemanding and romantic for a change and the producers had gone to extraordinary lengths to make it possible, even to the extent of planning to rehearse and record it during the gaps in the National Theatre's repertoire.

It was going to be very hard work, but Peter Hall had by now agreed to cast Margaret and all might have been well had not the technicians at the Teddington studios decided at this point to go on strike.

All the careful planning had to be abandoned. I had to rise soon after dawn, drive over to Hampton Court to a pub rehearsal room, work all morning and then drive to the National, pausing on Lavender Hill in Battersea for egg and chips, rehearse all afternoon with Maggie and appear at night, with the understudy recording *Let There Be Love* on Sundays. It is difficult to say how I survived.

On the much-postponed press night Maggie was superb and the management gave us a modestly festive party. I still have the voucher entitling me to one glass of wine, which for some reason I did not use.

The reviews were overwhelmingly good and Maggie got the Best Actress award for 1981. But at what a price! Soon afterwards I had an excruciating attack of arthritis which crippled me for several days. Perhaps it was not altogether surprising.

Sometimes, however, it is the director rather than one's fellow performers who creates the most difficulties. In the sixties and seventies Charles Marowitz made a considerable name for himself. Riding the crest of the New Wave were people such as Brook, Artaud and Brecht, whose names carried even more resonance, and Marowitz was swept along in the undertow; he became one of the trendiest of their camp followers.

To old-fashioned actors such as myself some of his experiments seemed rather pointless. One of the more surprising was chopping Shakespeare into small pieces and rearranging them – an exercise designed, I think, to throw new light on hackneyed old speeches. It may have been interesting for students but was less so for those of us who are always taken by surprise by every line of his anyway; my own feeling is that Shakespeare probably got it right first time and that to do one of his plays better than it has been done before is innovation enough.

Nevertheless I was intrigued by Marowitz, and I knew trendiness when I saw it, so when Donald Albery asked me to be in a play directed by him I took the plunge. At least we would get serious critical attention. I decided that if I were to get anything at all out of the exercise I must sink my prejudices and approach it with rigorous objectivity. The play, *Blue Comedy*, was in fact two one-act plays, *Madly in Love* and *Hank's Night Out*, by Paul Abel.

When I met him and Charles for the first time my prejudices had to be given another sharp talking to. Abel was short and oily with a nervous air as of someone expecting to be arrested at any moment.

Charles was a tall and cadaverous ex-New Yorker with a sparse beard, lank black hair and adenoids. He had an absinthe complexion and was one of those people who, although scrupulously clean I am sure, always looked as though he could do with a good wash and brush-up. Had he auditioned for the part of Fagin, the other candidates would not have stood a chance.

The play was to be tried out at the Yvonne Arnaud Theatre in Guildford, but for everyone's convenience we rehearsed in an airless, neon-lit games room beneath the YMCA in Tottenham Court Road, where for four weeks my open mind was tested to destruction. We played a lot of games, some of which were designed to emphasise various aspects of the plays or the characters in them, but most to break down our inhibitions – although they tended to reinforce mine.

Some days we sat in a semi-circle and spoke our lines and, instead of doing 'business' – that is, moving from one place to another, opening a door or pouring a drink – we slapped our knees vigorously. On other days we sang our lines instead of speaking them, making up the tunes as we went along. Another time we spoke and moved fairly naturally but added our inner thoughts, as though we were cartoon characters with balloons hovering over our heads. One day when I was particularly tired mine said, 'What a bloody silly game!'

I went through several stages, starting with total commitment and a refusal to listen to doubting voices. As these grew more insistent I started to pay some attention to them and found I had reservations. Eventually I decided that Marowitz had feet of clay, to say the least. Some people took much less time than I did.

We actors found ourselves in a familiar situation. Putting on a play is a huge collective effort and imponderables abound. It is easy to make a mistake with a director or a colleague, a management, the designer, even a play. Few actors have outside sources of income and this makes them particularly vulnerable. It is only in the last few years that I have had the luxury of being able to pick and choose, which means that I have had to retrain my critical faculties.

So you may find yourself lacking faith in the director and having doubts about the play. No matter, it is advertised as opening on a certain date and you just get on with it and, should the director find you unsatisfactory, he or she is in the same fix. A week after you have opened, however, the author is back in his study and the director and designer are busy with their next production. The actors are there at the cutting edge, night after night, wooing the customers. Naturally I view things from the actor's perspective, but how many productions have I seen rescued by a gallant cast!

The plays we were doing, while risqué, were not all that outrageous. But they were amongst the first to be produced after stage censorship had been abolished and Charles was not about to let the opportunity slip to astonish the bourgeoisie.

In the cast was Madeleine Smith, still in her teens, a sensationally pretty girl, serious-minded and with a most attractive air of virginal purity. One day Charles said, with a wolfish sidelong glance at Maddy, 'At the end of this scene I think you all ought to take your clothes off and fuck each other.'

Women at that time were assumed to have delicate sensibilities and he waited eagerly for her response to this assault. I could see that at the very least he was hoping she might run from the room in tears. But he had picked entirely the wrong victim. Maddy's air of virginal purity was genuine.

'Oh, do you think so Charles? I see.' She nodded wisely. Charles's disappointment was tangible. At one point he directed her to stand on a chair and jump up and down solely in order, I felt sure, to see her generous bosom bouncing. I advised her privately not to do it, and she did not.

By this time I must have been spoiling the fun rather and, perhaps predictably, the production was not much more than fairly good. One night over supper in Guildford, while we were doing it there, Donald Albery asked me whether or not we ought to bring it into the West End. I gave it the thumbs down.

While I was still busy playing *Who's Afraid of Virginia Woolf?* and *Let There Be Love* was still running on television, Michael Codron sent me a script of a new Michael Frayn play. *Noises Off*, it was fairly clear, was an extraordinarily funny comedy, verging on farce. I say 'fairly clear' because it was based on a device which made it, for me, a complicated read.

It starts in a second-rate repertory theatre where the company is doing the dress rehearsal of a sex farce called *Nothing On*. In the second act the entire set is turned round with its back, as it were, towards the audience which then sees the first act being performed again, only from behind the scenes, with all the company's jealousies, love affairs, missed entrances and assaults woven into the play which is being rehearsed. In the script the words are written on one page and the backstage action on the one opposite. I gave it to Tricia to read and tell me what it was about. Luckily she confirmed that it was indeed extremely funny, and I began to make plans.

There were two snags: I had already agreed to do another series of *Yes, Minister* in the New Year. Michael Codron, the producer of *Noises Off*, said he did not mind if I were to do the series at the same time as his play, but what if *Virginia Woolf* were offered a transfer after all? It looked as if there might be a grand collision. Luckily the National Theatre decided not to transfer *Virginia Woolf* and I breathed again.

At the end of an interview with Sheridan Morley I said, 'off the record', that I was grateful for the wonderful reviews and extremely pleased about Margaret Tyzack's Society West End Theatres' award, but that until she had arrived my time at the National had been the most anxious and unhappy of my career. 'A thoroughly hateful experience,' I said. He courteously shut his notebook and buried my indiscretion. As I left the theatre on our last night I ceremoniously shook the dust from my feet. Standing there, looking at me with some curiosity, was Michael Blakemore, who was going to direct *Noises Off*.

The Michaels, Blakemore and Frayn, had apparently spent weeks with wet towels round their heads working out the complicated moves, but their thorough homework had paid off. They both radiated a quiet confidence which transmitted itself immediately to the cast, added to which Michael Codron had gone to the considerable trouble and expense of having the main part of the set erected in our North London rehearsal room. I have never before, or since, been in a production where everything ran on such well-oiled wheels. Not once did I hear anyone say, 'Oh, my God, we do this in two weeks' time!' in the sort of panic that almost always seizes actors as a first night approaches.

I very nearly got off on the wrong foot with Patricia Routledge, though. I said to her lightly, 'You're so lucky to be in a play with me, you know – they always run!' I thought she would have a seizure.

'I have never in my life,' she fulminated, I think is the word, 'heard such unmitigated arrogance! Of all the disgraceful ...' etcetera, etcetera. It took quite a while to calm her down.

We started off with a five-week run at the Lyric Theatre, Hammersmith and did so without any pre-publicity: no radio or television interviews, no articles in the papers, just a handwritten notice on the theatre door. On the first night the small theatre was about half full. The audience seemed to enjoy the play and there was a good deal of hearty laughter. We were pleased.

On the second night we shared what I think was a unique experience. We were called on to the stage or into the wings at Beginners and stood waiting for the Stand By. We waited for perhaps five minutes. Not unusual on a busy night. We waited for ten minutes and then for fifteen. That was unusual. At length the stage manager apologised and asked us to go back to our rooms. 'There's been some sort of hold-up,' she said.

Back in our rooms we sat and wondered. I became convinced that someone must have had a heart attack and that St John's Ambulance people must be dashing about everywhere. Then the stage manager's voice came over the public address system: 'This call really is Beginners,' it said. 'So sorry about the delay, but there's such a crush in the foyer that the box office has been unable to cope.'

Everyone who had been in the audience the previous night must have rushed home and telephoned all their friends to tell them to get straight on down to the Lyric and book seats for *Noises Off*. The enthusiasm was almost of Broadway proportions, except that in New York theatregoers usually wait to read the reviews first.

From then on we hardly had an empty seat. Michael Codron had arranged for us to transfer to the Savoy, which seats about eleven hundred, and after five weeks of sell-out business at Hammersmith I could not believe that there was anyone left in London who hadn't seen it. It ran for over three years.

The play opened with Patricia Routledge as a 'daily' in the play within the play and myself at the back of the auditorium as its director. To begin with I was very nervous about appearing amongst the audience, but the first taste of blood cured me and it was not long before I was hoping for crowds of latecomers amongst whom

I could insinuate myself. If I was lucky I would shout my first line to Patricia from their midst, causing a mild wave of panic in those of a nervous disposition. I could imagine what would happen in a New York theatre. People there would swing round and say, 'Shut up! There's a play going on!' Here I could hear them saying, 'For God's sake don't look round, darling. I think there's a lunatic behind us.'

The reviews were ecstatic. One even said that *Noises Off* was the funniest play this century. People certainly were ill with laughter, and more than one person told me that they were praying for it to stop because they were in pain.

I do not on the whole warm to plays which gratuitously use bad language, but in *Noises Off* I had to burst in at one point and, for reasons too complicated to go into, say, 'What the fuck is going on?' The line is so entirely apt at the moment it is uttered that the audience gives a laugh like a broadside from a man-of-war. The manager of the Savoy was very nervous of his customers' possible reaction and begged me not to say it. 'Why not say "What the hell is going on?"' he suggested. The line as written got the biggest laugh I have ever heard in a theatre and it would be cut, I told him, over my dead body. I regularly got letters of complaint, but I knew I was right and dismissed them. One I did treasure. It was from a woman who wrote that it was such a pity that I felt I had to use four-letter words (she must have thought I had written the play) because it was quite funny enough without. 'However,' she concluded, 'I have to say that the man next to me was lying on the floor, barking!'

For some actors a curious love-hate attitude exists towards audiences. If they laugh or cry when they are meant to, remain pin-drop silent at other times and applaud vigorously at the end, with perhaps an occasional cry of 'Bravo!', all is well. If, however, an audience fails to come up to expectations a marked coolness can descend on the actors. They are inclined to criticise the customers' lack of intelligence or to believe them all to be Japanese tourists – or, if the house is only a quarter full, to resent even those who have come. Siren voices urge them to scamper through the play giving an off-hand performance, go home to bed and hope for better things tomorrow. It is, of course, a temptation to be resisted at all costs, but it was many years before I learnt the hard lesson that the only way for an actor to combat boredom and irritation is to give the best performance of which he is capable. I believe that I have given some of my best performances at sparsely attended matinées and I am convinced now that a production is in fact only as good as its matinées.

Having said that, I myself can hardly afford to be too censorious. In my youth I am afraid I gave many an off-hand performance, and in *Noises Off* I actually assaulted a member of the audience who I thought was not paying sufficient attention. During part of the play I had to appear in the dress circle, calling out occasional directions to the actors on the stage. One young man, I noticed, was sprawling across a couple of seats on the end of a row, one foot in the aisle, apparently asleep. Childishly vulnerable, like so many actors, I immediately assumed that he was only pretending and was simply making a discourteous exhibition of boredom. I was incensed and more or less shouted my last line in his ear, managing as I made my exit to catch his foot with mine in such a way as to jerk him violently awake. I hastened back to the stage, amazed at what I had done, and emerged nervously from the stage door at the end, narrowly escaping, I felt, a justifiably angry confrontation.

Acting on the wrong side of the footlights has other hazards, too: while standing at the back of the stalls one night I was waylaid by a woman who told me a long whispered story about how she could not get back to her seat, having popped out to go to the loo, but that she was having a wonderful time, it being her wedding anniversary and her husband having booked them into the Savoy Hotel and the theatre as a surprise. Given half a chance she was clearly going on to tell me all about her family and no doubt other holidays she and her husband had taken. She must have thought me very rude when I tore myself away to continue the play.

One woman demanded angrily why this was not the Olde Tyme Music Hall which she had seen advertised. Put like that, I really could not say. Another man shook me warmly by the hand and told me he was from Denmark. I was careful to keep on the move and avoid eye contact after that.

Another series of *Yes, Minister* was soon in the making. It meant another six weeks of learning the lines during the intervals, in the times between performances and recording on Sundays.

One of the unexpected hazards of making television is that one's mistakes are recorded as faithfully as are one's triumphs. Ex-film actors are sometimes led into a false sense of security because this hardly ever happens in films. Film stock, the actual photographic material of which films are made, is very expensive and unless a shot has a fair chance of being used it is not printed. The video film used in television, however, can be used many times over and there are now whole programmes devoted to showing (with their permission, of course) actors making silly mistakes.

With a live audience in front of you, mistakes have to be treated as the most tremendous fun. You are concentrating furiously on getting the words right, and if they go wrong the four-letter expletive rising to your lips must be forced back down and replaced with a good-humoured chuckle.

The three of us in *Yes, Minister* knew each other well both on and off the set, and it was fatally easy to get the names muddled up. I regularly called Derek 'Bernard' in the canteen and more than once during a recording called 'Bernard' Derek. At various times we all made that sort of mistake and provided the material for countless *Auntie's Bloomers* and similar programmes.

There were rapped knuckles all round on one occasion. We had finished the recording one night and were waiting for the tape to be checked before the audience could be released and we could all go home when someone doing the checking noticed a slight mistake in one of Nigel's long speeches.

The poor man came back with it all to do again, took a deep breath and did it, perfectly. We got our clearance and shot off home. But what no one had noticed was that since Nigel recorded the speech the first time there had been intervening scenes with costume changes, and Nigel was wearing the wrong tie. It was a viewer who spotted the mistake when the episode was shown. Reruns of *Yes, Minister* are infrequent, but that mistake seems to be shown quite often. We were professional actors and all of us, on both sides of the camera, knew what we were doing. We did not make very many mistakes and most of the curious things that happened to me were seldom in the studios, rather they were outside and in consequence of the two series. One of the most bizarre, however, came about while we were actually filming.

When, as Jim Hacker, I became Prime Minister, Mrs Hacker and I were about to celebrate our wedding anniversary; we had decided to spend a romantic weekend at the country hotel where we had spent our honeymoon. As the story went, the head of the secret services had meanwhile told me that for some reason I had become the target of an international terrorist gang. As you may imagine, he thoroughly put the wind up me, but I decided to try to forget it and go to the hotel anyway.

Things did not work out as we had hoped, though. Much of the romance was dispelled by the fact of our arriving with a police car in front of us and another behind us. The bushes were full of armed detectives, and romance took another blow when we realised that two of them were stationed outside our bedroom door all night.

The hotel the BBC chose for the filming was in Ross-on-Wye. Ross-on-Wye is not far from Hereford, and Hereford is where the SAS have their headquarters. It was just before Christmas, and it so happened that on the night of our arrival the SAS had chosen our hotel in which to hold their annual Christmas party. We were quite unaware of them – they are, after all, secret – but I believe consternation in their ranks was extreme. Descending on them out of the blue were all these limousines and police cars. Half the armed detectives in the bushes were BBC extras and half were actually armed detectives. Some of the waiters had bulges under their armpits and were not in fact waiters at all. I believe that GCHQ Cheltenham was busy that night as messages sped to and fro.

No sooner had we finished making that series than I was made another offer which I felt I could hardly refuse. This was an ATV film of Richard Harris's wonderfully accurate comedy about an amateur cricket team, *Outside Edge*. With Prunella Scales as my wife, Maureen Lipman and none other than Jonathan Lynn, the co-author of *Yes, Minister*, in the cast it was clearly not to be missed; I was evidently still foolhardy enough to say yes to an offer straightaway and to work out afterwards how I could possibly fit it in.

For once, knowing that filming traditionally takes place from dawn to dusk, I exercised a little foresight and demanded a location near to where I was living in North London, a district where there are more cricket grounds than you could shake a stick at. The location turned out to be near Banstead, many miles to the south and about as far from my house as one could get and still be within reach of London. The stipulation should, of course, have been written into my contract, but I have long since come to the conclusion that one does not live and learn, one simply lives.

I fell back on my second contingency: having a car at my disposal at all times. This worked reasonably well, particularly as my driver was Keith Tillotson who had driven me on many previous occasions. He is endlessly accommodating and considerate and was at my door at seven sharp every morning with rugs and pillows so that I could catch a little more sleep *en route*. He was outside the cricket ground every evening to ferry me to the Garrick Club for a pot of tea and toast, and waiting in the Strand to take me home after the evening performance of *Noises Off*. I wasted no time getting out of the theatre, sometimes treading on the heels of the departing audience. 'If you stick close to me,' my dresser Cliff said firmly, 'no one will look at you!' He was quite right; in his cut down British Warm and his trapper's hat, ear-flaps down and tied with a bow under his chin, I was invisible.

Michael Codron had for some time been pressing me to lead the cast of *Noises Off* in America, with a month in Washington and five months on Broadway. Looking back, I suppose that professionally speaking I ought to have done so; but in spite of the fact that Tricia gallantly urged me to accept, the thought of all the hassle over visas, the swingeing taxes and union dues, the loneliness I had previously felt in New York and above all the idea of six months' separation from my family seemed too big a price to pay. In any case, I had committed myself to a further series of *Yes, Minister* later in the year, and commuting from New York to do it was something that even I realised was hardly practical.

My original contract for the rather depressing 'romantic' comedy *Let There Be Love* gave ATV the option of doing another series, and this they took up. The original cast of *Noises Off* withdrew on New Year's Day 1983, and after a two-day break I started on the series. I suppose with writers such as Bob Larbey and John Esmonde in *The Good Life* and Jonathan Lynn and Anthony Jay in *Yes, Minister*, I had been grossly spoilt, but apart from the income there were huge compensations in my colleagues, who became and remain friends. By normal television standards it was a perfectly acceptable series and both ATV and my colleagues begged me to do yet another, but with money already in my pocket and the promise of more to come, I rose grandly above it.

A most remarkable phenomenon had in the meantime begun to emerge: my own metamorphosis into an International Celebrity. *The Good Life* had been shown all over the world, and still is, but a leap forward had been made with *Yes, Minister* and later its offspring, *Yes, Prime Minister*. I had assumed at the beginning that the theme, engrossing though it was to me, was probably somewhat parochial so far as the rest of the world was concerned. I was, of course, entirely wrong; the world was clamouring for it. Every regime, authoritarian or democratic, every conglomerate, every organisation which depended for its operation on the interpretation by managers of orders given from above, instantly recognised in *Yes, Minister* their own situation. In every country I visited during the next few years I was asked how on earth I knew about them.

The first, after a one-day break at the end of *Let There Be Love*, was Australia. I was invited to speak at a conference of advertisers in Sydney. Henry McGee had worked in Australia and I asked him what it was like. He said that there was really only one word to describe it, 'Paradise!' Tricia, ever supportive, encouraged me to go – cancelling a holiday we had planned for ourselves in Madeira, by the way. Although she has travelled the world, Tricia does not care for flying and was not keen to go on such a long journey. She suggested that I should take our middle son, Hugo, to look after me and act as my secretary. I have to say that, as long as someone else is paying, first class is the only way to travel. The lounge at Heathrow, though, did become very familiar to us as take-off was delayed for an hour or two, and when we were finally invited aboard, standing beside my seat was a group of large men in overalls grouped round a trapdoor. Two or three floors below I could see other men in overalls pulling banks of instruments out of the panelling and puzzling over them.

Halfway over the Indian Ocean the captain invited us on to the flight deck, and I was able to ask him what the trouble had been. He told me to look at one of the dials, which had two wires in the form of a cross. 'Now,' he said, 'when I switch this off those wires disappear. Or they should. Actually, only one of them does, as you see.'

'Is that,' I enquired tentatively, 'important?'

'Well,' he said, 'it's one of the navigation instruments.'

I looked out of the window. Ocean, in every direction.

'Don't worry,' he said. 'There's plenty of back-up.'

We stopped everywhere – Oman, Kuala Lumpur, Singapore – and took every advantage of the hospitality offered in all the first-class lounges across the world.

A long journey by air is a great leveller. Passengers stroll aboard with their Gucci handbags and Armani suits and within hours are reduced to crumpled heaps, unshaven or covered in layers of face cream and tissues. After a thirty-four-hour journey, at what should have been 6.20 a.m. local time we staggered off the plane semi comatose and liberally sprayed with the Immigration Department's insect repellent. It was in fact now early evening, and being the Southern Hemisphere, the end of a lovely summer's day. Not quite the end for me, however: I was rushed somewhere to make an immediate unscheduled speech to a gathering of British Airways executives, which in a dream I did. What I said I cannot imagine.

We were then installed in a superb, all-white seventeenth-floor apartment with a balcony overlooking the famous harbour with its bridge in the foreground. The blue water, the inky sky and the throngs of yachts with their brightly coloured sails recalled a picture by Australia's Dufy, Ken Done.

The next day one of my hosts (I became a little confused as there seemed to be so many) asked me if I would like to meet the Prime Minister, Malcolm Fraser, so that balmy evening we went down to the Regent Hotel where the ballroom was thronged with the Liberal Party faithful. Australians very sensibly have a moratorium on political rallies for several days before a general election – in order, I imagine, to allow the rhetoric to die down and to give voters a chance to make up their minds away from all the noise. I knew that an election was in the offing, but only gradually did it dawn on me that the one I was attending was the culminating rally of the campaign. The lights dimmed, and the spotlit Prime Ministerial party entered to a fanfare of trumpets. I was asked if I would care to meet Mr Fraser and was led up on to the platform. While he and I were exchanging pleasantries an introductory announcement was made over the public address system, detailing the treats that were in store for the evening. Amongst these I just happened to catch the fact that the first of them would be a speech by me.

When the red mist had cleared I saw that I had two choices: I could fall down in a faint and claim jet-lag, or I could make a speech. I felt that the first option had little to recommend it. I could imagine the next day's headlines: BRIT STAR FAINTS AT LIB RALLY – BLAMES JET-LAG. The second, appalling though it was, seemed the lesser of the two evils.

I mounted the podium, which was decorated with the Liberal Party logo, and saw thronged before me the nation's media, radio microphones and television cameras at the ready. A huge Australian flag hung over my head. I had thought beforehand that the press might well waylay me and ask me to comment on Australian politics, and knew that I was entering a minefield. One false step and I could be blown straight back to London.

I took a deep breath. After the usual courtesies I said that, as an occasional employee of the BBC, I could not of course express a political bias. I could, however, confidently predict that the winner of the forthcoming contest would not be our host tonight. There was a sharp intake of breath from wall to wall. 'Neither,' I said, 'will it be Mr Hawke.' Breath was held. 'It will be,' I ended triumphantly, 'the Public Service!' which is Australian for the Civil Service. Roars of applause. I felt that I could now faint in comfort.

Full use was made of me, and I lost count of the radio and television interviews I did over the next few days. To save time some radio interviews were done in the limousine that whisked me from studio to studio.

Australian hospitality is famous, and the most generous friendship is offered on all hands and in all circumstances. One of the first things my son did on arrival was to go out to find a pub. When he came back he told me he had nearly got into a fight. I went white, but he said that when someone had called him a Pommie poofter or some such he had offered to punch the man's face in. They all thought that was marvellous and bought him a drink.

I made the speech I had come to make to the Australian Federation of Advertisers. It was not too bad but was very much outshone by one made in reply by Sir John Mason, the retired British High Commissioner, one of the most popular speakers in the country. I was then flown to Canberra to speak to the Press Club – a daunting occasion because previous speakers had been people like Mrs Nehru and Henry Kissinger. Already some confusion was arising as to my actual identity. Was I really a British cabinet minister? I myself remained fairly sure that I was not, but I could tell that others were not so certain.

Canberra is a city built round a large artificial lake, Lake Burley Griffin, named after the architect who planned the capital. I suggested it might be renamed Lake Humphrey Appleby, but the civil servants who make up a large proportion of the population were not amused.

As I was checking in at the airport to return to Sydney, I noticed a sober-suited group of men standing near the desk. One of them detached himself and came over, introducing himself as Barry Cohen, Federal Minister for Arts, Heritage and the Environment. He was one of Bob Hawke's senior ministers, just coming away from their first cabinet meeting. When we were all back in Sydney Barry invited me to lunch with him and his wife Rae at their home in Gosford, about one and a half hours' drive north. The ministerial limousine collected me, we picked up an Australian senator and swept up the Pacific

Highway to Barry's constituency – which Australians confusingly call an 'electorate'.

Barry's house was set on a wooded hillside. The steep garden was filled with the silvery sound of bell-birds and two young wallabies were playing in it. We saw where they slept, in a shelter slung from a beam in two sacks made in imitation of their mothers' pouches.

Social distinctions are happily blurred in Australia and Barry's driver, Kerry Ternan, joined us for pre-lunch drinks.

'Oh, by the way, Kerry,' said Barry, 'after lunch would you take the senator back to Sydney and then come back here and collect Paul, who's staying for supper?'

Kerry registered incredulity. 'Fuck me, Barry,' he said, 'that's a three-hour drive, man. Jesus Christ!'

'Please don't mind me,' murmured the senator.

'Oh, all right,' said Barry, and we all stayed and went out that evening for a Chinese meal.

The Palace of Westminster seemed a long way away.

At this time I was beginning to have a little trouble with my heart; my pulse was more rapid than normal and not quite regular either, and it was not helped by the fact that I had had a bout of bronchitis. This had started the day before we had set out and, as it was blazing hot in Australia and freezing cold in Europe, I had very sensibly packed a thermal vest to wear on the way home.

We landed at Muscat at 6 a.m. It was already ninety degrees outside but I knew we would only be down briefly so I slipped into the loo, had a wash and brush-up and put my vest on. We were there for four hours. The doors were open, the air conditioning turned off and a very smart-looking policeman with a machine gun was posted at the bottom of the steps, presumably to discourage anyone from taking too much Muscat air.

The captain invited me on to the flight deck for a chat. Ironically, it seemed that the de-icing equipment was faulty, and this would be very necessary by the time we reached Heathrow. He had been in touch with his bosses in London, where it was still the middle of the night, and they were having an emergency meeting about the situation. He would let me know the outcome.

Meantime, we sat and sweated. I reflected that I must be amongst the very few people on the Persian Gulf that morning wearing thermal underwear. The captain said that it was a typical *Yes, Minister* situation; his bosses had decided eventually that it was safe enough to take off – 'captain's responsibility'. I was not entirely reassured.

11

'You'll be Marvellous!'

⤳⧽⧼⤶

Not long after my return from Australia I was asked by the doyen of London's charity fund-raisers, Martin Tickner, and the critic Jack Tinker to take part in a rehearsed reading of a compilation of excerpts from Terence Rattigan's plays, which they had called *In Praise of Rattigan*. I admired Rattigan as much as they did, and since the cast included Dorothy Tutin and Denis Quilley and we were to do it for Prince Rainier and his family in Monte Carlo, it did not take me long to agree.

Monaco, with its high rise apartment blocks shouldering each other aside for a view of the sea, is not the prettiest part of the Mediterranean, but we certainly enjoyed ourselves. Even though it was only excerpts and even though we only wore evening dress and read our texts, Rattigan's genius, only now being rediscovered, shone out. Patricia Burke, who had been one of the Maids Marian in *Robin Hood* all those years ago, brought to my dressing room her mother Marie, a famous musical comedy star in her day who was now living in the South of France. Tricia was delighted, as she had been with her in pantomime at the Bristol Old Vic. Marie, old and now blind, touched our faces. 'Ah, yes. Now I remember you!' she said.

Having paid our respects to the royal party we thought it might be fun, as we were all dressed up, to stroll down to the casino and see if there were any ruined playboys shooting themselves in the shrubbery. The gardens were undisturbed. No doubt the Salle Privée is very glamorous but the Grand Salon was a sad let-down, crammed with people in torn jeans and grubby tee-shirts working rows of fruit machines. We returned next day and were shown the theatre, which was a bit more like it. With its worn plush seating, its rococo proscenium and gilt cherubs it was crowded with the ghosts of Diaghilev and the Ballets Russes.

After a holiday in Italy it was time to earn some money, and unluckily the opportunity that presented itself was a play called *Lovers Dancing*, by Charles Dyer. Dyer is a very considerable writer; he had had a great success with *The Staircase* some years previously and as a young man had written a thriller which has more or less kept him and his family ever since. It was called *Wanted One Body*. He had in gratitude called his house 'The Old WOB'.

Whether it was the cast, the management or the direction I do not know, but certainly Georgina Hale gave a performance as eccentric as I have seen and Donald McWhinnie directed it through an alcoholic haze. I suspect that it was just not a very good play and that my need to earn some money and the fact that Colin Blakely would be sharing the top billing with me had over-ridden my judgement. Certainly the reviews were lukewarm. Some critics wrote that it was obscene.

I had a premonition of failure when I came in to the theatre to do the dress rehearsal. The American producers and the company manager were standing in my room with pattern books in their hands, and invited me to help them choose some new wallpaper and some coverings for the furniture. I felt distinctly uneasy. We had not yet even opened, and a better time to think of redecoration might have been when we had enjoyed a month of general acclaim and the advance was a couple of hundred thousand pounds. I feel much more comfortable with a producer like Michael Codron. With him you have to storm into his office and shout or burst into tears and threaten not to go on that night unless your dressing room walls have an instant coat of whitewash. You do feel he has probably got his priorities right.

I still had no answer to my skin problem and, as with everyone who was likely to see me at any rate partly clothed, I told Colin about it and showed him the unsightly red patches. '*You've* got a skin problem!' he said. 'Look at this!' He showed me his knuckles. They were swollen and cracked and looked as if they might recently have been bleeding. 'It's something called "mycosis fungoides". Nothing to do with fungus,' he chuckled. I was to remember our conversation later.

Some time previously, before we had opened, Nigel Hawthorne and I had had supper with some mutual friends. Princess Margaret was another guest. After we had eaten, the Princess had entertained us by singing the whole of *Guys and Dolls*. She knew it well, and had even restored the cuts which had been made in the National Theatre's production. By 3a.m. we all knew each other pretty well, so I was not altogether surprised that when she came to see *Lovers Dancing* she indicated that she would come and say hello to us afterwards. I was even less surprised when a message came during the first interval to say that one of her ladies-in-waiting had felt unwell and that, much to Her Royal Highness's regret, she had been obliged to accompany her home.

We had been living in our North London house for seventeen years. It stood in a pleasant, tree-lined street, it had served its purpose nobly and we had brought up four children there, but in spite of the fact that the district was gradually being gentrified (I have no objection to this process) we had got bored with it. It was getting shabby and needed constant repair; besides which the children were all leaving home and it was getting too big for us. We needed a flat.

For a long time I had been saying to Tricia how happy I had been as a child when my mother and I lived near the river in Chelsea. 'What would be ideal,' I had been saying, 'would be to get an empty box somewhere on the Thames and let Max design something inside it. I must have a balcony from which I can spit into the water,' I added. Max Clendinning had redesigned the inside of our retreat in Suffolk which we had bought many years before. One Sunday morning Tricia was reading the paper. 'Is this the sort of thing you mean?' she asked, pointing to an ad.

Taking Hugo, I drove straight to Bermondsey. The flat was part of a nineteenth-century warehouse, beautifully adapted and with many of its most interesting features preserved. The walls were two feet thick and it included a balcony overhanging the water. I spat into it just to make sure. That afternoon I went back with Tricia, collecting Max en route. We said yes straightaway! That was the extent of our flat-hunting, and we put the house on the market.

One of the tabloids rang the next week and a reporter asked why we were moving. We told him. The following Sunday there was an item which said that we were moving because we were 'sick of being gawped at by the neighbours'. If I see something in print, my first inclination has always been to start off by believing it. The neighbours proved to have the same instinct, and as we had been living there perfectly amicably for twenty years I had to spend quite a lot of time placating them.

* * *

Patrick Garland, who had directed the original production of *Forty Years On*, told me that he was going to revive it at the Chichester Festival Theatre, of which he was now the artistic director, and asked me to play the role which Gielgud had created seventeen years earlier, that of the headmaster. I agreed eagerly. I loved the play as much as any I had ever done, and could remember vividly the previous production. To follow Gielgud would certainly be a challenge, but, as I have said, challenges may not be avoided. There was not a lot of money to be earned in Sussex, but it is a lovely place to work and a major attraction was that I would be able to stay with our friends Michael and Caroline Marshall. We had first met them at Penelope Keith's wedding reception. Michael, the MP for Arundel, one of the safer Tory seats, has a lovely house near there and, although we seldom agree politically, we have always been close friends.

Lovers Dancing finished its run at the end of January and I emerged with relief. In my diary there is a sharp reminder to myself to read proposed plays more carefully in future.

Rehearsals in Chichester were not due to start until April and I plunged into a flurry of foreign travel. I went to Dublin to appear on *The Late Late Show*, hosted by Gay Byrne, who asked me if I had any children. When I said that I had three sons and a daughter there was a thunderous round of applause. I could not think why until I realised that we were in a Catholic country. I went to the Algarve to advertise lawnmowers. I think it was Olivier who brought respectability to TV advertising when he endorsed a cigarette that bore his name. He did the profession a great service and every actor gave a sigh of relief, took what money was offered and ran. Then there was a weekend in Belfast to open a travel fair. I was put up at the Europa Hotel, 'The most bombed hotel in Europe', as it was known, and thought it a piece of luck the moment I arrived to see an armoured patrol go down the street. I saw one go down the street every five minutes after that.

In the South of France I took part in an entertainment for IBM. The big conference centre in Cannes is concrete and windowless, but I did manage to stroll round the marina and look at the millionaires' luxury yachts. I sat for an hour on the beach and got into conversation with an elderly American, who told me that he lived in one of the better parts of Cannes and complained bitterly of the outrageous tax demands made of him by the wicked socialist government.

'Well,' I said, 'look at it this way. If you've got ten million and they take nine, you've still got a million left.'

He looked at me strangely.

'Mind you,' I continued, 'there certainly is a lot of money down here. Half those vast yachts are flying the Red Ensign.'

The American looked startled. 'No!' he said. 'Russian yachts!'

Back in London I met Gielgud on the steps of the Garrick Club. He was in his best brick-dropping form. 'I hear you're going to do *Forty Years On* at Chichester,' he said. 'I'm so glad, you'll be marvellous. Of course they asked me. I didn't want to do it.'

I was getting to an age when I was beginning to be uneasy about my memory, but I had little difficulty with *Forty Years On*. Phrases and even whole passages had stayed with me over the years, and I put the fear of God into the rest of the cast by knowing it on the first day of rehearsals. It was a delight to do it in those handsome surroundings, and the pleasure spread through the whole company. On the first pay-day I was walking across the lawns which surround the theatre. Just ahead of me were two of the small boys whom Patrick Garland had recruited from the Cathedral Choir School, skipping along clutching their pay packets.

'Cor!' said one. 'You get paid for it as well.'

'Better than sex!' replied his friend.

Halfway through the first night I happened to be standing next to one of the boys in the wings. He smiled at me encouragingly. 'Well, Mr Eddington,' he said, 'so far so good.'

The repertory system at Chichester, which provides occasional days off, allowed me to accept an invitation from Carol Martys, a drama teacher at Parkhurst, to visit a group of lifers at the prison. I was simply required to go and chat with them and give them a breath of ordinary life for an hour or two. It was an unsettling experience. One is, of course, accompanied by a prison officer all the time, and at each door and checkpoint through which one goes permission is asked on a radio telephone for the party to proceed to the next. The way ahead is unlocked before you and locked again when you have passed through. To visit what are considered the highest-risk prisoners you go from barrier to barrier, deeper and deeper. Crossing the last courtyard, I glimpsed between two buildings a green hillside and the end of a white bungalow, and realised that if you were confined there that was all you would see of the outside world.

The first person I saw was unmistakably Reggie Kray. It was

strange to be sitting chatting to a man who, I had to remind myself, had stabbed a man through the eye while his brother held him. I was very privileged, I was told; Reggie did not meet just anyone.

Only ten men were allowed in the room at a time. There did not seem to be a type of murderer; each one was quite different. A jolly red-faced car dealer from South London sat at the end of the table, and next to me was a young man who could have been my son. The son of a North Country headmaster, he had discovered that his wife was being unfaithful to him. Instead of killing her immediately, which might have been seen as a mitigating circumstance, he had brooded for a few days and then killed her, so making it a premeditated crime. He was obviously a nervous and highly strung person, an expert conjuror apparently and a member of the Magic Circle. As I left the prison I took large gulps of air, feeling much as I had when, as a Catholic child, I had emerged from confession, liberated and absolved for another week.

I had a quick check-up at the Whittington Hospital where the head of the cardiac department was Roy Davies. Of necessity we saw each other regularly and had luckily become good friends. He saw to it that I took all the right pills to keep me going, since *Forty Years On* was transferring from Chichester to London and opened at the Queens Theatre in August. I have always thought of myself as a lazy person, but the evidence points the other way; on our opening night Nigel and Derek and I went to the BBC's Paris Studio in Lower Regent Street and recorded the first of eight consecutive days of *Yes, Minister*, this time for radio, and on the third of those days we moved house, or rather Tricia and some friends did. I went to the studio in the morning, did the recording, went back after the recording to the flat, went to the theatre in the evening to do the show, and returned to the flat to sleep. I imagine we all slept well.

We had good reviews and a respectable run, but never quite recaptured its original freshness. Transferring a play from Chichester can often present a problem. Chichester has an open, fan-shaped stage, with the audience almost surrounding the actors. It is a difficult theatre to play in but can be extremely effective, and the whole atmosphere of the place is wonderfully friendly. In most other theatres the stage is behind a conventional proscenium arch and there is seldom sufficient time, or money, to make the major changes which are necessary. In consequence sightlines are squeezed, the set does not look quite right and there may be sound problems as well.

With John Quayle in
Donkey's Years

Dressed for the pageant in *Ten
Times Table (John Haynes)*

Sir Oliver Cockwould in
Jonathan Miller's
production of *She
Would if She Could
(Frazer Ashford)*

'Very courageous, Minister' with
Nigel Hawthorne and Derek
Fowlds in an early episode of
Yes, Minister (Joan Williams)

A worried Prime Minister
(Joan Williams)

Christmas at No. 10 *(Press
Association)*

In Peter Jenkins' only play *Illuminations* at the Lyric, Hammersmith

With Margaret Tyzack in *Who's Afraid of Virginia Woolf (Zoë Dominic)*

With Roger Lloyd-Pack and Nicky Henson in *Noises Off (Morris Newcombe)*

Being briefed in
Urdu by the BBC
World Service
cast for the
Indian version of
Yes, Minister
(BBC)

A photo
opportunity.
Margaret
Thatcher
presents Nigel
Hawthorne and
me with an
award from the
National
Viewers and
Listeners
Association,
(PA News)

Two Prime
Ministers:
with Gough
Whitlam at
the launch of
HMS Pinafore
in Australia

As Sir Joseph Porter in *HMS Pinafore* at the Victoria State Opera House, Melbourne

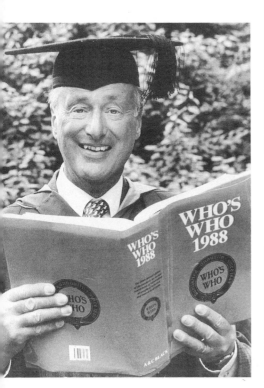

Collecting an honorary MA from Sheffield University *(Sheffield Newspapers)*

A full house for *London Assurance* at Bath's Theatre Royal, 1989

With John Sessions and Jennifer Ehle in *Tartuffe (Stuart Morris)*

With Harold Pinter in *No Man's Land (Stuart Morris)*

My 'coming out' photograph *(Express Newspapers)*

Relaxing at home in London,
at our cottage in Suffolk, and
with the family

Home (John Timbers)

Our main drawback was in having to replace all the small boys. The GLC regulations did not allow us to use players so young and we had to cast youths who just looked small, rather as though they had been kept on the gin in order to stunt their growth. If this was a drawback, it did not stop the Variety Club from giving me the Best Actor award.

Stephen Fry was playing the part that Alan Bennett had originally played. He said he was working on an adaptation of the old musical *Me And My Girl* and hoped that it would be produced. Soon after we closed it was, and made him a millionaire. Alan himself we saw less often. He promised to come to tea one day but failed to turn up. His excuse was that he was suffering a mild form of writer's block: he had just written, 'What has happened to your public lavatories? They used to be the envy of the civilised world.' 'And where do I go from there?' he complained.

I had been a governor of the Bristol Old Vic for ten years – I believe the first actor to serve on such a board. I very much appreciated the opportunity to give something back to a theatre which meant so much to me and to my wife, but I had become uneasy. Two or three years previously the board had decided to accept a small amount of sponsorship money from Imperial Tobacco. I argued as forcefully as I could against acceptance. There was always a quid pro quo, I said: we would have to publish our gratitude in the programmes and thus imply, to impressionable minds, a respectable partnership between a cultural activity such as ours and tobacco. It was virtually free advertising for Imperial Tobacco, I said, adding that, as the theatre is a notoriously overcrowded profession and actors always have great difficulty in finding work, occasions would inevitably arise when an actor like myself who objected to people being encouraged to smoke would be forced to accept work in a tobacco-subsidised theatre, thus making himself an indirect accessory. Of course I was voted down. 'Beggars can't be choosers!' I was told.

This year the subsidy offer was increased by a few hundred pounds and I made my annual speech against it. I had in the meantime been recruited by ASH, the anti-smoking organisation, and my profile as an anti-smoker was high. When my objections were rejected I felt I had little option but to resign and did so, with the heaviest of hearts. One of the governors, a representative of tobacco workers in Bristol, said he envied me the luxury of being able to indulge my conscience in this way.

PAUL EDDINGTON

* * *

Remarkably, almost uniquely, I have never been amongst those actors who have difficulty finding work. We recorded a Christmas edition of *Yes Minister* and, only sixteen days after *Forty Years On* closed in January, I was rehearsing a revival of Tom Stoppard's *Jumpers*, opposite my dear friend Felicity Kendal and directed by the wizard-like Peter Wood.

Once again I was placing myself under a considerable strain. Tom Stoppard shares with Jonathan Miller an apparently effortless intellectual superiority. Full of fun and generosity and in no sense condescending, they nevertheless make people of anything less than shining intelligence, and here I certainly include myself, feel distinctly inferior.

Tom's dialogue is notoriously dense, in the sense that a Dundee cake is dense. Every cubic millimetre (and of course it is three-dimensional) is loaded with meaning, allusion, poetry, history and anything else you care to mention. As the aging professor, the part originally played by Michael Hordern, I had an opening speech several pages in length and of stunning complexity in which I was attempting, I think, to prove mathematically the existence of God. The opening line is, 'To begin at the beginning; is God?' The professor is constructing the speech in order to deliver it at a later date. His secretary, who does not speak, is taking it down in shorthand, he is clutching some notes and his glasses are on the end of his nose.

I decided that the whole effect of his extemporising, making it up as he went along, would be spoilt if I had to keep pausing to glance at the notes or if the secretary were to prompt me discreetly, which she could easily have done. To put temptation out of my way I instructed her not to do so, had plain lenses put in the glasses and also made sure that the notes were, in fact, gibberish. Inevitably there would be a night when I would lose the thread or simply forget a word, but I thought that in that case the tension would be better maintained if I were to struggle out of the hole on my own.

There are several speeches in *Jumpers* of a similar density, if not quite as long. Michael Hordern told me that he had never bothered to try to find out what they meant, but I think he was being disingenuous. I doubted if I would be able to convey the meaning to an audience if I did not fully understand it myself, and thought that I had better have a very hard look at the text and perhaps even learn the first speech.

It was midwinter. Tricia and I thought it would be fun to get clean away, out of reach of everyone and into some sun. Neither of us had ever been to Africa, so we decided to have a couple of weeks in Malindi, on the coast of Kenya. As the small plane which had brought us from Nairobi to Malindi took off for its return I realised that I had left the script of *Jumpers* on board, so after a frantic telephone call to the Codron office I was forced to rest for the first week.

Malindi was the smart place to be during the heyday of Empire, but it had by now fallen on hard times. Our hotel, the Sinbad, once so grand, was in sad decline. There were one or two expensive-looking German-owned hotels, and the flavour of the place can be gauged by the fact that Malindi was advertised in Frankfurt as, 'Sea, sun and sex!' The public was only just becoming aware of AIDS and Malindi was apparently notorious as somewhere that couples could come and have sexual holidays from each other.

Our own prim aloofness was rescued by Bentley Tollemache, a scion of the brewing family. In his kikoi, the wrap-around skirt favoured by the locals, and his native beads he was colourfully extrovert, and entertained us generously at his beautifully cool house on the beach. A keen fan of *Yes, Minister*, he had a large collection of the videos – recorded illegally, of course. He knew the dialogue by heart, and it was his custom to round up all the ex-pats on the coast and hold a monthly *Yes, Minister* party, at which he would show the videos to his captive audience and his Arab butler would serve fish and chips wrapped in specially imported copies of the *News of the World*. The first time we dined with him the butler served us roast lamb, new potatoes and minted peas. Where he got them from I cannot imagine. As we ate we were entertained by the croaking of a frog from beneath a pile of stones in the otherwise empty fireplace.

Most of the second week we spent walking up and down the beach, with me muttering the lines as Tricia, who was holding the script, prompted me. Stout Germans, wallowing naked in sand pools, glanced at us curiously, as we did at them. We swam on the coral reef, thrillingly with barracuda and other wonderfully exotic fish. A pair of mating octopuses stared at me indignantly when I caught them *in flagrante*.

Our guide made us wear pyjamas. She said that even on an overcast day the ultra-violet rays, magnified under the water, could be extremely dangerous. We were not at that time used to seeing Australian cricketers with smears of sunblock on their faces and I allowed myself to become deeply sunburnt. One day the skin started peeling off the back of my thighs, almost in handfuls. I was mildly alarmed, but thought at the time (how wrongly!) that it was a small price to pay for such a handsome tan. And excessive sun was not the only hazard; one day I stood on a poisonous sea urchin spine which had to be surgically removed.

One night we dined with some other acquaintances; halfway through the meal Tricia excused herself and went to the bathroom. When ten minutes had passed and she had not reappeared, our hostess went to see if she was all right. She was not. Luckily our hostess had been a nurse and recognised the symptoms. When the doctor arrived, only minutes later, Tricia's blood pressure registered zero and she had no pulse. She was in fact clinically dead. She was given a massive injection of something or other and soon afterwards came to, feeling a bit feeble but otherwise not much the worse. We decided that the lobster she had eaten the previous night was the culprit. Her recovery was so rapid and complete that her true peril was disguised. But whenever I think of it now my blood runs cold. Future invitations to visit Africa were treated with caution. We had, we felt, been there and done that.

One of the first things that Tom Stoppard said to us when we started rehearsals was that he regarded the original text of his plays as mere blueprints, and any revivals as an opportunity to rewrite everything. I went white. I explained that I had spent two dangerous weeks in Darkest Africa committing his tortuous phrases to my fragile memory. If there were any significant changes, I said, I would cry. It was his turn to look alarmed, but I have to say that he respected my frailties – though I also have to say that I have not been invited to appear in a Stoppard play since.

With his ruddy cheeks and beetling brows, his slight air of menace and his magical sleight of hand, Peter Wood gives the air of someone in touch with darker powers. I am aware that some actors fear him, and for those who do he can be uncompromising. His style of directing is exuberant and robust and the secret, I found, was to give as good as you got. If he swore at you, rather than submit blushingly it was best to swear back; out of the conflict some tremendous work could be forged. Naturally, actors in the lesser parts and those fresh from drama school were reluctant to join in the game and they could get hurt. I can only say that for me every rehearsal was like a master class and I came away from them, not exhausted as I had expected, but refreshed and alert.

My role in *Yes, Minister* was still exacting its toll. One night during rehearsals I was asked to dinner with the Worshipful Company of Vintners in their pre-Great Fire of London hall. I sat between Count Tolstoy and someone who told me that he had won the hundred yard dash at Eton in 1928. The ex-sprinter begged me to use my influence with the Prime Minister of New Zealand to allow nuclear warships to use their waters. Not wishing to confuse him further, I promised to do what I could.

Jumpers has music, laughter, a chorus of dancers, a tortoise, a girl on a swing and archery, and is altogether an effervescent extravaganza. I do not think any but a professional philosopher could follow the many arguments fully at the time, but on the other hand I do not think that anyone could leave the theatre without a share of the sparkle. Certainly our audiences did not, and we had a long, happy and prosperous run at the Aldwych.

About halfway through the run I began to find I was having to visit the loo rather more frequently than seemed normal, and before very long this inconvenience had become, unmistakably, diarrhoea. It does not take a great feat of the imagination to guess just how inconvenient that condition is for an actor with, now, a particularly high profile, and not simply on the stage. By the time I had had my insides thoroughly investigated I was having to 'go' thirty or forty times a day. I was sure I must have picked up some tropical disease in Africa and for the next three months I trudged from one doctor's surgery to another. Eventually I was diagnosed as having ulcerative colitis, a condition which is often associated with the arthritic disease I had been suffering from for years but which was now, thankfully, in remission. I was told that mine was a comparatively mild attack. Like deafness, incontinence is to the unafflicted a subject for farce, but as John Cleese once said, 'Farce is what happens to you on the worst day of your life.'

Wherever I went, the first thing I had to do was to check where the lavatories were and to gauge my distance from them. After the first warning from my gut I usually had between fifteen and thirty seconds, and I never went anywhere without a nappy and spare underwear. I was given a powerful drug which would seize me up pretty effectively by the time I had to go on stage, but I could only take a limited amount on any one day and I usually saved it until the performance.

It took some years to get the evil thing fully under control and send it into remission, and while it lasted I used to think that I would rather endure anything else. The agonies of dread and humiliation were a nightmare, and I got to the stage where I felt that it would have been so easy simply to lie down and stop eating.

But I would hate to give the impression that gloom reigned; quite the contrary. Tricia cheerfully devoted her entire life to my wellbeing and the children – children no longer – were as thoughtful and loving as a parent could wish. Apart from that, the entire eighties were the busiest time ever, which is saying a lot.

The year ended with Richard Briers and me, amongst a hundred or so others, helping Princess Diana with her first public engagement – switching on the West End's Christmas lights. 'Aren't we lucky,' I remarked to Clement Freud, 'we could have been saddled with some night club floozie.' Then I remembered that he was a director of the Playboy Club. 'Sorry!' I added. 'Of course, you're a night club floozie yourself, aren't you!' He looked frosty, as well he might. My sense of decorum does sometimes desert me.

The worldwide success of *Yes, Minister* continued to have its effect. I was voted their favourite personality by Denmark's TV magazine, and Tricia and I were invited to collect an award. When the plane landed at Copenhagen the purser held the other passengers back and asked us to alight first. Awaiting us was one of the royal Daimlers, flying the Danish flag. This was the sort of thing we were beginning to expect and we descended the steps with aplomb, to be swept, without any fuss about passports or customs, to the Foreign Ministry where we had a chat with the Prime Minister and the Foreign Minister. At dinner that night I was presented with a copper saucepan, a certificate, a scarlet sash rather like that of a beauty queen and a laurel wreath as tall as myself. It was clear that there would be a diplomatic incident if we did not take all these home with us, especially the wreath. Our departure from Copenhagen was a good deal less dignified than had been our arrival.

Jumpers went on through most of that year and I continued to busy myself with many other things, mostly advertisements. I have said that a good living may be had from radio voice-overs, but to get into the real money one has to appear 'in vision'. So much money is involved that most actors who are lucky enough to be invited to do them often feel a little guilty. My own defence is that actors' work is casual and most have long stretches without any income at all. There are no pensions for actors, unless they save hard and set them up themselves. Another factor is that if an advertiser thinks that you are going to boost his profits, simply by being who you are, to him it can make a difference of millions. One couple I know bought a handsome villa in Spain and earned a large fee as well, simply from doing a series of short TV adverts.

My entrée to this world was again through Penny Keith. Together she and I did one for a brand of biscuit. Apart from the fee, which in my case was £22,000, an added attraction was the fact that it would only be shown in New Zealand. Over-exposure could quickly lessen your value, and for showing in Britain I never did more than one a year.

And there is no doubt that I was well known. I was walking through Green Park one morning when I noticed a large black police sergeant, a constable and a civilian standing by the railings outside the Ritz. 'Good morning, Minister!' cried all three. I waved graciously and the civilian added, 'Could you have a word with the Home Secretary? It might help!' Only then did I notice that he was handcuffed to the railings, and recognised him as a member of one of the three-card-trick gangs that work the West End, usually in Soho.

All the stage doors of the theatres on Shaftesbury Avenue open on to Soho back streets. When working there one automatically becomes an honorary member of the village, and any time of the day or night your fellow citizens will make sure that you come to no harm. On my way to the theatre one night I was waylaid by a posse of nubile black girls who took me by the arm and excitedly invited me home. 'Oh God, it's you!' they said when they saw who it was.

The villagers know your business better than you do. 'I hear your show's coming into the Globe, Paul!' a fruit vendor would shout to me in Rupert Street market. They were usually right, and more than once it was the first I had heard of the matter.

My perceived political status took me to all sorts of unexpected places. I seemed to have assumed a mysterious status as something to do with government – I mean in real life. I only gradually became aware of this after the British Council and the Foreign Office had asked me once or twice to meet ambassadors and other dignitaries. I dined with the Duke and Duchess of Gloucester, I welcomed the Chinese Ambassador, I bade farewell to the Danish Ambassador, I even attended what Alan Bennett called one of the Queen's 'All Walks of Life' luncheon parties at the Palace.

We had drinks in an ante-room and then, preceded by a flourish of corgis, the Queen and the Duke were amongst us. It was only two days after an intruder had managed to breach Buckingham Palace security and enter Her Majesty's bedroom. Anyone would have forgiven her for cancelling appointments for the next few days but the Queen seemed to me to be in remarkably good spirits.

When I got home I was telephoned by a woman who described herself as the Palace Correspondent of the Press Association. In my innocence I imagined that she must have some form of official accreditation and did not put the telephone down straightaway, as I should have done. By asking me leading questions, the reporter was trying to make me say that the Queen was in a furious mood about the lack of security at the Palace. This was, of course, not the case and most unwisely I told her that the Queen had simply thought that the 'intruder' was one of the servants who had come to draw the curtains, which I believe was the case.

The following day every newspaper from the *Sydney Morning Herald* to the *South China Times* and the *Toronto Evening Star* showed my picture with a story on the lines of 'Palace Guest Tells All'. I had suffered my first assault by media and felt as if I had been hit by a landmine. I wish I could say that it taught me a lesson, but it took me years before I was thoroughly able to harden my heart to what seemed a friendly approach from a journalist. Harold Pinter has told me that he actually experiences physical pain when confronted by one.

I understood from one of the Queen's biographies that she was not best pleased by my indiscretion. Although I naturally wrote an apology via her secretary, it was some years before we attended another royal garden party.

I was still, however, *persona grata* with the British Council, who invited me to help entertain a party of Soviet actors and dancers to dinner at a discreet Italian restaurant off St Martin's Lane. I was seated next to a young film actress and, through an interpreter, we had a conversation about theatre and film directors. Some, I said (and I had one or two in mind), liked to tease and bully their actors and, if they were female and good-looking, perhaps to make them cry.

As if she had been pierced by something sharp, my companion burst into a torrent of what sounded very like invective. The interpreter bent his ear towards her. 'She does not like such people,' he told me, and bent his head again. 'She is thirsty for their blood.'

On the home political front Robert Maxwell invited me to a party he was giving one night for the Labour leaders at the top of the Mirror building, possibly because I had just given a favourable review to a book by Gerald Kaufman. Harold Wilson said to me, 'Of course you know that it was me who suggested to the

BBC that they should do *Yes, Minister.*' Tony Jay smiled when I told him.

Mrs Mary Whitehouse, the self-appointed arbiter of 'taste' on television, decided that *Yes, Prime Minister* merited her organisation's top award that year, to be presented to us by her in the crypt of All Souls, Langham Place, next to Broadcasting House. The night before the ceremony I was in my dressing room at the Albery when I had a startling call from the BBC. They said that Mrs Thatcher had decided that she, not Mrs Whitehouse, would present the award. Moreover, she would like to take part in a little scene with Nigel and me.

. This would not so much be an honour for us, I realised, as a wonderful photo-opportunity for herself. We had all of us bent over backwards to avoid any connection being made with any particular political party. Now here we were, to be presented as part of the Thatcher administration! I rang Nigel and told him that, as a matter of principle, he must refuse to do it. Nigel felt that it was really my responsibility to refuse, since it was my name which came first on the credits. I rang Jonathan Lynn. He very much agreed with Nigel. 'You refuse,' he said.

A mixture of nervousness and vanity eventually won the day. Surely nothing like this could ever have happened before? I agreed.

The scene consisted of a firm, no nonsense, but kindly Prime Minister summoning a craven minister (me) and an obstructive civil servant (Nigel) to instruct the minister to abolish all economists, who all told her different things and who were always wrong.

I asked a press secretary who the author was and, after a slight hesitation, she said, 'Someone at No. 10.'

The crypt of All Souls was packed with members of Mrs Whitehouse's Viewers and Listeners Association, which had started life as the Clean Up TV Campaign. All no doubt fervent admirers, perhaps of us and certainly of Mrs Thatcher, they laughed loudly and often and gave us a standing ovation at the end.

I do not know whether her message about economists got across or whether her association with a popular show helped her own ratings, but it certainly planted in the public mind the curious idea that she had been recruited by the BBC to play a role in *Yes, Minister.* I told a journalist that it was all rather disappointing for us; we had toiled long and hard to make the series one that would offend everyone – clearly we had failed to do so!

*   *   *

As guests of the BBC we went to Montreux in 1986 for the international TV festival. We did not win an award, but there were some considerable compensations. Noël Coward's long-time companion Graham Payn swept down to our hotel in Noël's open white Mercedes and took Tricia and me up the mountainside to the villa he used to share with him. In a magnificent position, it was nevertheless surprisingly ordinary and could have been in a prosperous English suburb. I asked him what it had been like to live with Coward.

'Oh, it was such fun,' he said. 'For instance, I was dancing round the pool one day and he laughed at me rather cruelly. I said, "I'll have you know that people have paid good money to see me do this!"' (He had been a dancer.)

'Not very much, dear,' Coward had said, 'and not for very long!'

Jonathan Lynn and his wife Rita were in Montreux on their way back from Italy. The nuclear accident at Chernobyl had happened not long since, and Johnny said that as a result the Italians were refusing to eat red lettuce. When he asked them why not, they had merely shrugged expressively and said darkly, 'Red lettuce!'

April in the country filming Agatha Christie's *Murder in the Vicarage* sounded a most attractive idea. One of the great advantages of being an actor is that, so long as you keep your health and strength, there is never any need to retire. As Romeo sinks slowly in the west, King Lear rises in the east, and it was a great privilege to work with Joan Hickson, who was already in her eighties, difficult though that was to believe. Warm spring sunshine in the daffodils was absent, however, and I shivered and shook my way through the filming, most of which seemed to me to take place out of doors, with the stage hands having to sweep the snow out of the shot.

The schedule was organised to give me a few days off to compère, with Judi Dench, the gala at the Royal Opera House in honour of the Queen's sixtieth birthday. I detected the hand of Patrick Garland, the director of *Forty Years On*, who was the overall producer. Apart from anything else I expect he felt that Judi and I, as old 'legitimate' actors, might exert a steadying influence on a cast as potentially volatile as Mount Etna. Some of the world's greatest singers and dancers in the world had agreed to appear: Jessye Norman, José Carreras, Lucia Popp, Placido Domingo, Gwyneth Jones, Anthony Dowell, Gelsey Kirkland, Lesley Collier, Jennifer Penney – everywhere one looked there was a world star.

Some anxiety was felt when the great tenors met; it had been rumoured that they could not be in the same city together, let alone the same theatre, but this rumour was evidently just a symptom of the nervous excitement that was taking hold of everyone. The dancers displayed a good deal of fiery temperament despite John Copley's tactful handling, and there was a point when Judi Dench declared (to me) that she was quite prepared to bang their heads together. Two very distinguished dancers were having an affair and had been booked into a suite at the Savoy when it was found that they had fallen out. They never turned up at all.

On the night the police cordoned off the whole of Covent Garden, only letting in those of us with special passes. The Opera House looked superb, with hundreds of garlands of flowers decorating tier after tier of boxes. People with water sprays went round them all every hour to keep them fresh. Twenty-two members of the royal family were to be present, and the royal box and two boxes on either side had been made into one and lined with rose-coloured silk.

Judi and I were having a snack in Bertorelli's after the dress rehearsal when a policeman loomed over us. 'Your optician is here, Miss Dench,' he said. The man had not been allowed into the theatre and Judi had to have her new contact lenses fitted in the back of his car.

For the first item, Frederick Ashton had choreographed a ballet about the two Princesses, Elizabeth and Margaret. I was told to get Sir Fred off when it was over or he might go on taking applause all night. When the curtains closed (guided by two splendid footmen in powdered wigs) he led the girls on, took a bow and then another. He then thrust them firmly out of sight and continued to take several more. As an old pro myself I could sympathise with him – it's wonderful to feel you have really pleased an audience – but I could hardly let such feelings conflict with my evening's duties as compère. I cannot recall quite how we cajoled or coerced Sir Fred off, but we did, and the show went on.

12

G & S in OZ

The little I had seen of Australia had made me eager to see more, and I was thrilled to be asked to do Gilbert and Sullivan's *HMS Pinafore* at the Victoria State Opera House in Melbourne and afterwards to tour the country with it. It was to be a co-production with an impresario called Jon Nicholls. Some people said that Jon was a 'likeable rogue', but then so many theatre managers are simply rogues, and luckily, for the time I knew him, the likeable side predominated.

Despite my minor success in *Jorrocks* nearly twenty years earlier, I am no musical comedy star. It was clear that I was going to have to do a great deal of preparatory work, quite apart from what I would have to do when I actually got to Australia. One of our Sheffield friends, Elsie Orme, had introduced me to the famous singer Ian Wallace, who in turn very kindly introduced me to his own singing teacher, Mary Nash. For some weeks I paid regular visits to Mary's studio in Swiss Cottage in North London. I was hardly in that league; every time I drove up some great diva would emerge and climb into her limousine. But Mary was very tolerant, and at my final lesson Ian actually took the trouble to come as well in order to give me a master class, a kindness which reaped handsome dividends when I reached Melbourne.

Once again Tricia jibbed at the long flight and wanted to give herself a little longer to work herself up to it, so I asked our daughter, Gemma, to come with me for the first few weeks. I was going to be away for the best part of a year, but my contract generously included several return trips for the family which now included our first grandson, Tom, and most of them were able to make the journey. There was excitement two days before we took off when a letter arrived from the Prime Minister's office asking me if I would care to be made a

Commander of the Order of the British Empire, a CBE, in the New Year's Honours List. I wasted no time in replying that if that was how Her Majesty felt, it would suit me very well. As far as I was aware all that remained of what had once been the British Empire was Hong Kong, and then only until 1997, and the Falkland Islands – but any more, I felt, might be a bit unmanageable. We had heard horror stories of people who had boasted of honours that had been offered them and because of that they had not subsequently materialised, so apart from Tricia's sister, who was visiting us at the time, we kept mum.

Melbourne's Victoria State Opera House is an outstanding piece of work. It consists of the main auditorium, seating well over two thousand people, a comfortable drama theatre, a studio theatre and two or three spacious rehearsal rooms. When it was built, George Fairfax was the principal administrator. Before he emigrated, many years ago, George was an actor in England; with his specialist and practical knowledge of working in theatres he was able to act as the architect's adviser, and as a result the backstage parts of the Arts Centre, the parts the general public do not normally see, are as handsome – I am tempted to write 'luxurious' – as the parts they do.

In almost all the theatres I know (the Theatre Royal, Bath is an honourable exception) the money has been spent, understandably, where the customers can see it: on the foyers, the bars and the auditorium. In Melbourne, too, no expense has been spared on these; but what is exciting for the performers is that the financial structure has allowed this generosity to be extended to the other side of the footlights. There is wall-to-wall carpeting throughout the backstage area, bathrooms en suite in all the principal dressing rooms and showers elsewhere, silk wallpaper and pleasant prints on the walls, and, of course, air conditioning. As a performer, you feel you are being really looked after and appreciated. I am sure that this factor produces in turn an atmosphere in which people are eager to give their best.

Perhaps most remarkable of all is the fact that six of the eleven storeys of the Arts Centre, including the entire Opera House, are underground. Built on swampy ground on the banks of the river Yarra it was, in addition to everything else, a remarkable feat of engineering to avoid this huge space collapsing in on itself. Rising above it is a kind of Eiffel Tower. Floodlit at night, the tower can be seen from far away; round it a cloud of gulls drifts like moths.

I was on my mettle. Like Wales, Australia is famous for its singers, and on the bill with me were some of the finest in the country: Geraldine Turner, John O'May, Marina Prior and a host of others whose names would undoubtedly be well known in the rest of the world but for the barriers erected by our respective unions. I cannot blame Australian Equity for this; their theatrical, television and film industries have been ripped off by ourselves and the Americans for decades. It used to be common practice for us to send out second-rate companies in second-rate productions to clean up and take handsome sums of money back home with them. Australian audiences and players are wiser now, but the sad corollary is that only those deemed 'international names' can work both here and there, and how do you become one without doing that?

Mary Nash and Ian Wallace between them had done a good job on me. The numbers in *Pinafore* are not as easy as they may sound, and the harmonies in the ensembles are decidedly intricate; I think my colleagues were quite impressed. Less so, however, when it came to the dancing; dance numbers are something you simply cannot learn beforehand, and when you are out in front, trying to give the – in my case quite illusory – appearance of leading the others they can be testing indeed. I toiled and sweated.

One New Year's Eve I went to Melbourne Airport to meet Tricia, who, with my agent Michael Anderson, had come for the first night. Details of the CBE had been on the early morning news. There was a frenzy of press attention which started at the airport and went on all day. Michael gave me a bottle of champagne presented by the captain and crew which was a charming gesture. Tricia told me that, when the captain was congratulating them for me, she had asked Michael whether he had known. Apparently he had, and had been keeping as quiet as the rest of us!

After that night's dress rehearsal there was a call from London. It was the BBC, who wanted an item for the one o'clock news – it was then about midday there: they asked for a combined interview with myself and Nigel Hawthorne, who had been similarly honoured. While we were waiting for the radio to be set up Nigel and I took the opportunity to have a chat. The BBC producer cut in to say that he had been listening to us and thought our conversation had been very amusing. Could we do it again, 'spontaneously'? I can hardly think it sounded very spontaneous.

The first night was sensationally successful and everyone was very thrilled. The chorus was one of the star turns. Cut off, as

Australian artists sometimes feel, away there at the bottom of the world, their confidence wavers. It is a great and undeserved disadvantage. Michael, Tricia and I agreed that my colleagues were amongst the best in the world.

My first entrance was by hot-air balloon, which descended from the fly gallery to the deck of HMS *Pinafore*. I was not allowed to use the lift in case it broke down, so, accompanied by the chief mechanist, I had to climb the five storeys. Every night I would peep through a crack in the proscenium arch down into the auditorium to see, with a quickening of the pulse, two thousand three hundred people enjoying themselves.

Publicity in Australia was an eye-opener. PRs there are full of enthusiasm and fun and obviously love their jobs. Jim Macpherson looked after me at the Opera House and he and I were always plotting amusing stunts. He managed to organise a big press conference in the main foyer to launch the production and persuaded Gough Whitlam, the ex-Prime Minister, to do the launching.

I suggested to Jim that it might help if I were to do a book signing of *The Hacker Diaries* at the ABC bookshop (the ABC is Australia's BBC). By a happy coincidence Jim's wife was the manager, so between rehearsals one lunchtime I was picked up by a white Rolls Royce and driven to the shop through the pedestrian streets in the centre of Melbourne, which the police had cordoned off. The queue was a quarter of a mile long and I forget how many hundreds of books I signed before I had to go back to rehearsal. Jim had carefully slipped into each book an advertisement for *HMS Pinafore*.

Michael Shmith, the then arts editor of the *Age*, some say the best daily in Australia, asked me to do a weekly diary of my stay in Melbourne, and I came to enjoy doing it immensely. The press office lent me a laptop; I would write a few words in the coffee break or in the interval and more over breakfast, then take it to the office and, using a modem, telephone it straight to the *Age*.

I learnt the power of the pen. Before leaving London I had asked the BBC if I could have a box of the *Yes, Minister* desk diaries, which were great fun as well as being useful and which were selling well. These, I said, would come in handy as little gifts when I met people such as State Governors and Premiers, as indeed they did. I was astonished one day to get a bill for them from BBC Enterprises, and I wrote about this startling request in the *Age*. Within hours I received a grovelling message of apology.

Although it was midsummer in Australia my skin condition caused a considerable loss of heat, so I bought a duvet (called a duna there) in the Christmas sales. Several people came up to me in the street, having read my problem in the *Age*, to say how glad they were. 'We wouldn't like you to be cold,' they said.

Tricia stayed for a month, which was packed with social activity. The dozens of friends we made kept us on our toes with an exhausting round of lunches, yacht parties, weekends in the country and of course the more formal occasions such as visits to Government House (built in Melbourne's case to resemble Queen Victoria's Osborne House on the Isle of Wight), visits to Parliament House and to and with various politicians – all, I suspect, eager for a photo-opportunity. We went to Cruden Farm where Lady, or Dame, as she prefers, Elisabeth Murdoch, mother of the media tycoon lives. It is very like a large farmhouse in Sussex, with a pool, of course, and a sunken rose garden. Dame Elisabeth herself is a delightful woman, tirelessly engaged in a round of good works, and I am not alone in this view; it would be difficult to find anyone in Australia, of whatever political colour, who has a bad word for her. I once said to a journalist friend that it was hard to believe that such an obviously wonderful woman could have bred the monster so many people believed him to be. My friend agreed. 'But she did,' he added.

The next step on our tour was Brisbane. The city is in the tropics, and as you step out of the plane you are met by a blast of hot, greenhouse, wet-earth smell, like the Palm House at Kew. Lovely. All the commissionaires at my hotel were in smart white coats and pith helmets. I felt as though I had stepped back into the days of Empire, and because I was constantly losing so much heat I felt really comfortable for the first time in years.

Brisbane's sun is hot and strong, and the occurrence of skin problems is amongst the highest in the world. I concluded that, if medical people there could not diagnose my own problem, probably no one could. Wickham Terrace is Brisbane's Harley Street and there I sought out Dr Beardmore, whom I was told was the best of the skin men. After careful consideration he said he would take a biopsy and sliced off a piece of my back. After telling me that I must get confirmation from St John's Skin Hospital in Soho, which he described as 'the centre of the skin world', he informed me that in his opinion I was suffering from a condition known as mycosis fungoides. Ordinarily that would have meant nothing to me, but I was immediately transported a couple of years back to Colin Blakely's dressing room at the New Theatre. He had told me then that he was suffering from something called mycosis fungoides. I knew by now that MF is a form of cancer which is not curable, and that Colin had since died. Someone remarked that I had a slightly preoccupied air during the performance that night.

Canberra, the capital, was naturally a whirl of social, mainly diplomatic, activity. I visited Bob Hawke in his residence and we seized a 'photo-opportunity', apparently struggling for the prime ministerial chair behind his desk. Later I strolled round the lake on a charity walk with a group headed by Hazel Hawke. I liked Mrs Hawke very much; she seemed to be amongst the pantheon of distinguished women which Australia has produced in the face of the general assumption that it is a rigorously sexist society. Sadly, the Hawkes' marriage has recently come to grief in the wake of sensational revelations concerning Bob's sex life – revelations made largely by himself.

But sexual scandals, or indeed financial ones, seldom seem to do much lasting harm in Australia; rather the reverse. My own theory is that a habit, perhaps bred in penal times, of being 'agin' the government', or indeed almost anything else, has persisted. I have to say I find it rather refreshing after the dim conformity that prevails in the UK. There is another side to the coin too; there also persists a wonderfully invigorating optimism. If something new is suggested in Britain, even something as trivial as, say, fixing a dripping tap, there will be much in-drawing of breath and shaking of heads. I am sure that if you were to suggest building a new harbour or moving a hill from one place to another in Australia the immediate response would be, 'Give it a go, mate!'

On the day I was invited to be welcomed to Adelaide in South Australia by the State Premier, the morning papers were triumphant. The naval dockyard there had secured an order for six nuclear submarines from the Swedish Navy and the economy of South Australia would be rescued from the doldrums. As I was waiting in an ante-room the Premier's secretary came in and told me that they had had a wonderful idea. At the culmination of our interview, the Premier would tell me that he would name one of the submarines *Pinafore*. Good for him, good for me, good for the show, wonderful for everyone.

I said I did not want to embarrass him in front of the cameras, but that as I was a Quaker and a pacifist I was afraid I could not join in the fun. Perhaps it might not be such a good idea after all. It must have been very disappointing for them, but they accepted the situation with a good grace and the subject was not mentioned again.

The media, however, had no doubt already been briefed, and afterwards they descended on me like vultures on to a tasty bit of carrion. I explained my position as best I could, saying that some people would no doubt profit, but that when the contract had been completed nothing would in fact have been produced except a small inflationary boom and the world would be a slightly more dangerous place than it was before. Perhaps, I said, the money might be better spent on the countless starving people in the world. If there were no starving people there might be no need for submarines.

I have made public my views on these and other matters once or twice and the inevitable result is a small crop of abusive letters, anonymous, of course. They nearly always have the desired effect in that I become, at any rate temporarily, upset and depressed. However, on this occasion I received one that nearly cured me. I think it is worth quoting unedited:

Dear Sir,

We do like your performance in; *Yes, Minister* and *Yes, Prime Minister*. We thought you are in real life clever, observant thinking person who would care what happens in your country and in the world.

But we were shocked when you told on our TV that you think all money which goes to defence must be given for those in third world starving people. Why are almost all actors hell bent to support world disaster which is; overpopulation. If those people would be made to have BIRTHCONTROL there would not be anyfamine. But what they do, indulge in satisfying their sex lust produce countless kids with half a dozen women and expect other people to tighten their belts and support them. No way. We work hard and we have birthcontrol and we plan what we do or else we would have nothing. For Your information we also live in very dry country, but our men do not have sex any which way with countless partners. What those third world bastards do, they are heading for WORLD DESTRUCTION and the actors are shamelessly supporting this. Who spreads the AIDS, Where did it started, IN AFRICA, where they have no more moral and it seems to us neither the actors have any moral or feeling for humanity, they are ready to support the destruction and spreading of AIDS.

So the nine of us decided we would not be interested to go and see you if you are in real life as stupid as you are in your plays. And we will spread the word around.

There followed an indecipherable signature. I pinned the letter to our company notice-board, adding a note on my own to say that the writers were clearly keen theatregoers and that if there were a drastic falling-off at the box office I could only apologise.

During the tour I had become increasingly short of breath and a little wheezy, so when we arrived in Sydney I went to see a heart man. Henri Paolini examined me and asked if I was suffering from swollen ankles. 'It's funny you should ask that,' I said. 'It's getting to be quite difficult to get my boots on for the show at night and too fat round the waist for my trousers.' Dr Paolini, ever buoyant and reassuring, arranged to meet us (Tricia was with me again) at a suburban hospital the following morning where I was wired up and tested. Bleeps bleeped and printouts whirred and he told me that I was suffering from congestive heart failure.

My heart had clearly not quite failed, yet, but it was an uneasy moment. Henri, who with his family became one of the countless good friends we made in Australia, gave me the necessary pills and I soldiered on. On our last night in Sydney they all came to see *HMS Pinafore* and admitted cheerfully that they were among those who called, three times, for my last number to be encored. I concluded that my condition was not as frightening as it might have been.

We came home at last, spending a couple of weeks in Capri *en route* to recover ourselves and become Europeans again. The last few weeks, wonderful though they had been as they had included a trip to some of Australia's most beautiful sights, were tinged with anxiety for us over my heart. I did not care for the idea of spending any time in a Neapolitan hospital where Thatcherite reforms seem to have rather gone to their heads; the staff of one of the biggest, it was discovered, had gone into business and was keeping chickens in the surgical ward. So I confess that, when we touched down at Heathrow, I did brush away a tear of relief.

It was not until the following April that I was able to see a skin consultant. As she was examining me I heard her say to her students, 'Oh, yes. A classic case, classic,' but a classic case of what she did not say. A few days later, when I saw my own doctor, Roy Davies, he confirmed that it was indeed mycosis fungoides. 'It won't kill you,' he said. 'Just a bloody nuisance.' I was directed to St John's Skin Hospital (now no more) in Lisle Street, Soho and began the never-ending ultra-violet treatment. It was once a week then and I straightaway learnt that there are a few compensations, whatever hits you. On treatment days I treated myself to lunch at my favourite fish restaurant, Manzi's, which still stands on the opposite corner. Another compensation, when at last you are obliged to become bald, is that you can put after-shave on top of your head. I may think of some others.

I was appearing at the time in *The Browning Version*, that most perfect of Rattigan's plays, which has all the glowing perfection of a Persian miniature. We had a splendid cast, headed by Dorothy Tutin, John Duttine and Jack Watling, and had rehearsed in the amazing suite of apartments which Sir Herbert Beerbohm-Tree had built himself under the dome on top of Her Majesty's Theatre in Lower Regent Street. (It must have been the place where, Willie Armstrong had told me, Tree had once taken his handsome male ASM home to supper. Lady Tree excused herself early, turning at the door to say, 'And remember, Herbert, it's still adultery.')

The theatre at which we were presenting the play was less happily chosen. The Royalty, in Portugal Street, stands on the site of the grand old Stoll Theatre. Time had no doubt passed it by and so it was pulled down to provide the inevitable office block. However, in those days there was a London-wide authority, which was able to insist that the developers make provision for a theatre to replace the Stoll. But one only has to step inside the Royalty to sense the resentment the developers must have felt at the time.

The theatre is underground, the dressing rooms are poky and airless, and if you want to visit a member of the cast after the show you have to climb forty steps to reach Portugal Street, turn right and right again, walk a couple of hundred yards up Kingsway and, if you can find the stage door, climb another forty steps down. Actors who play there do not get many visitors. The front-of-house is not easy to find either, and I have known hardened cab drivers, schooled in many years of 'The Knowledge', hesitate over Portugal Street. There is, too, an insurmountable pedestrian barrier which runs down the centre of Kingsway, designed to deter the most dedicated playgoer. Good as the show was, we only ran a few weeks.

However, Jon Nicholls, my Australian producer, came to see it and was convinced that it would please audiences back home, and we began talks. He had made the flattering suggestion that I might like to direct *The Browning Version* myself and, although it is notoriously difficult to both appear in a play and direct it, I jumped at the chance. The taste of directing I had had in Rome had given me the feeling that I might be able to pass on some of my experience to actors, especially young and comparatively inexperienced ones, and to give them the confidence to develop their own talents. I am very far from being the inventive, avant-garde director of the kind that is so eagerly sought after; but after all I had been doing my job in the most practical and direct way for many, many years, and something might rub off.

Australian Equity adamantly refused to take anyone besides myself, even Dorothy Tutin, so I had to start with a clean sheet. This was not altogether a drawback because, ever since I had first done the play, years before in one of the Bristol Old Vic seasons, I had thought that it was really just as much the wife's tragedy as the husband's, and I had never seen this idea fully realised. The play is about a public school master who marries a younger wife, he from mild and passing infatuation, she for social status; and because he is, I suspect, a closet gay the marriage falls apart in increasing bitterness.

We did it as it is usually done, with another of Rattigan's short plays, *Harlequinade*, a much lesser piece. Sir John Gielgud told me that they had been written for him, and someone else told me that when Rattigan finally ran him to earth Gielgud had said, 'I'm not going to do those little plays of yours, Terry. I don't think my public would accept me in something second-rate.' It was some moments before Rattigan got his breath back.

With two plays, it was a large cast. Jon Nicholls was in Melbourne and I was in London, so his ingenious solution was to short-list the candidates for the supporting parts, video the auditions and send them to me. Surprisingly it worked very well, and I am sure I would not have done better any other way.

I cast Lewis Fiander, mercurial and nervy; Michael Craig, splendid as the head; handsome Jeffrey Hardy and beautiful Glenda Linscott. But above all, I had the greatest good fortune in getting Julia Blake as my leading lady; she was not required to audition. Julia is not only one of Australia's finest actresses but also one of the most beautiful, and if that sounds as if I were seriously smitten, well, I suppose I was. The evidence for her talent and beauty can be checked objectively by anyone who sees the film *Travelling North*, with Leo McKern.

We started rehearsals at ten o'clock one morning in a chilly church hall in Melbourne. As I have mentioned earlier, I have never belonged to the puritan, self-denying school of acting. Not for me the early morning workouts, the trips to Golders Green to see how Jews behave, the evening rehearsals and the Sunday word runs. I climbed on to a bench and called the actors to order. I apologised for their having been called at ten. In future, I told them, it would never be before ten-thirty. There would be lengthy luncheon breaks, and I said, echoing William Armstrong's philosophy, we would stop early. In between there would be frequent breaks for tea, coffee and discussions. Anecdotes, even. I concluded by saying that it was my firmly held belief that there are some actors who would much rather rehearse than give a performance in front of an audience. My whole objective was to get on to the stage and do the show. The job was simply not worth doing, I finished, unless it was thoroughly enjoyable.

The effect was remarkable; we had four weeks in which to produce the two one-act plays. It was a brief period by any standards, but the cast seemed to revel in the liberal regime, as my experience with William Armstrong and later with Geoffrey Ost had suggested they would. They arrived punctually in the mornings, were eager to discuss all aspects of the plays, cut their lunch breaks to the minimum and left in the evenings still discussing. The net result was that we were ready a week before we need have been and coasted easily to the first night.

In Melbourne we appeared at the Comedy Theatre, on the opposite corner to Rockman's Regency Hotel, where we were living. Tricia was with me at the time and we, or rather I, had got tired of living out of suitcases and told the manager one day that I was thinking of moving to an apartment. We were suddenly surrounded by chefs, housekeepers, chambermaids, laundry personnel and doorkeepers. 'Why, oh why?' seemed to be the question on everyone's lips. I said that I wanted my own front door. But I could have one, they said. A kitchen? Yes, that too. A private cinema? Of course! I left Tricia to it and went to the matinée.

'The Flat', on top of the hotel and over the top in every other respect, was the suite occupied by Rex Harrison when he was playing at the Comedy. There was a huge sitting room, divided from the bedroom by a sliding bronze partition and a cinema-sized screen which descended at the touch of a button. At the touch of another button the curtains wafted to and fro, and there was indeed a fully equipped kitchen. A private sauna, bathroom and shower and an extra cloakroom at the other end of the flat completed the facilities, with the exception of a hall at either end. When we were shown this luxurious piece of accommodation my objections to the hotel died on my lips. A limousine had also been part of Harrison's deal and he used it to go to the theatre – about thirty yards as the crow flies. At the end of the show the car would collect him and return him to the hotel. Luckily I found I could walk it.

After our by now tearful farewells to our increasing numbers of Australian friends we arrived back home in a freezing December, but almost immediately I was off again on another *Yes, Minister* mission, this time at the invitation of Turkish state television to meet Turgut Ozal, the Prime Minister. The Turkish Airlines plane was almost empty and I spent much of my time with the very attractive air hostesses, whom I graciously permitted to take it in turns to have their photographs taken with me. The captain invited me on to the flight deck when we were now only a couple of hundred miles from Istanbul and asked me if I would like to stay there while we came in to land. Of course I said yes, and the co-pilot showed me how to strap myself into my seat. All round me and over my head were those complicated banks of instruments that one sees in films.

A yellow light winked on above me. I peered up. 'Flaps,' it said. 'System One, Fault.' I pondered, and glanced at the pilot. He and the co-pilot were talking urgently to ground control. I thought I would not interrupt them. No doubt they would get things sorted out in a moment and the light would wink out again.

Instead, a second light came on. 'Flaps. System Two, Fault.' I tightened my seat belt slightly and made myself invisible.

We came in very fast indeed, Istanbul Airport going past in a blur. Before we slid off the end of the runway the captain, with great skill and using maximum reverse thrust, managed to bring us to a halt and we breathed a collective sigh of relief.

As a member of Amnesty I knew that there were at least ten thousand political prisoners in Turkey and I wondered whether Amnesty would expect me to confront Mr Ozal. I hoped not; even in the face of some great wrong little is gained, I have always felt, by angry confrontation; besides which, the net result in this case would no doubt have been the arrest of my hosts and my instant deportation.

What I was not prepared for was the astonishing popularity of *Yes, Minister* and its sibling. I was severely mobbed. I was taken to the famous Topkapi Museum but saw very little of it for the crowds of reporters and photographers, to say nothing of the general public. Small boys selling tourist postcards outside the Blue Mosque knew me by name: I do not mean 'Jim Hacker', I mean 'Paul Eddington'. On one occasion I was forced to jump out of my limo, run through an arcade and hail a taxi on the other side, just as though I were in a movie.

Eventually I decided that the only thing to do would be to call a press conference and get all the interviews over at once, or I would not be able to move. The first question came out of the blue. I had expected to be asked my views on Topkapi Museum or the Blue Mosque. 'Mr Eddington, what is your attitude towards human rights?'

It had not occurred to me that in what I had been led to believe was a repressive regime a journalist would dare to ask such a question. Once again, I was uneasily aware that anything I said might well be regarded as the Voice of Britain.

'Well,' I replied carefully, 'we are ourselves sometimes criticised by our neighbours in the European Community on that score, particularly with regard to our handling of the Northern Ireland situation.' I was searching for my words, knowing that a good deal hung on my reply. I went on, 'I know that Turkey is itself very anxious to join the Community, and I am afraid that you might attract even harsher criticism than ourselves.' I felt I had done my duty, and we sat back and discussed the Blue Mosque.

I flew to the capital, Ankara – a much less impressive city than Istanbul – to meet Mr Ozal, who proved to be a jolly little man with a formidable wife who was said to be the real ruler of Turkey. I was neither interned nor expelled and returned home to face the agreeable task of doing *London Assurance* at the 1989 Chichester Festival.

Robin Phillips was the new director of productions at Chichester, having succeeded John Gale, and it was he who was going to direct. Although John had put the theatre comfortably in the black, it was felt by some that he might have done so at the expense of a certain artistic loss, playing safe to the comfortable bourgeois patrons. Robin, however, had a considerable artistic reputation, gained both in London and at the Bristol Old Vic, and latterly at the Festival Theatre at Stratford, Ontario where the Maggies Smith and Tyzack, amongst many others, had given some great performances under his direction. There was a keen air of anticipation amongst the cast, one member of which had come all the way from Sydney to work for him and another from New York. Angela Thorne had been persuaded to play Lady Gay Spanker. Both Robin and his designer, Daphne Dare, came to see me at various times to talk about their ideas for the production, which I liked very much. I, too, looked forward to starting rehearsals.

We were not due to do so until June, and as it was still only March I was able to respond to another *Yes, Minister* invitation to go to Jerusalem to open a new cultural centre for the British Council, and to visit Mr Shamir, the Prime Minister. The British Council put me up at the famous old American Colony Hotel which had, I believe, started life some hundreds of years previously as a very grand town house. I was in a large, airy room on the first floor from which one stepped on to a gallery overlooking the courtyard. The only drawback was that outside my window, almost within touching distance, was the minaret of the local mosque: at four o'clock every morning I rose from my bed like a rocket in response to the call to prayer.

Before my meeting with the Prime Minister I was entertained to lunch by the press. What, a journalist asked, was my solution to the Arab-Israeli conflict? I replied that I had only been in the country for a matter of hours and was hardly in a position to offer solutions. I said that I did think, however, that peace bought at the muzzle of a gun would only be a temporary one. 'I see,' he said ironically. 'You are going to shake hands with Mr Shamir this afternoon. Would you shake hands with Mr Arafat?' I remembered that during the time of the British mandate Mr Shamir had been a member of a terrorist organisation called Irgun Zvai Leumi, and I had a real struggle with myself not to say, 'Why discriminate between ex-terrorists?' Cravenly, I am afraid, I resorted to the Jim Hacker evasion: 'What a very interesting question, I'm so glad you asked me that . . .'

At the Cultural Centre I met Lord Goodman and the British Ambassador, who was escorting Anthony Eden's widow. I told them about my experiences with the refugee children at school, and to my pleasant surprise met several friends of friends of those children. I recalled a recent occasion when, still in my something-mysterious-in-government role, I was invited to lunch at Old Admiralty House in Whitehall to welcome the new Chinese Ambassador. What did surprise me was to meet there an old school friend, Hans Berg, another of the German Jewish refugees. Like me he had undergone a transformation and was now Sir John Burgh, head of the British Council.

Now, in Jerusalem, the Council officials asked me as a great favour if I would visit the Cultural Centre on the Palestinian side of the city; the people there were, they said, a little jealous and felt they always got left behind in the distribution of funds. Of course I agreed straightaway.

The other centre was in fact a good deal shabbier and had a somewhat improvised air. They were rehearsing a play, but although it was now nearly midday they had not started yet because, they told me, half the cast had been held up by Israeli police at the checkpoint outside the city. I was told by my host that, as the Palestinian Centre could not be diplomatically recognised as such, messages to the Israeli Centre, a few hundred yards down the street, had to be sent via London. Life was evidently full of pinpricks, if nothing worse. Arab number plates are a different colour from Israeli ones, so they can be instantly identified. On the motorway I saw an Arab car which had been stopped; its occupants were being made to clean the graffiti from a defaced Hebrew signpost.

I met Mr Shamir in the office one has seen so often on television and we sat on those brown leather sofas. Our conversation, as might have been expected, was so superficial as to evaporate as soon as the words were uttered. Only one question of his can I remember: 'What show should I see on my forthcoming visit to Britain?' Unless I am paid to appear, I am a reluctant theatregoer at the best of times – and in any case heads of state seem to be drawn to popular musicals, which are not usually my cup of tea. I had, however, been to the theatre recently and very much enjoyed it and so I suggested Alan Bennett's *Single Spies*. At least I got a laugh.

Soon after the Jerusalem trip Derek Fowlds and I, accompanied by Tricia, went to Barcelona to collect an award from Catalan Television. We seized the opportunity to visit Gaudi's extraordinary cathedral and spent a day by the sea at Sitges, where our driver showed us with pride the house in which George Sanders had committed suicide and the golf course on which Bing Crosby had dropped dead. If that was what Spain did to an actor I felt I was quite glad to be going back to rehearse in Sussex!

13

Home

❧◊❧

We started work on *London Assurance* on 5 June, sitting on
Chichester's wide open stage to read the play. At lunch I sat
between the director Robin Phillips and the actress Angela Thorne
and we chatted pleasantly about this and that. Afterwards we discussed
the play in a desultory sort of way, and Sarah Woodward read one
of the young girl's wonderfully over-the-top romantic speeches about
how she loved the early dawn. (To which Sir Harcourt Courtly's dry
rejoinder is: 'The effect of a rustic education!')

'What the hell are we going to do with these speeches?' demanded
Robin. I was startled, firstly because he had evidently wrestled with
the problem and failed to resolve it, and secondly because he had
admitted as much in front of his new company. I thought that maybe
he had meant it as a cue for discussion and said, 'Surely it's just a
send-up of the sort of romantic fiction that was popular amongst young
girls at the time?' With its rubicund squires, confidence tricksters,
absurd aristocrats and elopements many people with only a rustic
education assume *London Assurance* to be a Restoration play, but in fact
Boucicault wrote it nearly two hundred years after the Restoration, in
the first half of the nineteenth century.

'That's all very well,' responded Robin tartly, 'but she's got to speak
the fucking things.' I retired into my shell.

After we had played one or two of the sort of improvisation games
that brought Charles Marowitz vividly to mind, Robin said, 'Right,
we'll break there.'

I glanced at my watch. It was half-past three. 'What time would
you like us back?' I asked.

'No, break,' he said. 'Break for the day.'

We were all baffled. Never one to look a gift horse in the mouth,

I collected Frank Gatliff and we went upstairs for a reflective cup of coffee. Ten minutes later, John Gale's secretary came and asked me if I would come to John's office for a moment. 'He wants me to open his village fête,' I thought.

When I arrived, Robin was sitting on the sofa and John was standing behind his desk, white in the face.

'Robin's going,' said John.

'Going?' I said. 'You mean to London?'

'No. Going. Going for good.'

I sank into an armchair, unable for the moment to take in what was being said.

Robin started on a more or less coherent apologia. He said that things in this country were so different from what he remembered when he had left, actors were different, he did not think he could work in this kind of intellectual environment, he should never have left Canada, and a lot more.

I had read in novels how people who find themselves in an unbelievable situation pinch themselves to see if they are awake. I had always assumed that it was merely a figure of speech, but it is not. I actually pinched myself to find out if this were just a bad dream. Alas, I was awake. I was not dreaming.

John was within days of handing over the running of the Festival Theatre to Robin and taking his wife, Lisel, on a world cruise.

'How are we going to handle the press?' said John, anguished. 'They will obviously jump to the conclusion that we have had an almighty row.'

'How much more convenient it would have been,' I said to Robin 'if you had simply fallen under a bus.'

'Of course I'll stay if you'd like me to,' said Robin, 'until you've got someone to take over permanently.'

Suddenly my mind cleared. 'No,' I said firmly. 'If you're going to go, go now. At once.'

It was hardly my place to say that, but I had a vision of the endless mess and complications that would follow if Robin were allowed to stay and 'see the new man in'.

After he had left us, John told me that he had decided to ask Sam Mendes to take over the show. Sam, the possessor of a first-class degree from Cambridge and an impressive theatrical CV, was still only in his early twenties and had recently been made the artistic director of the new Minerva Theatre, a satellite of the main one. Over supper we told him he had to drop everything and direct *London Assurance*; with admirable nerve, he agreed. John Gale was forced to abandon the world cruise which he and Lisel had been looking forward to for years so that he could sort out the succession once again.

We decided that the first thing we must do, as a matter of courtesy, was to telephone Angela Thorne and break the news to her. Then, I suggested, we must ring the other senior members of the company, John Warner, Frank Gatliff, Bille Brown and Jonathan Elsom, and call them in half an hour before we told the rest of the cast. So at half-past nine the following morning John and I met, to be joined by Robin, furious at having his farewell speech pre-empted by our having called the seniors early. He said he had a good mind to go immediately, without making a speech at all.

'Do,' said John, lowering his voice in the intensity of his feelings. 'Fuck off.' And he did.

After the meeting the actors had the rest of the day off to give Sam the opportunity to collect himself and to have technical discussions with Daphne Dare, the designer. I ran into Peter McEnery, who was appearing in Sam's current production of *Summer Folk* at the Minerva and he told me that I need have no misgivings about him: his opinion was that Sam was an extremely fine director and absolutely to be trusted. That night I went to see *Summer Folk* myself and any reservations I may have had about a new young director were instantly dispelled. It was a magical production and I was entirely carried away by it.

The next day, before Sam appeared, I was able to say what I felt to the rest of the cast and I think we set off on the right foot. It had been an extremely delicate situation and in their changed circumstances we could hardly have prevented anyone from going home had they wished to do so. Luckily no one else defected.

After all the excitement, the success of our production came almost as an anti-climax. It was wonderfully stylish and funny and people who saw it then, its later London run at the Haymarket, tell me now how much they enjoyed it. I had played Sir Harcourt some years before at Bristol, in the wake of Donald Sinden's exquisite revival, and on that occasion I had copied as much of Donald's performance as I could remember. I did so again – I have no conscience when it comes to artistic theft. My only regret was that, as we were dressing the play in a slightly later period, with the men in trousers instead of breeches, I had to do without the old dandy's strap-on false calves.

The Theatre Royal, Haymarket, to which we then moved after a short national tour, is one of the loveliest in London, and has dressing rooms which are equally pleasant. I was asked whether I wanted the one down by the stage or the upper one which had a retiring room with a fireplace and chandeliers. With what seemed like a gallant gesture I allowed Angela Thorne to have the one near the stage. I then discovered that mine was fifty or sixty steps up. My dresser, Robin Cartlidge accepted the situation without demur and made me as comfortable as he could, which was very, and kept me entertained with all the scandalous gossip of our world, which was hair-raising and enthralling. I hardly noticed the stairs.

Our daughter Gemma, who is now a very successful teacher of drama, was at Chichester herself a little later, gaining experience as an assistant director. One night she did an entertainment of her own, a one-act play by Brian Friel followed by some accomplished singers. I was unable to get away that evening and therefore did not see it, but I am told by those who did that it was excellent and it attracted a good deal of favourable attention.

Things were nevertheless going rather too slowly for her and I asked her if there were a play that she particularly wanted to do. Immediately she said, 'Congreve's *The Double Dealer.*' She had seen it some time previously and had been thinking about it ever since. The play, first performed in 1693, just falls into the bracket of Late Restoration and, although it has plenty of the chracteristic affectations of the age, it is informed throughout by a cold cynicism and even a savagery which lies nearer to Jacobean tragedy.

'Is there a part in it for me?' I wanted to know. There was: a small one, that of Sir Paul Plyant, an uxorious husband who was led a considerable dance by Lady Plyant. 'Why don't we see if someone will put it on for us?' I said.

Dick Tuckey, an old friend and colleague of mine from Bristol days, was running the Wolsey Theatre at Ipswich (where, coincidentally, our third son was joint master carpenter) and I got in touch with him to see if he were interested. By a stroke of luck, *The Double Dealer* was on the shortlist to begin the following year's season. Dick took up the idea eagerly and in April Duncan Weldon, who had been co-producer of *London Assurance*, rang me to say that he was interested in coming into the deal. Gem and I tucked it away in our respective bosoms and began to think about casting.

In July of that year the British Council invited me to take part in the last, and perhaps most unusual, of my 'diplomatic' missions; would my wife and I, they asked, care to attend the Patras Arts Festival in western Greece? Every year it had a different national emphasis and this year it was to be British. We could think of no good reason why not, so we said yes.

When we arrived in Athens we were treated to the full diplomatic courtesies. I cannot remember a red carpet, but the Ambassador gave us a splendid reception to which he had invited the *bon ton* of Athens. Next day he asked me into his office to explain the delicate situation in which the British Council found itself. The conservative government of Greece hung by a thread and often had to depend for its survival on the vote of one of the right-wing members of the opposition. The governor of the province of Patras, or 'nomarch', was a government appointee, but the mayor was a member of the socialist party. The nomarch had accused the mayor of using the festival for his own political purposes, so the central government had withdrawn its financial support. Unfortunately the British Council had already commissioned the Early English Opera Society, the Scottish National Orchestra and two or three jazz groups to appear, and unless the Greek government chipped in with its share it was going to leave us about a million pounds in the red.

What I could do about this was not made clear. Tricia and I were to sit with the Ambassador and his wife at these events, flanked by the nomarch and his wife and the mayor and his wife, and my own theory is that people would recognise me and say, 'Oh look, isn't that the man in *Yes, Minister?*' and then think, 'Aren't we being rather silly?'

The concerts took place in the Roman amphitheatre and were followed by a magically atmospheric reception in the grounds of the Venetian palace above the town. We managed to get in a little sightseeing before this happened. The Ambassador took us to see a Crusader castle overlooking the sea, obligingly wine-dark, and we went, too, to see the original Olympia, the general shape and outline being quite well enough preserved to provoke a ghostly shudder. On the way I had mentioned to my host that the scenery was Arcadian. 'Yes,' he said, 'Arcadia is about a mile over there.'

Whether or not my presence at the festival helped I do not know, but about a week after our return the Greek government relented and the Treasury was able to relax.

Frank Gatliff, who had played the genial squire in *London Assurance*, had just died. I mention it only because his was the most moving funeral I have ever attended.

He was a modest man, and it was not until then that I discovered in what distinguished circles he had moved in his native Australia. I believe that his brother was a general. Amongst the small circle of friends that sunny morning at Mortlake crematorium were the Earl and Countess of Harewood. Frank was a non-believer and the ceremony was entirely secular. It started with a scratchy old recording of the music hall song 'The Good Ship *Yackihickidoola* – so I set my sail and sailed away', then half a dozen of us read brief eulogies. It finished, as the coffin glided away, with another antique recording, this time of, 'Pack up your troubles in your old kit bag'. There was not a dry eye in the chapel.

One of the inevitable consequences of becoming a 'celeb' is that one becomes the target of charity fund-raisers, usually nowadays professional ones. The public perception is that anyone who appears in public, particularly on television, is by definition a millionaire. Confusingly some celebrities are in fact millionaires, but the vast majority live fairly modest lives, most of them wondering where on earth the next job is coming from. I have no idea of the statistics, but I am willing to bet that most top lawyers and businessmen earn astronomically more than do most actors.

However, a celebrity name looks good on the letter heading and potential contributers can immediately identify them, so through the average celeb's letter-box comes an average of at least one appeal for money, personally addressed, per post. What does one do? Broadly there are three methods. Tear them all up, write back and say that you can only concentrate your efforts on one favourite charity (this must be true or *Private Eye* will find out), or contribute to every one. This last was Sybil Thorndike's method; she gave a modest sum to anyone and everyone who asked her, and she died a poor woman.

My own method has been a highly inefficient mixture of all three, leaving me either racked with guilt or worried about my old age. Some years ago I made up my mind that for most appeals it had got to be the waste paper basket. I thought I should suffer agonies, but instead a wonderful feeling of liberation stole over me every time I aimed one of those brown envelopes at the bin, and now I feel I can give mature consideration to just a few.

Something which distresses me a great deal is that current government policies make it very difficult for potential drama students to
get help from their local authorities, so many of the appeals which
I get are from students. I am afraid I have had to harden my heart
to the 'Oh, Mr Eddington, so you don't want to help the Ethiopian
Wheelchair Fund!' I made a, modest I admit, contribution to a school
building fund and the chief fund-raiser wrote back to say that they
were a little disappointed as they had been expecting something rather
more generous. I make an exception for local causes and, as a member
of Amnesty, I was very willing to appear one evening at the local
branch at Cavendish, a village near our East Anglian cottage. As I
was preparing to leave the house I had a call from my friend Dr Roy
Davies. Some time previously, an American-owned French mustard
manufacturer, Grey Poupon, had asked Ian Richardson and me to
advertise their product on television. This was big money, and one of
the attractions was that the advert was to be shown only in America.
For the manufacturers so much money hangs on these operations that
everyone vitally concerned has to be medically examined for insurance
purposes.

Roy said, 'Ah, so you're in the country, are you?'

'Well, yes,' I said.

'I see. That medical exam you had the other day . . . in the country,
you say?'

'Yes.'

'I'm not terribly happy about it . . . the country, I see.'

'Would you rather I were not?'

'Well, yes, I would really.'

'Can I drive?' I asked.

'Oh . . .,' he paused, worryingly. 'Oh, yes.'

Staying only to do my duty at the Amnesty meeting, I hastened
home.

Apparently my blood-sugar count was unacceptably high; I had, in
fact, developed diabetes. It was not the very serious kind that can be
contracted in youth – 'mature onset' is the tactful way they described
mine – but it was just one more thing; another handful of pills and
keep off the sugar.

The extra insurance money they must have had to pay did not
deter the mustard people, and next month Ian and I set off. The
intention was to shoot four or five small scenes in glorious English
countryside in high summer. As it was now November that idea

was hardly practicable and New Zealand was proposed. When we arrived in Auckland it was in fact a little overcast and the producers had a conference. Someone suggested that we move on to northern California, which had been the original idea. In my naïve British way I wondered whether that might not be rather expensive, but I was assured that that was not an insuperable problem; the budget for the shoot was nine million dollars.

Many actors will say that one of their principal objectives in earning a large sum of money is to enable them to do more interesting and satisfying work – work which will almost inevitably be underpaid. Often they are unable to realise their dreams because of tax or other problems, but in my case, especially as Duncan Weldon was prepared to fund a national tour, I was able to join Gemma to do *The Double Dealer*. To join us Duncan had managed to recruit a first-rate cast, headed by Nichola McAuliffe and a very old friend, Jerome Willis. We started work at Ipswich, where, he being the resident master carpenter the set was built by Dominic. Gemma and the cast made what I felt was a superb job of the production. I myself found it easy to be under the guidance of my daughter, as I had expected I would. We agree on most things, certainly all important things, and her method of work is imaginative and dynamic yet humorous and sympathetic in just the way that I have tried to work. To be acting in a play directed by my daughter in a setting built by my son was a unique and thrilling experience.

Ipswich playgoers, out for a decorous evening's entertainment, came in for something of a shock as Vanbrugh's cruelty and eroticism was revealed. The reviews were excellent and, but for the fact that Nichola McAuliffe was contracted to do another play after the tour, I believe it would have had a London run. Duncan was understandably reluctant to risk remounting the production for the West End but some months later, when it was really too late for me to go backwards, Michael Codron asked me if I would like to do it in the West End under his management. So I am driven to think that, although I was naturally extremely eager for Gemma to do well, my judgement had not been entirely knocked sideways by fatherly pride.

Part of the tour took us to Belfast and its magnificent Opera House. I and two or three other members of the cast stayed at the Europa Hotel, which is just across the road. One morning, at about half-past eight, I received a rather puzzling telephone call. A young man with a Belfast accent said that he had been to see the play the previous night and had very much enjoyed it. There was nothing very puzzling about that, perhaps, except that such a thing had never happened to me before, nor has it since. It is a statistical fact that most playgoers are female, middle-aged and middle-class, and this person was none of these things. I was very pleased and mentioned it to the Opera House manager that night. He was equally intrigued. I dismissed it from my mind.

I was naked from my bath at eight-thirty the following morning, one foot raised to put on a sock, when there was an almighty bang in the corridor outside. 'Now if this were Belfast,' I thought, 'I would have said that that was a bomb. Oh, my God, it is Belfast!'

The television, which was not switched on, suddenly sprang to life. Everyone was ordered to leave the hotel immediately. We were told not to stop to pick up anything, but just go.

A strong streak of vanity in my nature prevented me from immediately obeying orders; I hastily put on the minimum amount of clothing, gathered up the rest into a bundle and made my exit down the fire escape, joining my fellow guests across the road. None of them was naked, I noticed.

It appeared that the bomb had been placed just round the corner from my room in a service recess and that only the detonator had gone off. Had the bomb itself exploded, the whole wing would no doubt have been blown out. The Europa, after gaining a reputation as 'the most bombed hotel in Europe', had not had an incident for eight years and was just beginning to recover.

A journalist from the *Irish Times* told me that the bomb was intended for me; a fresh round of London–Dublin talks was due to start the next day and I would have been an amusing distraction. I found this very difficult to believe, but the theatre manager reminded me of the curious call I had received the previous morning. 'They were checking up to see which room you were in,' he said, 'and whether you were likely to be there at that time.'

I had been joking for years that the ultimate accolade for the success of *Yes, Prime Minister* would be for someone to attempt my assassination. Tricia had always thought it a joke in poor taste, and I saw her point. I also felt very uneasy about the fun I had made a decade earlier at the expense of Joan Plowright, when she had objected to our going with the National Theatre to Dublin.

Mary Wesley's novels, constantly in the bestseller lists, are obvious material for television and an adaptation of one of them, *The Camomile Lawn*, was proposed that summer. It would be directed by Peter Hall, mostly in Cornwall. Peter asked me to play one of the central characters and, after only the hastiest skim through, I agreed. When I read it again, a little more carefully, I realised that Uncle Richard was a one-legged child molester. I wondered what had made Peter think of me. But since I would be acting with my dear friend Felicity Kendal, however, together with Jennifer Ehle, (Rosemary Harris's daughter), Toby Stephens (Robert's son), Oliver Cotton, Nicholas le Prevost, Claire Bloom and Richard Johnson, I was not going to make any objections. Rebecca Hall, Peter's enchanting eight-year-old daughter, fully justified what I expect many people must have seen as nepotism by giving a most wonderful performance, with a maturity of understanding far in advance of her years.

We spent some days in the studios and then a few days in Oxford; this was followed by six weeks in Cornwall, mostly on top of a cliff in a howling gale with squalls of rain. By some miracle of lighting and directing Peter and his team made it all look like the serene and sunny place I had loved as a child, even to the extent of bathing-party scenes which half killed the actors.

On a day off I risked having a look at Polperro. It was a mistake. I had a cup of tea at the Piskie's Pantry and thought I would walk up the cliff path instead. On the approach to it I spotted someone who looked as if he might be a native, and had the cheek to enquire of him if this were so. He replied warily that he was and I asked him if any of the Puckey family still lived there. He said they did and that he was himself one of them. When I had recovered from my surprise I told him how, sixty years before, we used to pass away a dull day sometimes by going out in their boat with the Puckey brothers. 'Yes,' he said, 'that would be my father and my uncle.'

The day trippers melted away as I climbed higher and higher up the path, and soon I was alone. I had gone a mile or so when I thought I recognised what looked like the beginnings of the path over the cliffs to 'our' cove. It was, and I scrambled down. The 'smugglers' cave at the back of the cove had partially collapsed, but further down the beach something caught my eye. Someone standing with their back to the sea had evidently written something in huge letters. I went down to have a look. It was my daughter's name, GEMMA.

Back on the location, I sat in Peter's caravan in my muddy boots while Peter told me how he intended to form his own company. The opening production, at the Playhouse Theatre, would be Ranjit Bolt's new translation of Molière's *Tartuffe*. He asked me to play Orgon.

I hesitated. My health was worrying me a little; I had not been able to get to a hospital for the appropriate treatment as often as I should have, which was twice a week now. I was deceiving myself, though. The reason I was hesitating was because I was nervous; Ranjit Bolt's adaptation was, I knew, written in iambic pentameters – and, moreover, rhyming couplets. The thought of learning those reams of verse, remembering it night after night, and the ghastly penalties for a moment's inattention made my blood run cold. I played for time. Could I read it? But of course.

Reading it did nothing to calm my nerves. 'Why are you hesitating?' asked Peter at our next interview.

'I'm frightened,' I said.

'Well, you'll just have to get over that, won't you!' he replied bluntly.

Yes, I thought, I see what he means.

He leaned forward and said, 'I think your acting is Mozartian.'

Peter clearly knows how to handle people and his description of my acting, coming as it did from one of the world's great Mozartians, left me clay in his hands.

The BBC had previously arranged with him that I could be released from filming for a few days to join a small group of actors and broadcasters to go to St Paul-Minneapolis for a joint radio hook-up between their local station and London. An old friend, Hannah Gordon, came with me; we had a few days' fun and, of course, generous hospitality. From my hotel window I was excited to see, crossing the Mississippi below me, one of those freight trains which seem to go on mile after mile. Later there was some very foreign weather as a minor hurricane hit Minneapolis, with branches of trees torn off and billboards being hurled about the street. I looked forward to returning to the rigours of a Cornish summer.

To get me back in time I had to fly Concorde. Accounts of flying Concorde are not very original, but I was sufficiently unsophisticated to enjoy reading the statistics which appeared magically printed out on the bulkhead, the tremendous speed and the stratospheric height, and, even where there was almost no atmosphere, to feel the window warm to the touch from friction.

The deal for *Tartuffe* was tied up in July, and on 1 September we started to rehearse in the hall attached to Chelsea Old Church. Peter

Hall had managed to retain many of the cast of *Camomile Lawn*, and it was a happy reunion. Felicity, Jennifer Ehle, Toby Stephens, Nick le Prevost were now joined by the superb Dulcie Gray and by Jamie Glover, Julian's son. John Sessions was cast as the confidence trickster Tartuffe himself, all sanctimoniousness and hypocrisy. Retaining his native Scots accent, black-clad and with his tremendous natural energy, he cut a chilling and hilarious figure.

Ranjit Bolt's text was racy and witty and accelerated by the rhyming couplets. It was, as I had suspected, extremely difficult to learn, but once learnt, like Shakespeare, its own rhythm kept it skimming along.

The play posed one or two difficult technical problems. A central scene, which is both tragical and farcical is the famous one in which Tartuffe, who has been posing as my best friend, attempts to rape my beautiful young wife (Jennifer) on top of the table under which I am hiding. There is a cloth over the table concealing Orgon and the table is on runners because at various times it has to be moved. I have to say that at that point Peter seemed to slip into a neutral mode, with a tendency to look into the middle distance, hoping for inspiration. In the end I organised that part of the scene myself and at its climax, when the table is pushed roughly to the other side of the stage and the audience is certain that Orgon will be exposed, I managed to climb on to the stretchers under the table and be transported with it. Instead of Orgon on his hands and knees in the middle of the stage, there was an empty space. The effect was all one could wish. A friend told me that when Jennifer was pushed by Tartuffe on to the table, in momentary danger of exposing her generous bosom, there was a snapping of handbags all round her as dowagers dived for their distance glasses.

For me, one of the most moving experiences of that production was the confirmation of a conviction which had been growing on me for some years: a conviction that, in spite of all the obstacles set against them and all the hardships which actors in general, and student actors in particular, endure, a generation of players is coming along which is as talented and as exciting as any which have preceded them. People are always saying such things as 'We've seen the last of the great actors', which is not true. It is thrilling to know that the torch is in safe hands.

For various reasons *Tartuffe* had to end prematurely. It was with mixed feelings, therefore, when I came into the theatre for the last matinée, that I saw the queue for returned tickets stretching down the street.

That bitter winter I was telephoned by my friend Roy Davies who said that a patient of his was on remand in Brixton Prison. He was a Malaysian businessman called Lorrain Osman who was alleged to have committed a financial crime in Hong Kong for which that government wanted him extradited. He was fighting this demand, not only because he denied the allegation but because if he were to lose his case he might well before long find himself in Chinese Communist hands.

Roy said that Osman, a middle-aged man, had a serious heart problem and felt that the prison authorities were not taking it seriously enough. Every time he got his patient up to the Whittington Hospital (in handcuffs) there was some difficulty – the officers had to return or there were traffic problems or something else which prevented Roy giving his patient the attention he required. Roy was under the impression that I was acquainted with certain people in high places and wondered whether it was possible for me to have a word with someone. He was right and I did; within hours, I am happy to say, Mr Osman was receiving the proper care.

I was appalled to learn, during all this, that Roy's patient was the longest-serving remand prisoner in British history. He had been in prison for something like six years, untried – presumed innocent in fact – in one of our most notorious jails. I naturally joined the campaign to get him, at the very least, let out on bail. Eventually Mr Osman gave in to the extent of allowing himself to be extradited, pleaded guilty to a minor charge and was finally allowed home to London.

I knew, and know, nothing of the legal, financial or political background to the case, much as I suspect that the latter, *vis-à-vis* Hong Kong, the Malaysian Government and our own, looms large. What dismayed me were the repeated refusals in the High Court, one or two of which I attended, to give this ailing, elderly and above all innocent man bail. In some ways we have not yet emancipated ourselves from eighteenth-century thinking.

Tricia and I had met Jeffrey Archer in Melbourne and, although to say that our political views are not shared would be an understatement, a fact of which he is well aware, this has not prevented our remaining on friendly terms. His enormous energy and enthusiasm are very infectious, particularly his enthusiasm for the theatre, which he loves.

One of the consequences is that I have occasionally been a guest at his celebrated luncheon parties, which are given in his penthouse on the Thames overlooking Westminster.

Early in 1992 I was present at one of them and the talk, naturally, was all of the coming general election. Kenneth Baker was a fellow guest and several other Conservative leaders were present. The talk was tough and cynical. They thought that Kinnock ought to be emphasising the tax issue and they themselves were very keen on winning favour amongst voters by lowering taxes. Politically I am sure they were right, but I felt I could not remain silent. I piped up nervously to say that, as a non-aligned layman – an ordinary voter, in other words – I myself would be willing to pay higher taxes if it would do something to remove the people living in cardboard boxes barely a stone's throw from where we were sitting at that moment.

I waited for the ceiling to fall. There was a scrape of chairs as they all turned to look at me. 'Oh, how true!' they chorused. 'How right you are – wouldn't we all!'

Halfway between Jeffrey Archer's flat and my own is the home of one of the many good causes which I have been happy to be roped into. It is not concerned with compassion or humanity or anything heart-tugging in that way, but is about something at least as large: civilisation.

Some years ago, when the site was still a few weed-grown acres on the bank of the Thames opposite St Paul's, Sam Wanamaker – a Chicago-born Jew, it should be remembered – seduced me and many others into sharing his vision of building a replica of Shakespeare's Globe Theatre only a few hundred yards from the site of the original one. A few months before this was written Sam died, prematurely and tragically: tragically because this magnificent building is now nearing completion and he will not now see his dream realised.

How he managed to bully, cajole and charm money out of a multiplicity of individuals and organisations both in this country and all over the world is to me a mystery; he had a magic touch. This did not extend to the British government, however, which has not contributed one penny.

At the time of which I am writing Sam was still alive and his latest fund-raising effort was to gather some of us together – Rosemary Harris, Keith Baxter, Janet Suzman, Victoria Tennent, Peter McEnery, Amanda Waring and Mollie Sugden on the British side: quite a bill! – to go to Dallas and give some Shakespearian readings in the great concert hall there in the hope of raising some cash from the generous citizens. This they did, and we returned to London, dizzy with hospitality and a very handsome cheque for the Globe. The building is being funded in tranches, and I believe the Dallas money was earmarked for the rush thatching – the first thatching to be allowed in London since the Great Fire in 1666.

Soon after my return the BBC asked me to take part in a mini-series in the coming summer called *The Riff-Raff Element*. It was written by a much admired young writer and set in a large country mansion in the most glorious country. There would be a limousine on hand, Tricia and I would spend several weeks in a charming country hotel and arrangements could be made for regular hospital visits. The billing would be top (naturally!) and the money was excellent. The part itself was the sort of character I had played many times before and would require little effort on my part.

Perversely, I felt dissatisfied. I did the sort of calculation I had done many times before. The live stage was my real home and if I were to live even as long and as healthily as Sir John Gielgud (too late for that now!) I could only fit in three or four more plays at the most. Should I be wasting my time doing run-of-the-mill television? Clearly the answer was no.

I thought it was worth having a proper discussion on strategy, so I made a date with Michael Anderson, my agent, and went into his office to air my worries. Michael was entirely sympathetic, despite the fact that the route I was proposing, that of doing good work even, if necessary, for little money, would bring the agency a smaller commission. I was halfway through my grumble when the telephone rang. It was Ian MacDiarmid who, with Jonathan Kent, runs the small Almeida Theatre in Islington. Harold Pinter, he said, wanted to revive his play *No Man's Land*, which had originally been produced in 1974 with Gielgud and Richardson. Harold himself wanted to play the Richardson part; would I consider playing the Gielgud one? Michael told Ian MacDairmid that I was actually sitting there in the office and that he would talk to me and ring back.

It was clearly what Quakers call a 'leading' – although I thought more of a vigorous shove. It was precisely the sort of thing I had been explaining to Michael, and if I had tried to imagine an ideal scenario for myself I could not have done it as well. I asked Michael to ring back straightaway. The Almeida said it was the fastest acceptance they had ever had. A polite rejection was conveyed to the BBC.

I had been a client of Michael's for over thirty years and we had enjoyed a most happy professional and personal relationship. To my dismay, he had told me that he was about to retire and the deal he struck then was the last service he did for me. In many ways it brought me as much pleasure as any he had negotiated for me over the years.

Douglas Hodge and Gawn Grainger were cast to play the two 'heavies', and David Levaux was the director. Gawn I had known many years previously at the Bristol Old Vic, but I had never met Douglas or David. David and I got on well over dinner at the Garrick Club, which was just as well: David had made few concessions to the conservatism of the place. Ties are obligatory, and I think David's was painted on to his polo shirt. His hair was long and he wore trainers. (What was he training for? as Alan Bennett would say.) Altogether he cut a striking figure in the candlelight and amongst the Zoffanys.

We rehearsed in the awful Almeida rehearsal rooms in Upper Street, Islington. This is no reflection on the Almeida – all rehearsal rooms are awful: dirty, cold and bearing the scars of innumerable boys' club activities and mothers' meetings. The toilet facilities are up an uncarpeted stairway and through a junk room and one hardly likes to enquire how cups of tea and coffee arrive. It was a cold, wet autumn and the room was heated by gas fires, elevated on stalks like motorway lighting. Not that that mattered: for much of the time they were turned off since the roaring noise disturbed Harold's concentration. It disturbed mine for that matter, but it was a price I would have been willing to pay.

The importance of all that melted away, however, before the enthralling magic of the play, as the powers of light and darkness gradually exerted their influence on all of us. One of the critics wrote later that we were all 'in the presence of greatness' and it was a sensation of which we became keenly aware, obscure though the play appeared at first sight.

As for Harold, it was not much use appealing to him for the meaning of an enigmatic phrase or arcane reference; from the start he had ceased to be the author and became, as he said himself, just one of the actors. I was reminded of the story, possibly apocryphal, about T. S. Eliot, who, when asked by an actor whether a phrase of Eliot's meant such-and-such, was supposed to have replied, 'Well, yes, perhaps it does. I hadn't thought of that.'

Harold's formidable appearance – beetling brow, grim mouth and square jaw – is a very effective disguise unless you are perhaps a journalist or a critic. We four actors quickly became a closely knit team, sensitively responsive to each other's performances. Not for the first time, I was struck by the similarity of a group of actors to that of a group of musicians: the yielding, the assertiveness, the variations of pace and volume, the surprises and the carefully prepared revelations.

Once again I had let myself in for an heroic task. First, I was following Gielgud in what was acknowledged to be one of the most celebrated of his more recent parts and, I suppose (although of course it was far from being my intention), implicitly inviting comparison. The part itself is also a remarkably difficult one and requires a degree of absorption in the text called for by few others.

As every author and director should, and most do, Harold and David insisted on absolute accuracy, a fidelity to the text that extended not simply to the words and the inner rhythm but to the punctuation as well. Near the end of the play, as Spooner, I responded to a question with. 'No. You are in no man's land . . .,' and so on. One night I tried quickening the pace very slightly by saying, 'No, you are in no man's land . . .' Harold said to me as we came off the stage at the end, 'Oh, by the way, Paul, when you say "No. You are in no man's land . . ." that's a full stop, you know, not a comma.' And moreover he was right to insist. It did make a difference.

On the other hand, in the early stages, when we were inevitably making errors, Harold could not have been more forgiving. He would tell us that the sometimes egregious errors we made did not matter in the slightest, that it meant the same thing and that the audience would not know anyway. As an actor, he himself had never been nearer to London than Watford, he told us. The courage of someone of his stature, to perform in one of his finest plays in succession to Ralph Richardson, took the breath away.

At the end of the first half of *No Man's Land* one of the bullies, played by Gawn Grainger, turns the light out and leaves me sitting in the dark. When the play resumes it is dawn and he returns, bringing me some breakfast. The curtain remained up during the interval and it occurred to me that, if I were to slip off the stage after Gawn and to return when the play resumed twenty minutes later, it would make rather brutal demands on the audience's suspension of disbelief. I suggested to David and Harold that perhaps I might remain, silent and motionless, in my seat. They both gave a cry of relief; they had thought the same thing but had hardly dared suggest it. So that is what I did. In a curious way I think the fact that I sat there made an emphasis of its own. One thing it meant to me was that, after I had made my first entrance at the beginning of the play, there I was until the end of the evening.

People were kind enough to congratulate me on my stoicism, but in fact, having attended Quaker meetings from about the age of nine, I did not find sitting still as much of a burden as might be supposed. The greatest danger was of falling asleep, but the change of light, from the comparative brightness of the auditorium to the atmospheric gloom of Bob Crowley's wonderful grey velvet set, always, luckily, woke me.

Another of my tasks was the speaking of a superb speech – superb but several pages of text long – towards the end of the play. I could no doubt be heard reciting it at the hospital as I stood every two or three days in my ultra-violet cabinet.

Only two dressing rooms are available at the Almeida and we unanimously decided to use one of them in which to receive visitors while all four of us would share the remaining one. It is a measure of the comradely unity of our company that this worked extremely well: there was much friendly badinage and a good deal of chat about Harold's other passion, cricket.

When we opened it was to the kind of reception that only comes on a handful of occasions in a lifetime. Ian McKellen rang me with such fulsome praise that I could not really tell anyone about it. Some friends of Harold told him that it was one of the greatest theatrical experiences they had had in years. The newspapers made sure that the whole run was immediately sold out. I think that if my career were to be judged on a single performance, I would be happy for it to be that of Spooner in Harold's majestic play.

In response, possibly, to Gerald Scarfe's unkindly accurate cartoon of me in the *Radio Times* a woman once wrote to it, at the height of *Yes, Minister*'s popularity, to express her dissatisfaction because, she said, 'Every time I turn on the set, all I see is Paul Eddington's big nose!'

Every time I had looked in the mirror, just at that time, I could see what she meant. My nose was getting bigger daily, and my upper lip fatter. I was seized at the hospital one day and told that it was another manifestation of the skin complaint; I must go straight to radiotherapy. I knew that the consequences would not be pleasant, but a good deal less pleasant if I were to neglect matters; so down I went.

Sure enough, about ten days later I looked very much as though I had gone the distance with the champion. From close to, but only from close to luckily, my nose and mouth were in a most unsightly mess. If you change a piece of your costume during the run of a play, it is polite to warn your colleagues lest, by suddenly noticing it, their train of thought is broken. I had to go to mine and display myself for the same reason. They were most supportive, but it was not an enjoyable experience for them or for me.

Bill Kenwright is known to the public as a producer of the big blockbuster, a football fanatic and an effervescent showman, but there is another side to him too. It was he who took on the very risky business of transferring *No Man's Land* to the Comedy Theatre for a short season. It was risky because the logistics of theatre production mean that a manager must make a lot of money in the West End simply in order to break even and – I do not mean to sound invertedly snobbish – a play as fine as *No Man's Land* is not going to make anyone's fortune.

Shortly after we had opened, my new agent, Paul Lyon-Maris, telephoned me to say that I had been voted the Critics' Circle Best Actor of 1992. This is a particularly pleasing award to have because it is given by professional theatre people. I know that great nervousness is sometimes displayed by actors *vis-à-vis* critics but they are the arbiters of our work, the ones who, at their best, can explain and inform ourselves to ourselves and to our public. Hilarious mistakes can be made and great offence can be taken, but I have noticed in the past that on the rare occasions when there has been a newspaper strike and a first night is imminent, the actors get very anxious at the prospect of lack of publicity.

The critics' presentation was made in the Theatre Museum, mine by John Peter, the theatre critic of the *Sunday Times*. John made such a hugely flattering speech about my work that, had he not spoken it extempore, I might have been tempted to reproduce it. I am afraid I cannot resist saying that he told my friend Simon Cadell that my performance in *No Man's Land* was the best performance he had ever seen.

Backstage I had streams of interesting visitors: on one Saturday a double bonus with Jean Simmons after the matinée, 'like Niobe, all tears', and Arthur Miller in the evening. But one evening was not so happy. I woke that morning feeling not very well – nothing serious, but I just did not want to eat and Tricia was away somewhere and so was not able to make me. Because I knew I ought to eat something, I had a boiled egg before going to the theatre. Nearing the end of the first half I suddenly felt extremely dizzy and fainted. I came to very quickly, apologised to the audience and carried on.

The press knew that something was wrong with me but had never had the opportunity to confirm it. They went mad with speculation but after a few days, happily, the excitement died down. My doctor told me that it was a typical diabetic episode; a sweet drink was probably all I had needed.

I do not know the final figures, but I do not think we lost Bill Kenwright a great deal. I very much hope not, as he is a courageous man.

An unexpected bonus of Harold's having a happy time as part of a company again was that, after many years lying fallow as a playwright, he began to write again, and on a short holiday with his wife Antonia Fraser before we did the transfer he wrote *Moonlight*. He gave me a copy to read, saying that I was the first person to read it after Antonia.

I had a few moments of unease, as the only part I could possibly play was not right for me at all, but to my relief, and to his I expect, he disabused me over a glass of champagne.

Antonia was delighted that he was writing again and grateful to Doug and Gawn and myself for 'inspiring' him, as she supposed. She sent us her new book after we had finished the run and I thanked her for it. A few days later Harold rang and asked me rather sharply if I had read it.

'Well, no, not yet,' I said.

'Have you read the dedication?' he persisted.

It read, 'For Paul, Harold, Gawn and Doug. *No Man's Land* 1992–3.'

On 1 July the press decided it was time I was forced out into the open on the subject of my health. The *Sun*, of course, set the pace. A voice at the other end of my flat's entryphone said that there would be a feature in the next day's paper about my suffering from cancer, and would I like to put 'my side'? I made no reply, but from then on the pressure was relentless. Reporters and photographers seemed to be everywhere. The run of the play was by then over so they were not able to lie in wait for me at the theatre, but they did so everywhere else. I was horrified by the feeling of persecution and became absurdly nervous; we even put up a screen in the hall to prevent reporters peering through the letter-box. If I had to go out for some purpose I would spend minutes peeping out of the window in an effort to see whether the coast was clear before dashing to my car.

One day I was returning on foot and Tricia came out to meet me. We entered our courtyard arm-in-arm to be confronted by a photographer who, gratifyingly, fell backwards as he snapped. The result was a very odd picture in the *Express* illustrating an article about my supposed agonies, the caption to which read, 'No longer able to stand unsupported'. The *Mirror* reported that treatment had turned my face black and that my hands were 'covered in blisters'.

That weekend we were planning to flee to the country but our neighbours there rang to advise us not to; two men had been sitting all day in the pub car park, apparently watching our cottage. We took refuge with some friends in Essex, calling *en route* on Nigel Hawthorne and his companion Trevor Bentham who, ironically, were to receive much worse treatment a year or two later when Nigel was nominated for an Oscar and their relationship was 'outed'.

Richard Briers and I had first met as fellow members of our union's Council in 1972 and had been professional colleagues ever since. Not long after our first meeting we had begun to appear together in *The Good Life*. Each of us admired the other's work and we got on well together on a personal level. Without living in each other's pockets, we make a good team.

For some years, on and off and not very diligently, we had been searching for a play to do together. The repertoire did not seem very wide. There was Charles Dyer's *Staircase* about two aging gay hairdressers and Ronald Harwood's *The Dresser*, and after that we rather dried up. *The Dresser* was a most attractive idea but the trouble was that each of us really wanted to play the part of 'The Dresser' of the title. One solution, of course, would have been to play each of the major roles turn and turn about, but neither of us felt we had the stamina now to do that eight times a week. So there the matter had rested.

I cannot think why we had not thought of it before, but one day I suddenly remembered David Storey's play *Home*, which I had seen played by Gielgud and Richardson in 1970 in a production by Lindsay Anderson. It is a poignant story, if 'story' is not too crude a description, of two elderly men who sit in the sun chatting and are later joined by two somewhat younger women. That is all there is to it really, except that during the course of the play a world of anguish, pain and coarse humour is opened up in such a way as to touch the compassion of all but the numbest spectator.

After the enlightening experience of *No Man's Land*, and not knowing Anderson, I very much wanted David Levaux to direct it. David said he would like to do so and Duncan Weldon was keen to produce it, so I telephoned Dickie Briers and put the proposition to him.

'No, no old boy, couldn't possibly. Oh, no. Something else to do. Sorry, old boy. Love to do it. Well, there we are. Too bad!'

This was an entirely predictable response and I hung on for a week or two. The telephone rang.

'Hello, old chap. You mentioned *Home*. What sort of dates are we talking about?'

I knew it would be all right; he came over and we read the play together. Much of it is very funny and we found it quite difficult to get through it for laughing, something one is very rarely tempted to do when actually on the stage and hardly ever in the studio. The pressures are so enormous and the penalties for getting things wrong so draconian that laughter melts away.

Sometimes, of course, as with laughter in church, the pressure works the other way. When we were at Sheffield Rep together, Peter Sallis was delivering a very solemn speech in the midst of a silent crowd, just after the murder of Macbeth. 'In the great hand of God I stand,' he declaimed, pausing to give full effect to his next sentence. At that moment one of the courtiers farted. There was not a dry eye in the castle.

I told Richard that, following the recent fun with the press about me and cancer, I had had numerous letters of sympathy. One of them was from a faith healer in the Home Counties who absolutely guaranteed to cure all my ills if I would only place myself unreservedly in her hands. She enclosed an impressive file of testimonials from famous people and assured me that she had never offered her services to anyone before, having always depended entirely on personal recommendation.

I asked my specialist if he would be offended were I to consult her. 'Give it a try,' he said, enigmatically.

So I began a series of visits to Ramona, as I shall call her, who lived in a pleasant bungalow on the outskirts of a country town. She was clearly not in it for the money, although consulting her was not cheap. A constant stream of devoted acolytes was welcomed and sent away again to perform various errands, or entertained to excellent home-cooked oriental meals and, no matter how early or late in the day, extremely large tots of vodka, with or without tonic. She was on intimate terms with God, with whom she chatted at length, addressing Him as 'Pappa' and from whom came the therapeutic recommendations – or so one gathered from the side of the conversation one could hear.

Her method of treatment was interesting. She would snuggle up to one on the sofa and place a firm hand on the seat of the trouble: in my case, luckily, the back of the neck. She would then groan and appear to suffer mild paroxysms while from some source came a violent farting noise. After several such treatments she declared me cured. I was completely clear of the arthritis, the colitis, the heart problems and, above all, the skin cancer. But Pappa had not been able to do everything, and Ramona advised me to return in a few weeks to have the diabetes sorted out.

Alas, my faith was not strong enough. In a very few weeks there were sinister lumps in several places, my hair was falling out and my face looked 'like an old peeled wall', as Congreve put it. I went back to the radiotherapy room. Well, I had tried.

In fact I was in quite a lot of trouble. Parts that I had once thought of as private were bombarded from what seemed like all directions. To cap everything I was also beginning to endure the rigours of colitis once more, having thought that it had gone into permanent remission.

We spent Christmas in Amsterdam with two dear friends, John Sharman and David Wood, the painter: Tricia with asthma, John with chest trouble himself, me staggering along in grave discomfort and David with leukaemia and in a wheelchair. Christmas in Amsterdam is not to be recommended unless you live there; it is shut. The museums are closed and there are no exhibitions, except of an improper kind. We must have presented a curious group as, halt and lame, we tottered resentfully from one high-priced fixed menu to the next, wishing only to get back to our comfortable hotel and the Scrabble board.

The press were still hungrily sniffing around so, weary with all the subterfuge and well aware that it would all start up again in the run-up to *Home*, I thought I had better give in and 'come out'. On the advice of my agent I hired a publicity firm and had some photos taken, and did a couple of interviews over which we had some control for popular papers. Now that my problems were in the public domain the press magically lost interest and I was able to get on with my job.

Duncan Weldon had recruited Brenda Bruce and Rowena Cooper to play the two women in *Home* and there was one much younger member of the cast, Jason Pitt. I was acquainted with Rowena, having acted with her husband, Terrence Hardiman, some years previously, but I did not know the others personally. Both women are highly distinguished actresses and each has spent lengthy periods at the two great national repertory theatres, the Royal National and the RSC.

An entirely unexpected bonus which made sure that everything would run smoothly and that we could relax in the knowledge that we were in safe hands, technically speaking, was to have with us the prince of company managers, David Bownes. The company manager's is a job entirely unknown to the public. He it is who, after the producer and the director, is in charge of everything. When the show is launched and on the road he is, irrespective of actual years, very much the father of the company and in David's case, its servant. Any laziness or incompetence on the part of the manager is instantly reflected in the company's morale, and the reverse is also true. David was eager to help in any way he could: provide timetables, arrange hotels (including discounts!), buy tickets, supervise 'get-ins' and 'get-outs' – the sometimes all-night dismantling of the sets and their transport to the next date and then their rebuilding – the payment of wages in cash to those members of the company not paid in more discreet ways, even the organising of company parties and outings. He was also very ready to defend members of the cast such as myself who were having trouble with the press, and even ready with a bankroll for anyone short of cash. I wish we had met him years ago.

Halfway through rehearsals I begged a Saturday off to give my daughter away to another actor, Andy Greenhalge. As I am a CBE and Andy is a graduate of Clare College, Cambridge, they could have been married in either the crypt of St Paul's or Clare Chapel but, resolute in their agnosticism, they insisted on a register office. I was not, however, let off a sumptuous reception at the Garrick Club where the bride looked sensational, the groom made a moving speech and a hundred or so guests had a very merry time.

That event proved to be the last occasion on which I made a public appearance with hair. Treatment to my scalp had meant that one or two bald patches had appeared there, about the size of a large coin. In the vain hope that I might get away with it I had consulted one of the profession's top wigmakers who had provided me with fillers, as it were. Exquisitely made and perfectly blended, they were absolutely undetectable, even to myself.

I did not of course get away with it, and soon the one or two bald patches became three or four. Like Canute, I saw that I would not be able to stem the tide and decided that, for the play at any rate, I would have to have a complete wig.

I have always thought that there was something rather absurd about wearing a wig as an ordinary private person. I have worn dozens of wigs in the course of a long career but they had usually been for period pieces or under the very bright lighting we used to have in the theatre when everything was frankly artificial. When I tried on the one that had been made for me for *Home*, with the same art and expertise as the 'pieces' I had had made and in fact by the same maker, I could not reconcile myself to it. We were, in the play, straining for an appearance of complete naturalism and every time I glanced in the mirror my coiffure said, loudly and distinctly, 'Wig.' I discarded it and shaved off what remained of my hair.

I did not, however, possess the courage to display my affliction in public and decided to wear throughout the play the straw hat I wore for my first entrance. David Levaux and the author, David Storey, immensely kind and affectionate, were very disappointed and, although they repeated several times that it was entirely up to me, they were clearly upset.

I had met David Storey many years previously when Tricia and I had gone backstage to see one of the actors in *The Contractor*, one of David's earlier plays. David told me that it was during rehearsals of that play that he had had the idea for *Home*. He had arrived early and sat waiting in the stalls for the others. On the stage were a table and two chairs; idly, David visualised two men sitting there and began constructing the sort of conversation they might be having. Only gradually did it emerge to him, as it only gradually emerged to its future audiences, that the pleasant, sunlit terrace upon which they were sitting was part of a secure home for the criminally insane. The two men struggle throughout the play and with increasing difficulty to avoid admitting their situation to themselves. It could, if one so wished, be an allegory of the human condition.

On the eve of our opening I discovered a small, bullet-shaped lump under my jaw which I had not previously noticed. My consultant advised a 'needle biopsy', which is exactly that, and arrangements were made for me to have another course of radiotherapy.

We opened the play at the charming Yvonne Arnaud Theatre in Guildford. It is built on a small bend in the river and is surrounded by trees, so through the open window of one's room comes the sound of birdsong and running water. Its charm, and possibly the prospect of a jolly night out with their old sit-com friends Richard Briers and Paul Eddington, brought customers in their multitudes. If so, they were rapidly disillusioned, and some were not too pleased – although, happily, the numbers did not diminish throughout a considerable tour.

By good fortune the second week of the tour was in the handsome Frank Matcham-designed theatre in Richmond, within reach of my home hospital. Every day while we were at Richmond I had radiotherapy, which meant that it was quite an endurance test. Then we went to the ever-delightful Theatre Royal in Bath. On the first afternoon we gave a press conference to a very small group of local journalists, at which the fact that I was bald did not, apparently, go unnoticed. The next day I was opening a Quaker housing project in a nearby village. My hosts were gratified by the remarkable media coverage; it was not, alas, the housing project which was exciting them, but my darkened skin and my baldness. I was clearly in the freak-show business. A friend in Australia sent me a cutting from a Sydney tabloid which described the scene and reported me as having waved my hat to the crowd (elderly Quakers!) and cried, 'It's nice to see some white people here!'

I received a rather disagreeable letter from a woman member of the audience who complained, amongst other things, that my hat obscured my face. I was able to reply that the results of treatment for cancer had made me shy about my appearance, and I confess that I do hope I gave her an uncomfortable moment. Actors are just like other people; to paraphrase Shylock, when you prick them, do they not bleed? I added in my letter that perhaps she had given me the courage to appear as myself, and indeed she had. Much to the relief of the Davids, Storey and Levaux, I removed my hat. The skies did not fall.

Our London run took place at Wyndham's. Faithful to the deal we had made, Richard allowed me first billing and I allowed him the number one dressing room. This had been home to innumerable star actors and actresses, one of the ones Richard most admired being Sir Gerald du Maurier. Richard showed me a key which had been given him by the veteran theatrical producer Harold French who had said that it was the key to du Maurier's dressing room. The old lock was still there but its function had been superseded by a modern, Yale type one. 'Look at this,' Dickie said. He put the key into the old lock, which turned perfectly. On the outside of the door, he also showed me where, under the many subsequent layers of paint, some raised lettering was faintly visible: 'Gerald du Maurier'. Richard decided to hire a signwriter to repaint the name, but William Ingrey, Wyndham's manager, generously did it for him, and it is there now.

Two months after we closed I celebrated fifty years as an actor and soon after that, having had to resign from my favourite committee, Equity's Committee for Artists' Freedom, Equity made me the handsomest gesture within their power by making me an honorary life member. It is no small gesture, as there are fewer than twenty amongst a membership of forty thousand. It would be difficult to feel more pleased than I was.

I was also delighted to be honoured by Sheffield University. They followed up the MA they had awarded me in 1988 with the Maisie Glass Associate Professorship in Theatre. Maisie and her husband I had known well as generous patrons of the theatre and on her death they had endowed this chair of which I was happy to be the first occupant.

A film-maker whom I have always admired is Verity Lambert. She asked me to appear in a P.G. Wodehouse film she was making in the summer – in deepest Shropshire, of course. Having discovered Wodehouse for myself in the school library nearly sixty years previously, and having been a devoted fan of his ever since, I was delighted. I was also somewhat apprehensive, because the last time I had met Verity had been several years previously and I wondered whether she knew how much my appearance had changed. I asked if we could meet, and she came and had tea with us.

She did not seem unduly put out but I was still a little unhappy; I would not have cared to walk on the set and for everyone to take a sharply indrawn breath and the make-up department to resign. I asked her if, just to make absolutely sure, she could arrange a make-up test, which she did a few days later. Sadly for me, the verdict was no. Evidently very upset to have to tell me, Verity said that the cameras would not be able to come in close, and as I clearly could not play a leading role in long shot I bade farewell as I thought to my television career.

No regrets. I have had a wonderful time and, unlike some people who have had a wonderful time, I have also been richly rewarded for it. The theatre, with all its magic and its artifice, is still available to me and it is, after all, my true home. I am even now making plans.

A journalist once asked me what I would like my epitaph to be. I took the question seriously and thought long and hard. It is an interesting exercise. How difficult not to sound mock-modest or boastful. I cannot remember what I said at the time, but long after she had closed her notebook and gone I thought of one. It treads, I think, a delicate path between the options.

'He did very little harm.'

Index

Abel, Paul 162
Absurd Person Singular 127, 131–5
Ackland, Joss 113
Acton, Mr. (Lewis's window dresser) 34–5
Actor's Equity *see* Equity
Adelaide, Australia 200–1
Adelphi Theatre, London 113
advertising
    Australian Federation of Advertisers 171–3
    television 128, 151–2, 180, 188–9, 217–18
    tobacco industry sponsorship 183
    voice-overs 151–2
Age newspaper 198
Albee, Edward 155, 158
Albery, Donald 105, 129, 162, 163–4
Albery Theatre, London 113, 191
Aldridge, Michael 78
Aldwych Theatre, London 125, 126, 187
Algarve 180
Allen, Sheila 78
'Allo 'Allo 129
Almeida Theatre, Islington 225–6
Ambrose (ENSA manager) 39
Amnesty International 206, 217
Amsterdam, The Netherlands 233
Anderson, Lindsay 231
Anderson, Michael 151, 197, 225–6
Ankara, Turkey 207
Ansell, Nora 33
Apple Cart, The 100–1
Archer, Jeffrey 223–4
Armstrong, William 53, 55, 56, 57, 203, 205
Artaud 161
Arts Theatre, London 86
ASH anti-smoking organisation 183
Ashcroft, Peggy 125
Ashton, Sir Frederick 193
Athens, Greece 215
Atkinson, Ella 79
Auckland, New Zealand 218
Auntie's Bloomers 168
Australia 171–4, 195–206
Australian Federation of Advertisers 171–3
award ceremonies 149–50
Ayckbourn, Alan 127, 139

Aylmer, Sir Felix 86

Bailey, Robin 71–2, 109
Baker, Kenneth 224
Baker, Stanley 93
Barcelona, Spain 209
Barkworth, Peter 68, 136, 137, 151
Barnes, Sir Kenneth 76
Baron, David *see* Pinter, Harold
Barron, Keith 114
Barton, John 126
Bates, Peggy Thorpe 59
Bath
    Assembly 71
    Theatre Royal 158, 196, 236
Baxter, Keith 224
Beardmore, Dr 199
Beckett, Henry 79
Beddgellert, North Wales 123
Beerbohm-Tree, Sir Herbert 55, 203
Belfast 180, 218–19
    Opera House 218
Benjamin, Christopher 103–4
Bennett, Alan 117, 119–21, 142, 183, 189, 226
    Forty Years On 117–22, 180, 181, 182, 184
    Habeas Corpus 120–1
    Single Spies 209
Bentham, Trevor 231
Berg, Hans *see* Sir John Burgh
billing 121–2
Billingham, Forum Theatre 146
Billington, Michael 145
Birmingham
    Crescent Theatre 36–8
    Edgbaston 33
    Holy Child convent, Moseley 8
    Lewis's Ltd 34–6, 38
    conscientious objection tribunal 49–50
    Rep 51–60
Birthday Party, The 95
Bit of Fry and Laurie, A 130
Blackman, Honor 86
Blake, Julia 204
Blakely, Colin 178, 199–200
Blakemore, Michael 164

Blick, Newton 78
Bloom, Claire 220
Blue Comedy 162
Boalth, Amy 74–5
Boddington, Diana 156, 159, 160
Body in Question, The 145
Bolt, Ranjit 221, 222
Bond, Gary 123
Boucicault, Dion 211
Bowen, Elizabeth 105
Bownes, David 234
Brand 102–3
Brecht, Bertolt 161
Brien, Alan 104–5
Briers, Richard 121, 127, 128–9, 135, 146, 148, 152, 188, 231, 232, 236, 237
Brighton 119, 147
Brisbane, Australia 199–200
Bristol
  BBC 83–4, 94–5
  Little Theatre 144
  Old Vic 77, 99–108, 144, 177, 183, 207, 226
  Rep 77–9, 83, 113
  Theatre Royal 78
British Council 190, 208, 209, 214–15
Brixton prison 223
Broadway, United States 107, 108–11
Brook, Peter 54, 58, 161
Brown, Bille 213
Browne, Coral 85
Browne, E. Martin 57
Browne, Miss (RADA bursar) 73
Browning Version, The 71, 203–4
Bruce, Brenda 234
Bruce, Nicky 56
Burgess, Miss 28, 29
Burgh, Sir John 208
Burke, Marie 177
Burke, Patricia 177
Burrell, Sheila 104
Butchner, Pam 160
Byrne, Gay 180

Cadell, Simon 229
California 218
Camomile Lawn, The 220
Campbell, Mrs Patrick 55, 57
Canberra, Australia 173, 200
cancer 228–37
Cannes, France 180
Canning family, Sibford Ferris, Oxfordshire 28–9
Capek, Karel 54
Capri 202
Carey, Denis 77
Carreras, José 192
Cartlidge, Robin 214
Castle, Barbara 63
Cavendish, Suffolk 217
CBE, Eddington awarded 195–6, 197
charity fund-raising 216–17
Charlie Girl 113
Chasen, Heather 104, 105, 108, 110
Chayefsky, Paddy 97
Cherry Orchard, The 68
Chichester

Festival Theatre 180, 181–2, 207, 211–14
  Minerva Theatre 212, 213
Christadelphianism 49
Christie, Agatha 192
Cleese, John 187
Clendinning, Max 179
Cliff (dresser) 148, 170
Codron, Michael 97, 132, 136, 163–5, 170, 178, 218
Cohen, Barry 173–4
Colchester 38
Collier, Lesley 192
Collins, Joan 77
Colombe d'Or restaurant 108
Concorde, flight on 221
Congreve, William 214, 218
Contractor, The 235
Conville, David 52
Cooper, Rowena 234
Copenhagen, Denmark 188
Copley, John 193
Cornwall 12–13, 14, 220
Cotton, Oliver 220
Courtenay, Margaret 143, 144, 145
Coward, Noël 48, 74, 83, 95–7, 96, 150, 192
  Hay Fever 95–7
  Private Lives 29
Craig, Michael 204
Craig, Wendy 79, 127
Criterion Theatre, London 105
Critic's Circle Best Actor award 229
Crosby, Bing 209
Crosland, Anthony 150
Crowley, Bob 228
Culshaw, Bernard 145
Cushing, Peter 114–15

Dallas, United States 225
Danziger brothers 88
D'Arcy, Father 6
Dare, Daphne 208, 213
Davies, John Howard 127, 135, 139, 140
Davies, Roy 182, 203, 217, 223
Dench, Judi 192, 193
Derwent Award 114
Desert Island Discs 160
Devine, George 95
Dews, Peter 114
Dixon of Dock Green 84
Domingo, Placido 192
Donat, Robert 105
Done, Ken 172
Donkey's Years 136–7
Double Dealer, The 214, 218
Dowell, Anthony 192
Dr Zhivago 111
Dresser, The 231
Dromgoole, Patrick 94
du Maurier, Sir Gerald 236
Dublin, Ireland 180
  Gate Theatre 87–8
Dunbar, Major Sir George 49
Duncan, Archie 90
Duttine, John 203
Dyer, Charles 178–9, 180, 231
  Lovers Dancing 178–9, 180

The Staircase 178, 231
Wanted One Body 178

Early English Opera Society 215
Eddington, Albert Clark (father) 1–3, 5, 81
Eddington, Sir Arthur 26, 76
Eddington, Dominic (son) 98, 218
Eddington, Frances (mother) 1, 3–4, 5, 6, 7, 8,
   14–15, 17, 24, 83, 94
Eddington, Gemma (daughter) 105, 195, 214,
   218, 234
Eddington, Hugo (son) 92, 158, 171, 173, 179
Eddington, Patricia (wife) 6, 8–9, 78, 79, 80, 81,
   83, 85, 92, 93, 103, 107, 108, 136, 158, 164, 171,
   179, 184–6, 195, 197, 199, 205, 209, 215
Eddington, Paul
   acting career 35–7
   agent 85, 225–6
   ankylosing spondylitis 92–3, 98, 137, 150–1, 187
   anti-nuclear campaigning 103
   birth 1
   CBE 195–6, 197
   childhood 1–15
   children 79, 93, 98, 105
   comic roles 127
   congestive heart failure 202
   Critic's Circle Best Actor award 229
   Derwent Award 114
   diabetes 217, 230
   education 7, 8, 10–11, 14–15, 17–32
   faith healer, Eddington visits 232–3
   health 25–6, 92–3, 47, 98, 109, 137, 150–1, 174,
     178, 187, 199–200, 202–3, 217, 228–37
   IRA bomb attack 218–19
   Labour Party membership 63
   leads Bristol Old Vic company 99
   marriage 69, 78, 79, 80, 108
   music, love of 14, 28
   mycosis fungoides 178, 199–200, 202–3,
     228–9, 233
   National Service, call-up for 59–60
   pacifism 35, 42–3, 46, 48–50, 59–60, 103,
     200–2
   parents' divorce 8, 14
   Shakespeare, love of 28
   smoking, attitude towards 29–30, 58, 101,
     129, 183
   stagefright 106–7, 112
   tuburculosis 25–6
   ulcerative colitis 187–8, 233
   Variety Club Best Actor Award 183
Eddington, Shirley (sister) 3, 7, 8, 9, 13, 22,
   34, 36, 49
Eddington, Toby (son) 79–80, 83, 101
Eddington, Tom (grandson) 195
Eddington, William Clark (grandfather) 1–2
Edinburgh, Prince Philip, Duke of 189
Ehle, Jennifer 220, 222
Eliot, T. S. 57, 226–7
Elizabeth II, Queen 131, 189–90, 192
Elsom, Jonathan 213
Entertainer's National Service Association
   (ENSA) 37–50
Epstein, Jacob 7
Equity 53, 85–6, 128, 145, 237

Australian 204
Committee for Artists' Freedom 237
Derwent Award 113–14
Esmonde, John 127, 170
Essel, Eileen 68
Etherege, Sir George 142
Evans, Dame Edith 95–6
Evans, Laurence 15–7, 8
Evans, Monica 104
Evening Standard newspaper 129
Express newspaper 231

Fairfax, George 196
Fall of Eagles, The 114
Family Reunion, The 57
Farebrother, Violet 66
Farr, Mike 23–4, 25
Farrer, David 39, 44
Fiander, Lewis 204
film making and television compared 89
Finch, Scott 112
Firstborn, The 68
Fitzgerald, Geraldine 87
Fletcher, John 6, 17–18
Fontaine, Joan 110
Foot, Freddie 122
Forbes, Hugh 85, 86
Forty Years On 117–22, 180–4
Fowlds, Derek 140, 168, 182, 209
Foxwarren 90
Franklyn-Robbins, John 100, 102
Fraser, Lady Antonia 230
Fraser, Malcolm 172
Frayn, Michael 136–7, 146, 164
   Donkey's Years 136–7
   Noises Off 164–6, 167, 170
French, Harold 236
Freud, Clement 188
Friel, Brian 214
Froeschlein, Mr (fencing master) 74
Frontier 123–4
Fry, Christopher 68
Fry, Stephen 183
Full House 37
Fulwood, Sheffield 79

Gachet, Alice 74
Gage, Alexander 90
Gale, John 146, 147, 150, 152, 153, 207, 212–13
Garinei, Pietro 131, 132, 133
Garland, Patrick 117, 122, 180, 181, 192
Garrick Club 170, 181, 226, 234
Gatliff, Frank 212, 213, 215–16
George and Margaret 37–8
Gerard, Mother 7, 8
Gerhardt (refugee) 21
Gibson, Chloe 83
Gielgud, Sir John 53, 117–19, 120, 121–2, 122, 180,
   181, 204, 225, 227, 231
Gilbert, W.S. 195
Giovannini, Alessandro 131, 133, 134, 135
Globe Theatre, London 224–5
Gloucester, Duke and Duchess of 189
Glover, Jamie 222
Goddard, Willoughby 113

Good Life, The 127–31, 135, 136, 140, 150, 170
Good Neighbors see Good Life The
Goodbody, Buzz 126
Goodman, Lord 208
Gordon, Hannah 221
Gosford, Australia 174
Grade, Lew 124
Grahame, Gloria 160
Grainger, Gawn 226, 227, 230
Gray, Dulcie 222
Greene, Richard 89–90
Greenhalge, Andy 234
Greenwich 143, 145
Guildford, Yvonne Arnaud Theatre 162, 236
Guys and Dolls 178–9

Habeas Corpus 120–1
Hale, Elvi 79
Hale, Georgina 178
Hall, Peter 155, 160, 161, 220–2
Hall, Rebecca 220
Hall, Roger 146, 149
Hank's Night Out see Blue Comedy
Hardiman, Terrence 234
Hardy, Jeffrey 204
Hardy, Robert 104, 105
Harewood, Earl and Countess of 216
Harlequinade 71, 204
Harris, Richard 169
Harris, Rosemary 220, 224
Harrison, Rex 205, 206
Harry (RADA pianist) 75
Harwood, Ronald 231
Hawke, Bob 173, 174, 200
Hawke, Hazel 200–1
Hawkes, Jacquetta 109
Hawthorne, Nigel 140, 142, 168, 178, 182, 191, 197, 231
Hay Fever 95–7
Haymarket Theatre, London 213
Heaton, Geoff 58
Her Majesty's Theatre, London 203
Hickson, Joan 192
Hilda ('auntie Hilda') 25–6
Hine 124, 127
HMS Pinafore 195, 197–8, 202
Hobson, Harold 95
Hoddinott, Diana 142
Hodge, Douglas 226, 227, 228, 230
Holy Child convent, Cavendish Square 7
Home 121, 231–2, 234–7
Hordern, Michael 184
Horniman, Miss 51
Huddleston, Father Trevor 85

Ibsen, Henrik 102
Illuminations 150, 151, 152–3
Illustrated London News 123
Imperial Tobacco 183
In Praise of Rattigan 177
Ingham, Barrie 124
Ingrey, William 237
Insect Play, The 54
Ipswich
    Rep 79–81, 124, 127

Wolsey Theatre 214, 218
Irgun Zvai Leumi 208
Irish Times newspaper 219
It's a Green World see The Good Life

Jackson, Sir Barry 51, 53, 54, 56–7, 58, 72
Jay, Anthony 139, 140, 170, 191
Jeannie 38, 39–40
Jenkins, Peter 150, 153
Jennifer (actress) 53, 57, 58, 59, 60, 62–3
Jerusalem 208–9
Jetstream 93–4
John ('uncle John') 26
Johnson Over Jordan 111
Johnson, Richard 220
Johnstone, Arthur 17, 19–20, 24, 26, 27–8, 29–30, 31–2
Jones, Barry 114
Jones, Brian 127, 128, 142, 148
Jones, Gwyneth 192
Jones, Ursula 145
Jongh, Nicholas de 146
Jorrocks 113, 195
Julius Caesar 114
Jumpers 184–7, 188

Karsarvina, Tamara 56
Kaufman, Gerald 190
Keith, Penelope 127, 128–30, 135–6, 137, 149, 151–2, 180, 189
Kendal, Felicity 127, 128–9, 184, 220, 222
Kenilworth 94
Kennedy, John F. 103, 105
Kent, Jonathan 225
Kenwright, Bill 229, 230
Kidd, Robert 146–7
King Lear 66
Kinnock, Neil 224
Kirkland, Gelsey 192
Knight, Laura 56
Komuso 86–7
Kray, Reggie 181–2
Khruschev, Nikita 95–6, 103

Labour Party, Eddington's membership 63
Lamb family, Sibford Ferris, Oxfordshire 18–19, 20–1
Lambert, Verity 237
Langtry, Lily 5
Larbey, Bob 127, 170
Late Late Show, The 180
Laughton-Matthews, Peter 9
Laughton-Matthews, Dame Vera 9
Laye, Evelyn 3
Leek workhouse 3, 6
Leigh, Vivien 77, 156
Leigh-Hunt, Barbara 104
Lerwick Military Hospital 47–8
Let There be Love 160–1, 163–4, 170, 171
Levaux, David 226, 227, 232, 235
Lewis, Gwynedd 9, 36–7
Lewis's Ltd, Birmingham 34–6, 36, 38
Life With Father 80
Lindsay-Hogg, Eddie 87
Linscott, Glenda 204

Lipman, Maureen 169
Liverpool Rep 55
Lloyd, Bernard 113
London
  Alexandra Road 5–6
  All Souls, Langham Place 191
  BBC's Paris Studio 182
  Bermondsey 179
  Bertorelli's restaurant 193
  Boundary Road 5
  Buckingham Palace 189–90
  Charing Cross Hospital 98, 137
  Chelsea Old Church 221
  Chesil Court, Chelsea 24, 31, 49
  Crouch Hill 86
  Ebury Street 74
  Grosvenor House Hotel 149
  Holy Child convent, Cavendish Square 7
  Kettner's restaurant 120
  Manzi's restaurant 203
  Montesson School, Regent's Park 10
  New End Hospital 81
  Old Admiralty House, Whitehall 208
  Old Brompton Road 83
  Parliament Hill 84–5
  Percy Street 21
  Quex Road R C church, Kilburn 11
  St John's Skin Hospital, Soho 199, 203
  Savoy Hotel 5
  Sloane Square 31
  Soho 189
  Swiss Cottage 195
  Theatre Museum 229
  theatres *see under individual names*
  West End theatres 97–8, 139
  Whittington Hospital 182, 223
  YMCA, Tottenham Court Road 162
London Assurance 207, 211–13, 214
Lotterby, Sidney 142
Lovers Dancing 178–9, 180
Love's Labour's Lost 78
Lumsden, Geoffrey 123
Lyceum Theatre, London 55
Lynn, Jonathan 139, 140, 169, 170, 191, 192
Lyon-Maris, Paul 229
Lyric Theatre, Hammersmith 95, 102, 151, 165
Lyric Theatre, Shaftesbury Avenue 147
Lyttleton Theatre, London 155–61
McAuliffe, Nichola 218
Macbeth 55, 69, 99, 101
MacDiarmid, Ian 225
McEnery, Peter 213, 224
McGee, Henry 161, 171
McGoohan, Patrick 68, 102
McKellen, Ian 228
McKenzie, Julia 139
McKern, Leo 204
MacNaughtan, Alan 70, 107
Macpherson, Jim 198
Macready, William 72
McWhinnie, Donald 97, 178
Madly in Love see Blue Comedy
Maguire, Ruth 33
Malade Imaginaire, Le 74
Maldon, Essex, Warren School 14

Malindi, Kenya 185–6
Malleson, Miles 81
Malvern 26
Malvern Festival 56
Man and Superman 159
Manchester Opera House 119
Manning, Hugh 53, 86
Mansfield, Nancy 79
Margaret, Princess 178–9
Marguerite (actress) 70
Marie 12–13
Marowitz, Charles 161, 162–3, 211
Marshall, Michael and Caroline 180
Martys, Carol 181
Mason, James 38–9
Mason, Sir John 173
Mason, Pamela 38
Massaini, Alessandra 133
Massey, Anna 136, 137
Matcham, Frank 236
Matthews, Jessie 3
Maxwell, James 123
Maxwell, Robert 190
May, Val 79, 99, 103–4, 112, 114
MCA agency 85
Me and My Girl 183
Meckler, Nancy 155, 156, 157, 158, 159
Medina, Patricia 89–90
Melbourne, Australia 195, 196–9, 205–6
  ABC bookshop 198
  Arts Centre 196
  Comedy Theatre 205
  Government House 199
  Parliament House 199
  Rockman's Regency Hotel 205–6
  Victoria State Opera House 195, 196
Mendes, Sam 212–14
Merrick, David 108
Meyer, Michael 102
Michell, Keith 114
Middle Age Spread 146–7, 149, 150, 151
Midsummer Night's Dream, A 78, 145
Miller, Arthur 229
Miller, Hugh 75, 77
Miller, Jonathan 142–3, 144, 145–6, 184
  The Body in Question 145
Mills, Ralph 160
Minneapolis, United States 221
Mirror, newspaper 231
Miss Mabel 70
Mitchell, Warren 77
Molire, Jean-Baptiste
  Malade Imaginaire Le 74
  School for Wives 81
  Tartuffe 221–3
Monaco 177–8
Monica, Luigi la 133
Montessori school, Regent's Park 10
Month in the Country, A 68
Montreux Festival 192
Morley, Robert 122
Morley, Sheridan 164
Morrell, Lady Ottoline 120
Morris, Lana 93
Moseley, Holy Child convent 8

Mountbatten, Earl 124
Mower, Patrick 127
Murder in the Vicarage 192
Murdoch, Dame Elisabeth 199
Murdoch, Iris 103–6
Muscat 174–5

Nash, Mary 195, 197
National Theatre, London 96, 102–3, 155–61, 164, 178–9
Neagle, Anna 113
Neville, John 78
New York, United States 108–11
Newman, Nanette 161
New Wave 161
News of the World newspaper 185
Nicholls, Jon 195, 203–4
Nicholson, Nora 117, 119, 120
Nimmo, Derek 113
No Man's Land 225–30
Noises Off 164–7, 170
Norman Conquests, The 127
Norman, Jessye 192
Northwood, Greater London 127–8
Nottage, Doug 141
Novello, Ivor 37
Nunn, Alan 79
Nunn, Trevor 80, 124–6

Observer newspaper 85, 146
O'Connell, Dr 137
O'Connell, Patrick 123
Of Mice and Men 78–9
Oliver Twist 127
Olivier Awards 149
Olivier, Sir Laurence 36, 55–6, 90, 155–6, 159, 160, 180
Olivier Theatre, London 159
O'May, John 197
On the Buses 142
Orme, Elsie 195
Oscar, Henry 49, 50
Osman, Lorrain 223
Ost, Geoffrey 63, 65, 67, 68, 69, 71, 79, 205
Oswestry 42
Oulton, Brian 58–9
Our Town 57, 58
Outside Edge 169–70
Owen, Dr David 152
Oxford 220
Ozal, Turgut 206, 207

Paolini, Henri 202
Parkhurst prison 181–2
Parkin, Eric 19, 48–9
Patras Arts Festival, Greece 215
Payn, Graham 152, 192
Payne, Laurence 58, 78
Pearman, Philip 85
Peet, John and Eirene 34
Penna, Tarva 76
Penney, Jennifer 192
Pentland Firth 43–448
Penzance 14
Peter, John 229

Phillips, John 123
Phillips, Robin 207, 208, 211–12, 213
Philpot, Eden 83
Pinter, Harold 95, 190, 226–7, 230
    Birthday Party The 95
    Moonlight 230
    No man's Land 225–8, 229–30
Pitt, Jason 234
Pioneer Corps 40
Playhouse Theatre, London 221
Plomley, Roy 160
Plowright, Joan 155, 156–7, 158, 159, 160, 219
Polperro 12–13, 220
Poor Clares, order of 7
Popp, Lucia 192
Portman, Eric 39
Portrait of a Queen 112–13
Powick Lunatic Asylum 5
Present Laughter 150, 151, 152
Prevost, Nicholas le 220, 222
Priestley, J. B. 103–5, 109, 111
    Johnson Over Jordan 111
    Severed Head. A 103–7, 108–9
Prior, Marina 197
Private Lives 29
Puckey brothers 12–13, 220

Quakerism 1. 6. 17–21, 38, 144–5, 200–1, 225, 236
    meeting for worship 20–1
    pacifism 19, 35
    Sibford School 17–32
Queen's Theatre, London 182
Quilley, Denis 177

radio 94–5, 151–2, 182, 221
Radio Times magazine 228
Rainier, Prince of Monaco 177
Ramsey, Peggy 131
Rattigan, Terence 204
    Browning Version, The 71, 203–4
    Harlequinade 71, 204
    In Praise of Rattigan 177
    Ross 102
Rawsthorne, Anne 108
Redgrave, Michael 55
Regents Park Open Air Theatre, London 52
Religious Society of Friends *see* Quakerism
Revill, Clive 79
Reynolds, Dorothy 117
Richardson, Sir Ralph 55–6, 101, 111–12, 225, 227, 231
Richmond 236
Riff-Raff Element, The 225
Rivals, The 71–2
Roberts
    Alice (grandmother) 4–5
    Frances *see* Eddington, Frances
    Roland (grandfather) 4–5
Robertson, Toby 114
Robin Hood 88–92, 177
Roman Catholicism 4, 5, 7, 8, 11–12, 17, 20
Rome, Italy 131–5
Romeo and Juliet 57–8
Ross 102
Ross-on-Wye 169

Routledge, Patricia 165
Rowland, Toby 117
Royal Academy of Dramatic Art (RADA) 35, 73–7
Royal Family 77
Royal National Theatre, London 234
Royal Opera House, London 192–3
Royal Shakespeare Company, 53, 57-8, 125–6, 234
royalties 130, 132
Royalty Theatre, London 203
Ruby, Thelma 113
Rudman, Michael 136, 155, 158, 159
Russell, Bertrand 120
Rusty (dog) 13–14
Rutland, John 71

Sackville-West, Vita 120
Sailor Beware 84
Sallis, Peter 68, 232
Sanders, George 209
Santarelli 5
Savoy Theatre, London 165
Scales, Prunella 169
Scapa Flow 40, 44
Scarfe, Gerald 228
School for Wives 81
Scofield, Paul 54, 58, 72
Scott, Miss 76
Scott, Patricia *see* Eddington, Patricia
Scottish National Orchestra 215
See How They Run 80
Selby, Nicholas 79, 95
Sessions, John 222
Severed Head, A 103–10
Sewell, George 127
Shakespeare, William 28, 161–2, 224–5
    Julius Caesar 114
    King Lear 66
    Love's Labour's Lost 78
    Macbeth 55, 69, 99, 101
    Midsummer Night's Dream, A 78, 145
    Romeo and Juliet 57–8
    Tempest, The 51–2
    Timon of Athens 58
    Twelfth Night 59, 119
Shamir, Yitzhak 208, 209
Sharman, John 233
Shaps, Cyril 124
Shaw, George Bernard 58, 100
She Stoops to Conquer 51–3
She Would if She Could 142–6
Sheffield 65
    Rep 63, 65–73, 79, 232
Sheridan, *The Rivals* 71–2
Shrubland Hall 151, 152
Sibford Friend's School, Oxfordshire 17–32
Sidcot Friend's School, Somerset 2
Simmons, Jean 229
Sinden, Donald 152, 213
Sitges, Spain 209
Sitting Duck, The 101–2
Sitwell, Edith 120
Smith, Madeleine 163
Smith, Maggie 95, 96, 207
Smith, Michael 198
Sokolova, Lydia 74

Southport 79
Southsea 41–2
Spanish Civil War 21
Special Branch 127
Spinetti, Victor 111
Staircase, The 178, 231
Stephens, Robert 220
Stephens, Toby 220, 222
Stilgoe, Richard 113
Stoppard, Tom 184, 186
Storey, David
    Contractor, The 235
    Home 231–2, 234–7
Strachey, Lytton 49
Stratford, Ontario, Festival Theatre 207
Stratford-on-Avon, Shakespeare Memorial Theatre
    53, 57–8
Streuli, Peter 51
Stromness 43–4
Sugden, Mollie 224
Sullivan, Sir Arthur 195
Sumburgh Head, 47
Summer Folk 213
Sun newspaper 230
Sunday Telegraph newspaper 104
Sunday Times newspaper 229
Sunderland, Scott 54
Suzman, Janet 224
SWET Awards 149–50
Sydney, Australia 171–3, 174, 202

Tartuffe 221–3
Teddington Studios 124, 161
Teddington, Surrey 84
television 83–4, 89, 94, 95, 123, 167–8, 170
    advertising 128, 151–2, 180, 188–9, 217–18
    comic roles 127
    series 130–1, 149, 170
Television Centre 83, 114, 131
Tempest, The 51–2
1066 and All That 54
Ten Times Table 139, 141
Tennent, Victoria 224
Tenth Man, The 97
Ternan, Kerry 174
Thames Television 123, 124, 160–1
Thatcher, Margaret 141, 191
Thaw, John 132, 135
Theatre Royal, Drury Lane 37–8, 42–3, 50
Theatre Royal, Haymarket 214
Third Man, The 98
Thorndike, Dame Sybil 93, 216
Thorne, Angela 208, 211, 213, 214
Thorne, Garry and Patty 107
Thurso 43
Tickner, Martin 177
Tillotson, Keith 169–70
Timon of Athens 58
Tinker, Jack 177
Tollemache, Bentley 185
Tolstoy, Count 187
Townley, Toke 52–3
Travelling North 204
Tuckey, Dick 214
Turkey 206–7

Turner, Clifford 75–6
Turner, Geraldine 197
Tutin, Dorothy 112, 177, 203, 204
Twelfth Night 59, 119
Tyzack, Margaret 160, 161, 164, 207

Upcher, Peter 39
Variety Club Best Actor Award 183
Vaudeville Theatre, London 112–13
Vaughan, Peter 112–13
Venus Observed 78
Verney, Guy 60
Viewers' and Listeners' Association 191
Villa Terre de Sienne 107
St Vincent de Paul, order of 7, 8, 10
voice-overs 151–2

Wales, Princess of 188
Wallace, Ian 195, 197
Walton-on-Thames Studios 88–9
Wanamaker, Sam 224
Wanted One Body 178
War and Peace 100
Waring, Amanda 224
Waring, Derek 112
Warner, Jack 84
Warner, John 213
Warre, Michael 86
Warren School, Maldon 14
Watling, Jack 203
Wattis, Richard 95
Way of the World, The 58–9
Weinstein, Hannah 88, 90
Weldon, Duncan 214, 218, 232, 234
Wesley, Mary 219–20

Weston-super-Mare 22
Wheatly, Alan 90
Whitehouse, Mary 191
Whitlam, Gough 198
Who's Afraid of Virginia Woolf? 155–61, 163–4
Wilder, Thornton 57, 58
Williams, Emlyn 122
Williamson, Kate 60–4
Willis, Jerome 101, 218
Wind in the Willows, The 28
Wilson, Harold 190–1
Windsor, Barbara 111
Wisley Common 89
Wodehouse, P. G. 237
Wolfit, Sir Donald 66
Wontner, Sir Hugh 5
Wood, David 233
Wood, Peter 184, 186
Woodward, Sarah 211
Worcester 1, 26
World War I 2, 19
World War II 21, 25–6, 30–1, 33, 35, 42–8
Worshipful Company of Vintners 187
Worthing
  Connaught Theatre 6–1
  Kate Williamson's theatrical lodgings 60–2, 64
  Rep 60–4
Wrede, Caspar 95
Wyndham's Theatre, London 121, 236

Yellow Sands 83
Yes, Minister 139–42, 147–9, 150, 164, 167–9, 170–1, 182, 184, 185, 186–7, 188, 191, 206–7, 208, 228
Yes, Minister desk diaries 198
Yes, Prime Minister 170–1, 191, 219